RECOLLECTIONS OF JERUSALEM

Recollections of Jerusalem

Anya Berezina Derrick

Holy Trinity Publications
The Printshop of St Job of Pochaev
Holy Trinity Monastery
Jordanville, New York
2014

Printed with the blessing of His Eminence,
Metropolitan Hilarion First Hierarch
of the Russian Orthodox Church Outside of Russia

Recollections of Jerusalem
© 2014 Anya Berezina Derrick

HOLY TRINITY PUBLICATIONS
The Printshop of St Job of Pochaev
Holy Trinity Monastery
Jordanville, New York 13361-0036
www.holytrinitypublications.com

ISBN: 978-0-88465-359-2 (Paperback)

ISBN: 978-0-88465-274-8 (ePub)

ISBN 978-0-88465-373-8 (Mobipocket)

Library of Congress Control Number 2014934054

CONTENTS

FOREWORD

⳩

The Psalmist exhorts us to "Ask now for things regarding the peace of Jerusalem" and goes on to assure us "that there is prosperity for those who love you" (Ps 121(122): 6 OSB). We also know that the earthly city of Jerusalem is intended to point us toward "the Jerusalem above . . . which is the mother of us all" (Gal 4:26).

Through the providence of God, Anya Derrick's life has been intimately connected to the earthly city of Jerusalem in Palestine. It was there as a young person that she was raised in the spirit of Holy Russia, as manifested in the life of the Russian Ecclesiastical Mission, the Mount of Olives and Gethsemane convents, and the Bethany School. Her spiritual life was nurtured by the wandering English Orthodox hieromonk Lazarus (Moore) and the many other churchly luminaries of the twentieth century she encountered such as St John (Maximovitch) of Shanghai and San Francisco, Archbishop Antony (Sinkevich) of Los Angeles, and Mother Mary (Robinson) of the Bethany School. All of this was to provide her with a foundation that would sustain her faith during wilderness years later in her life when the Church was geographically distant from her and her burgeoning family.

This short but vivid work will open up a world very different from our own that will seem historically distant to many readers. So it is all the more remarkable that these influences and experiences spanning three continents are contained within the life of one human being who is still very much alive with us on this earth today. It is also of the utmost importance as we strive to understand the world in which we live and the past events that have shaped its course such as the Russian Revolution and its aftermath, and the Arab–Israeli conflict.

These recollections also offer a window into the struggles, life, and aspirations of the Russian diaspora after the Communist takeover of the ancestral homeland. For all these reasons, we commend it to you, the reader.

Holy Trinity Monastery
Jordanville, New York, January 2014

CHAPTER 1

⊹⊹⊹⊹

Beginnings

Belgrade

I was born in a Serbian hospital in Belgrade, Yugoslavia, nearly a decade after the 1921–1922 great exodus of Russians from their homeland, which was being devastated by the Bolshevik Revolution. By that time, the Soviet government was becoming firmly positioned for what seemed an indefinite time. The Russian intelligentsia fled in terror from the Communists, whose murderous motto was "Those not with us are against us." They were stripped of what they had and fled to locations all over the world, desperately plunging into the unknown. Looking longingly backward to the happiness and security of the past, they hoped that their exile would be temporary.

While travelling by whatever means they could, they witnessed indescribable scenes of cruelty perpetrated by the revolutionaries and arrived in countries some of which were painfully recovering from World War I. Among these Russians were my future parents who were united in their homesickness, in their loyalty to Russian culture, and in a shared form of religious patriotism. My father was one of nine children, born in 1903 in St Petersburg to a military family. His father was Major General Nikolai N. Dubrova, who met his death at the hands of the revolutionaries. His mother was Anna von Kazenkamph, whose ancestors were from Bremen, Germany, a major port and one of the old free Hanseatic League towns. My father's older brothers completed the Third Moscow Cadet Corps,[1] but my father and his brother Alexei had to finish in Yugoslavia. Three younger sisters survived and remained in Soviet Russia, where they married and raised their children, and whose grandchildren I met for the first time after the fall of the Soviet Union.

Father was a nineteen-year-old cadet in the White Army when in 1922 it retreated from Russia to Belgrade. Toward the end of World War I, my mother became a trained Red Cross nurse and stayed on through the revolution in the Volunteer Army, later known as the White Army. My mother arrived in Belgrade at the same time as my father, but it was not until several years later they met at the Russian Orthodox Church there. At that church, a highly revered priest, Father John Sakal, gave lectures on Orthodox spirituality, which they both attended and by which they were deeply inspired. My mother was several years older than my father, and it was in this church that their lives merged in a spiritual sense as well as in an earthly marital bond, later torn asunder by the devastating events of World War II.

According to Russian Orthodox tradition, a child was usually named after the saint of the day or close to the day on which the child was born. As children grew, parents would tell them about their saints who had been faithful followers of Christ. Children would also hear about their saints in church and have their name days celebrated on the feast day of their saint, as birthdays today are celebrated.

Both of my parents wanted to name me after their mothers. Conveniently, both of their mothers were called Anna. The feast day of St Anna the prophetess was closest to my birth date, and so during my baptism I was given her name. She was the prophetess mentioned in the Gospel as having been present in the Jerusalem Temple when the baby Jesus was taken there to be presented to God, His Father. My mother hung over my bed a small icon of this event. When occasionally I was left alone in our mansard room on top of the red brick roof of the building in which we lived, I looked at this icon on the wall beside my bed and forgot about feeling alone. I slept at one end of the room in a child's wooden bed with my little icon above it, and when the window across from me was open, a black cat often sat on the sill. When my mother returned, she would begin to cook *mannaya kasha* (cream of wheat) in a tiny, red enameled pot on a small kerosene stove. The door of our room opened to a *cherdak* (attic), a dark place with cobwebs and large, frightening objects standing here and there. I remember passing through it when going down the stairs to go outside on the porch, where near the exit steps sometimes sat a little boy next to his mother. They were Serbian and spoke to each other in that language, which I soon began to learn.

On the upper level of the building across the street lived the doctor who delivered me and was my godfather. I remember being in his large apartment during a party with many people. It was what Serbians call *Slava*, the feast of families' honor day, and all families had one on some date. Lots of sweets such as baklava were served, and I was the center of attention while my godfather gently caressed me. I loved this place and how the Serbian language sounded. We were living at that time on a street named Krunska

Ulitsa, and Yugoslavia became my parents' adopted second homeland. I think I was around three or four years old when I started to observe and remember events and knew that I was born in Belgrade where Serbian was spoken, and I sometimes asked my mother, as she later told me, "Is this fly Russian or Serbian?" so accustomed was I to hearing daily comparisons.

The other place that left a strong impression in my memory was the Russian Orthodox church in downtown Belgrade. I remember climbing up stone steps to the church, which was painted white on the outside and was bright with candlelight on the inside. Small votive oil lamps called *lampada* were burning before the many icons, and I liked the way it smelled of incense. In Russian churches people usually stand throughout the service, and so did we, at times as long as two or three hours. We stood on the left side in front of a life-size icon of Christ sitting in the lap of His Mother. She was crowned and sitting in a regal pose, while He was holding the world in His hands. The icon had a lot of blue color, and Christ was older than on the icon above my bed at home. One time my mother did not notice that I had a small ball in my pocket just before we left for church. Then during the evening service, I suddenly threw the ball in the direction of the icon where Christ was holding the world in his hands. My mother spoke about this incident later, saying I must have thought the image of the world in the hands of the boy Jesus was a ball and so I wanted to play with Him.

Mother and I spent many mornings and evenings in church. I liked to watch the incense smoke rise and listen to the a cappella singing of hymns. No organ or musical instruments were played in Orthodox churches. Perhaps this was the time when the seed was planted within me for the love of singing in a choir, which later in my adult life continued to give me joy. This is where I developed my love for classical music as well, because church is where I first heard works of some of the best Russian classical composers who started their musical careers by composing church music. Later my love for folk music developed from hearing Mother sing Russian folk songs. I also was shown photographs of Mother and Father singing together in a large choir that not only sang in church, but also gave concerts of Russian music locally. In this choir, Mother and Father met and fell in love, and I was the product of this musical encounter.

At that time I did not know much about my father because he was not always home and spent most of his time at the military base of the Russian White Army, which survived until World War II. Later Mother told me that Father was an officer and that he was the son of a general. Of course, I did not understand what this meant and gave it little thought; I was totally immersed in my love for Mother as we did everything together. Often on the way back from church we passed by King Alexander of Yugoslavia's palace on our way home to Krunska Ulitsa. I remember the elaborate wrought iron fence, the big beautiful gate, and the booth of the military guard where we used to stop. I spoke Serbian to the handsome guard in uniform, and he took my hand in his and smiled at me, leaving another positive impression of Serbians.

Memories of War and Peace

Kral (King) Alexander, as the Serbs called him, was benevolent to the Russian imperial refugees or White Russians who fled to Yugoslavia after the takeover of their homeland by the Red Forces of the Bolshevik Revolution. This tragedy engulfed Russia from the moment of Tsar Nicholas II's forced abdication from the throne. Thus the revolution followed under the leadership of persons to whom Russia and its ideal of sanctity were alien. The internationally powered Bolshevik Revolution flourished because of the availability of large monetary resources from abroad, enabling its seizure of the country's rule.

It appeared as if this Russian national catastrophe was desirable to certain foreign forces, who believed that Russia's greatness and economic development would be detrimental to their own development. The ensuing civil war was the last cry of Russia's national awareness, the intent of which was to maintain the country's greatness within the sphere of European states. It was at this point that volunteer military divisions faithful to the tsar began to function, becoming the White Army, which eventually failed and was obliged to retreat toward Crimea in the south.

Having received his military education in tsarist Russia, King Alexander was predisposed to help the retreating White Army. He made the Russian military intelligentsia, to which my parents belonged, feel at home in Belgrade and other cities of his kingdom. When later he was assassinated in Marseilles, France, I was still very young, although vaguely I remember how those around me grieved, and how Mother held my hand when she took me with her into the palace's great hall. I still visualize the shiny black floor and the big dark bier in its center where rested King Alexander's remains. We followed a long line of people, who were allowed time only to enter, view the bier, and walk around it to the exit. For a long time afterwards, my mother and others wore black bands around one arm as a sign of mourning.

Mother grew up in her grandmother's big house in Moscow, where her mother and sisters also lived. On Sundays, the family walked from their home to church in the Kremlin. They sometimes made pilgrimages to Holy

Trinity St Sergius Monastery, the historical seat of the Russian Orthodox Church, also called Sergiev Posad or Zagorsk, a town about sixty miles north of Moscow. They traveled in their *troika* (three-horse-drawn carriage) and on their way stayed overnight in a guest house. It was in this monastery that at age seven my mother made her first confession before communion. She was being prepared for this event by her pious *babushka* (grandmother) while her slightly older cousin was visiting. Noticing that she was quite perturbed about having to tell the priest her sins and that she stole a piece of candy when no one was looking, her cousin decided to tease her. He tried to frighten her by saying that as punishment for her sins, she would be forced to carry a big sack of potatoes to the top of the monastery bell tower. Of course, *babushka* scolded the cousin for teasing my mother and reassured her that this was just a joke.

Mother liked to tell me about pilgrimages they used to make at that time to various distant monasteries and how much everyone enjoyed them. During her school years, she attended the Moscow Mariinsky Institute for Girls as a boarder. While she was there one spring, an unusual flood of the Moscow River took place, flooding the bottom story of the building where there were piano rooms as well as the dining rooms and kitchen. The boarders had to be sent home, and parents were obliged to come by boat along the flooded streets of Moscow to pick them up!

In the prerevolutionary years, my mother sided with the *Narodniki,* the populists, who believed that Russia's future lay in the transformation of the illiterate masses of peasants into educated, progressive thinkers. She hoped to enter a pedagogic institute so as to become a teacher. She was friends with the two maids at her grandmother's house, Dunyasha and Feklusha, who were brought to Moscow from the village where Mother's family owned a country estate. In those days, my mother said that Moscow was like an overgrown village. Grandmother kept a cow and chickens in the huge garden they owned around the two-story house. There were stables for horses and horse-drawn carriages that stood in the yard. Feklusha and Dunyasha milked the cows and took care of most of the housework. My mother shared her idealistic aspirations with those two young peasant girls, also in their teens, and shared with them her love for "Mother Russia," telling them about ideas she read in her books.

The carriage driver at the stables, whom she also befriended, came from a village in the countryside. He would drive her out of the yard and then give in to her pleas to allow her to do the driving. This was something a *barishnya,* a young woman of good breeding, never did; it was *ne prilichno,* not in good taste, and therefore unacceptable. However, my mother did not care; she considered herself a progressive young woman, and taking the reins in her hands she sped through the snow-covered streets of Moscow feeling victorious. This, of course, caused the driver great consternation lest she run over the pedestrians or bring about some other disaster on the road.

Back at her grandmother's house, the huge *pechka* (wood furnace) was centrally located in the house so it could warm four rooms. It burned wood and kept most rooms warm except for the dining room. Mother told me that it sometimes got so cold in the dining room that water in a glass froze solid. There was always a dish of *gorokhovyi kisel* (cooked split peas) on the dining table to have a bite between meals if anyone was hungry. For the rest of her life, she often expressed a desire for a dish of the same kind of peas. "They always tasted so good," she said.

Of her two younger sisters, Mother's favorite was Lida, the middle sister. Good natured and an excellent student, she also was the prettiest of the three. During parades, some of the best students of Moscow's institutes for young women were presented to Tsar Nicholas II, who shook hands with them and asked them a few questions. My Aunt Lida was thus honored for her superior qualities: good character, brains, and good looks! It made my mother proud of her, and she believed in a great future for this sister.

However, after the Russian Revolution, life in Russia turned upside down, as Aunt Lida expressed it in her letters to Mother living abroad. She wrote of the changes that took place in people's lives and in human nature in general. People became too materialistic: they were envious and infinitely greedy, she wrote, and there was no real friendship; only utilitarian relationships existed. Several years later, this one-time achiever of Russia's highest honor, the tsar's personal attention, encountered great sadness. In addition to terrible physical deprivations during World War II and the ensuing Siege of Leningrad, when the whole city endured great suffering, Aunt Lida had to bear even greater personal losses. She lost her husband and their fourteen-year-old son who both went to the front to defend their homeland. Then she lost her younger son, Yurochka, to diphtheria. He was only six years old and there were no medicines or doctors available, as the city was under a long siege. The winter was exceptionally cold that year, food was scarce, and normal life ceased.

Her mother was at that time also caught in the Siege of Leningrad, because she happened to be staying at Aunt Lida's home on a visit from Moscow. Born into a property-owning family before the revolution, the new government did not allow her to have even a room of her own in the big house she grew up in and where she raised her own children. The house was turned into communal living, and she was forced to live with one or the other of her married daughters in their one-bedroom apartments. My mother was already long out of Russia, while Aunt Lida was married and lived in Leningrad and her other sister, Aunt Olga, lived with her two daughters in Moscow. Thus my grandmother traveled constantly from one city to the other, destined to die from cold and hunger during the Siege of Leningrad.

At the end of World War II, we received our last letter from Aunt Lida, where she wrote, "I lost everyone close and dear to me, my husband, two sons and my dear mother all in a matter of a few months; I have nothing to live for." In earlier letters, she described hardships as a result of the new life after the revolution and how she longed to have her own place with her family. Her husband was sent away to work at hard labor eighteen hours a day, so she could rarely be with him and they could not enjoy family life together. She wrote, "How could our ideal childhood and youth have turned into such a nightmare?"

My mother was not very pretty, but she had expressive light blue eyes and naturally curly hair, which she used to call "The poetic chaos on my head." Her innate kindness and sunny personality made her popular throughout her life. When she was a Red Cross nurse at the front, she was also brave and self-sacrificing. For this she was awarded a couple of medals, one of which was the St George's Medal for bravery that she earned during an incident when the notorious outlaw "Makhno" and his band of the Pink Party, as they were nicknamed during the revolution, viciously attacked and robbed both Whites and Reds. Mother was on duty in the field hospital where she stayed with the wounded soldiers under the cross fire, and consequently received shrapnel wounds to her head, leaving a scar for life. When as a little girl I would ask Mother to let me comb her hair, she would say "All right but be careful of the scar," and then she would tell me with pride the story of how she got it.

Another war incident Mother told me about was toward the end of World War I when poisonous gas was released by the enemy. The military field hospital, already treating wounded soldiers, was now overcrowded with gas-poisoned soldiers; they lay listless in their tents devoid of the will to live. She made a supreme effort to get flowers from someplace and arrived in the hospital with a beautiful bouquet in her hands. She walked into the tent cheering the suffering soldiers, one of whom was her own cousin. He and some others attributed their survival to my mother's timely appearance, which lifted their spirits out of the deeply depressive state of mind caused by the gas.

When the White Army began to lose its positions to the Red Army, retreating toward the eastern and southern borders of Russia became a necessity. My mother did her utmost to try once more to go home to Moscow on furlough. She had a friend Yasha, a young Jewish man, who on occasion smuggled for her loaves of bread with money hidden inside to her grandmother's house in Moscow where her mother and younger sisters were near starvation. All the men in the family were at the front. The Bolshevik government already had issued new passports to the new Soviet citizens, which were necessary for travel within Russia.

Mother, being with the White Army, had no Soviet passport, and there was no hope to ever return home, but Yasha again came to her rescue. He offered to take her along with him to Moscow, saying he would tell the authorities she was his sister. He had some kind of stamp placed in his own passport to indicate this, thus taking her to Moscow and back out to the front lines. He was a salesman of sorts, and travel was allowed in his position. He was accommodating both sides, the Reds and the Whites; Jews often played such a role in those days. When Mother arrived in Moscow, the city was in complete disarray: no fuel and no food except pickled herrings, which were being looted by people through the windows of a basement warehouse. It was nearly impossible to eat such salty fish with no bread or anything else available. Life was terrible with absolute chaos reigning. This was the last time Mother saw her family in Moscow. She returned with Yasha to the front by night train, and after this she never saw him again; he too disappeared in the chaos.

Once, during the final phase of the struggle between the White Army and the Red Army, her division had already retreated to Crimea in the south. The day before the final battle, an officer, a good friend and obviously in love with her, asked her to take a last walk with him, as he was to be sent the next day to the battlefield. They walked toward the sea and stood on a high cliff overlooking the beautiful blue water. Suddenly he took her in his arms and pleaded, "Marusinka, I love you, be mine today, tomorrow I may be killed!" Mother replied that in spite of her own feelings toward him, it would be dishonorable, and afterwards the last recourse left for her would be to jump off the cliff into the deep water. Mother told me this story to point out how honorable young people were before the revolution. She said the young man understood her and refrained from kissing her as he did not want to compromise her. However, she said that when they returned to the base from their walk and went to the mess hall, someone noticed on the officer's uniform a couple of her blond curls, and she thought everyone around knew they were hers and that they had spent time alone together.

By that time, several divisions of the White Army were in retreat. Admiral Kolchak's forces in the east collapsed. This brought about a great wave of refugees, carrying thousands of fleeing soldiers and civilians into China and Japan. Then followed the tragic defeat of Denikin's Volunteer Army in the Don Cossack country of the southeast, and the stampede of troops with their families and their wounded into Black Sea ports. There were not enough ships to care for them all, and many were left to their fate. The remnants of the White Army were transported to Crimea; the civilians were taken to Constantinople, Turkey, which became a concentration point for Russian refugees.

Finally General Vrangel's army with which my parents were stationed and which was the last hope of anti-Bolshevik resistance was routed. The last bit of Russian soil held by the White Army, namely Crimea, had to be given up and the army, together with my mother's Red Cross medical division, retreated through Sevastopol. I remember her descriptions of the shortages of life's necessities and overall difficulties. On the way, there was no sanitation and food supplies were inadequate. The harbor of Constantinople was a mass of refugee ships, so tightly packed with men, women, and children that there was scarcely any room on board to lie down to sleep. There was a lack of drinking water and food, and many were sick or wounded. In Gallipoli the Red Cross staff was given a choice to sleep on clean sheets, after using bathing facilities, or having a good meal instead of clean sheets. Mother was at this point so tired of the filth, it overpowered her hunger, and she opted for a bath and clean sheets instead of dinner. That night she slept clean but very hungry.

Belgrade, Yugoslavia, was the refugees' final destination while the Russian naval forces were unable to disembark anywhere on the Mediterranean shore. Thus, they stood in port starved and filthy because the surrounding countries turned them away, not allowing them on shore for fear of reprisals by other nations. Finally the French, who ruled Algiers, allowed the naval forces to disembark and move into tents on the hot sands of the North African desert. In return for this favor, the French took possession of the ships whilst the formerly affluent White Russian naval officers began to live a life of poor refugees. They had no language in common with the natives except for those who spoke some French, nor did they have practical skills for employment. The White Army division that fled to Yugoslavia was luckier; the Serbs, who were co-religionists and brother Slavs, helped them resettle with less hardship and more "soul." Both nations had the Orthodox Christian faith in common.

When my father met my mother in Belgrade, he had already completed the Officers Cadet Training Corps and was serving as an officer while she was working as head nurse in a local hospital. He was tall with dark hair and extremely handsome; she was a short, cheerful blond. I learned about my father's good looks not only from my mother but also from those who knew him at that time and through photos that I later acquired. I inherited my father's thick, dark eyebrows and my mother's blue eyes.

Until World War II, Father was on active duty at a military base near Belgrade. During the war when Germany occupied Yugoslavia, divisions of what was left of the White Army and their families were relocated to German concentration camps in Austria. When the war ended, my father was spared the betrayal of Russian troops at Liens, where the mandatory repatriation of Russian prisoners of war, per agreement by the Allies at Yalta, was tragically enforced against their will. Father died in 1944 in a military hospital in Vienna; he was forty-one years old and was buried in a Russian military cemetery in Vienna in which two soldiers were laid to rest under one tombstone, encrypted with both names over their graves. Mother died without ever finding out what happened to Father or where he was buried.

CHAPTER 2

✠✠✠

A Time of Innocence

The Holy Land and the Russian Mission

At the outbreak of World War II in September 1939, Mother and I were on a pilgrimage from Belgrade to the Holy Land (Palestine), which at that time was under the British Mandate. My father was still in Europe at a sanatorium being treated for tuberculosis, which flared up at the military base where he was serving. As a great believer in prayers and resulting miracles Mother felt that praying for Father at the Holy Sepulchre in Jerusalem and bringing back for him a garment to wear that had been blessed on Christ's burial place would help him recover. The onset of World War II in Europe made it impossible for us to return to Yugoslavia. We had no choice but to appeal to the British Mandate authorities for asylum in Palestine, which we received with temporary visas that were renewable yearly thereafter.

Here I grew up surrounded by a culture very different from the land of my birth. Women wore long dresses embroidered with colorful silks and had long hair covered by veils. From under these veils sometimes clinked strings of silver coins attached to the sunburned foreheads of the bashful Arab women. Arab men's outfits had nothing in common with the way Russian and Serbian men dressed. Life in the white, square stone houses went on day by day, slowly but not monotonously. Days of the year were marked by religious holidays or other special events like weddings and funeral processions. There were simple pleasures, such as going into the vineyard or orchard at daybreak to bring in fruit for breakfast. The morning dew would shine on the grapevines and the fig tree leaves. On approaching home, one would be greeted by the aroma of freshly baked wheat bread called *khubz taboon* in Arabic, because it was baked in an outdoor clay oven called a *taboon*.

Days went by with work in the fields or olive tree groves and ended at sunset, when the young girls of the neighborhood assembled at the well to fetch water. Long lines of maidens gracefully walked on the narrow paths, clay jars poised on their heads. Gaily chattering, they proceeded through the village square while groups of young men stood dressed in *combaz* (an Arab men's outfit) with checkered black or red and white *kaffya* (kerchiefs) on their heads and shiny curved knives in their belts. They watched the girls from a distance while the setting sun kindled their lively dark eyes.

Evenings were spent around a low, olive wood table with mats or oriental rugs on the floors. Everyone sat cross-legged on the rugs with backs supported by hard pillows. The men stayed together conversing and smoking the *argileh,* which made a certain bubbling noise in the glass water jar at the end of the pipe. Sometimes young men sang and played the *ude* while older women drank coffee and told the young girls sitting beside them their fortunes by reading the coffee sediment in the bottom of their emptied cups. The cups were first turned upside down and so formed coffee sediment trails that looked like pathways to a predictable future. Some of the men were sheep and goat herders but most of them were *fellaheen,* or peasants. They were not always literate and were making just enough of a living for the survival of their families. Most of these *fellaheen* were born to Islam, a religion whose name means "surrender," as in surrender to Allah (God). There were also Christian Arab villages with Orthodox or Catholic churches but these were a minority. On Fridays, Muslim men prayed in the mosque (house of prayer). Here they heard about the sacred text of the Quar'an and its author, the prophet Muhammad. For entertainment, men often went to the coffee house and *argileh* smoking center in the village square; it was not only to socialize, but also to hear the latest news, especially after the radio became available there.

This was the Palestinian Arabs' way of life; contrary to popular opinion, they were a domiciled and agricultural people, unlike the Bedouins who lived in black goatskin tents and traveled the desert, returning to Palestine to graze their goat and sheep herds in spring. Palestinians built stone houses with flat roofs on which the family slept in summer. The roofs were also a convenient place for drying certain kinds of vegetables and fruit for winter use. There was no electricity or running water in the houses; instead people drew water from their wells, which filled up during the rainy months. Clusters of these square, white stone houses were usually surrounded by groves of prickly cactus, which defined the border of a village. Dogs were kept strictly outside, not as pets but as faithful guardians of a household.

The other way of life around me was that of my primary nationality: Russian. It was a life among Orthodox Christian Russians, some of whom had come before 1917 on pilgrimage from imperial Russia. Others had come to work at the Russian Orthodox Mission but because of the revolution at home were unable to return. Some entered the monastic life by choice because this was the only safe and reasonable life open to them. One former officer of the Imperial Army who became a priest expressed it like this: "Having been in the service of the greatest ruler on earth, the Tsar of Russia, I was left with only one choice: to serve the Ruler of the Universe, Lord God Himself." Such Russians were the custodians not only of the various properties acquired for the activities of the Mission as beautiful monasteries and schools for Christian Arab children, but also for the Russian Palestinian Society. This organization conducted archeological digs and built buildings to house Russian pilgrims within walking distance from the ancient walls of Jerusalem. There was a large pilgrims' center with a library and a hospital that was close by the grand Trinity Cathedral with the main Mission buildings and a residence for the clergy. These places were meticulously cared for by their residents, who tried to preserve Russia's past greatness represented by its properties in the Holy Land.

Perhaps at this point I should give a brief historical outline of the Russian presence in the Holy Land that began in 1843. Religion was a strong factor in prerevolutionary Russia, and pilgrimages to shrines and monasteries across Russia as well as to the Holy Land were standard devotional activities. According to Nicolai Berdyaev, the well-known Russian mystic, the pilgrimage was widespread in Russia before the revolution to a degree unknown in the West. The Russian people have always produced pilgrims from their ranks, always on their way to some monastery. Writers who were among the most creative representatives of Russian culture, such as Gogol, Dostoyevsky, and others, were pilgrims in spirit; Gogol made an actual pilgrimage to the Holy Land.

As early as the fifteenth century, Tsar Ivan the Third dispatched a representative to Constantinople to maintain close diplomatic relations with the Sublime Porte (the government of the Ottoman Empire). In this way all matters concerning the Holy Land and those who traveled there were handled by the Russian envoy to Constantinople. In 1820 a Russian consulate was opened in Jaffa, which was the port at which pilgrims arrived in Palestine. During the Crimean War (1853–1856), all Russian subjects, mostly clergy, were expelled by the Turks. Upon the termination of hostilities, the Holy Synod of the Russian Orthodox Church sent a large mission to Palestine with the object of establishing a formal Russian representation at the Holy Sepulchre and other holy places. This move was welcomed by Russian pilgrims as well as Christian Arabs, who had no formal national, political, or religious status in Palestine. Thus, the Russian Ecclesiastical Mission in Jerusalem was established, and its activities as well as the purchase of land were financed exclusively from funds raised privately among the people of Russia. Several years later, when Grand Duke Serge visited the Holy Land, he was impressed by the Mission's extensive and varied activities, and decided to endorse support for it. He founded a society to collect funds from private sources in Russia to assist the Russian Mission in the Holy Land called the Russian Orthodox Palestinian Society, the same name it bears today.

After the Bolshevik Revolution and the establishment of a Russian Orthodox Church outside Russia, the Mission represented the Russian Orthodox Church Abroad. The following sites were some of those acquired at various dates: (1) the Russian community on the Mount of Olives and Church of the Ascension, (2) a hill in Ein Karem (Gornia) where another Russian community was built, (3) the Russian community of St Mary Magdalene in the Garden of Gethsemane and a community in Bethany, (4) orange groves in Jaffa, where a school building and church were erected, (5) Wadi Faran by the Dead Sea, with a chapel and hermitage, (6) a guest house and orange and banana groves in Jericho, (7) vineyards near Hebron, Abraham's Oak, and a church and monastery, and (8) the threshold stone of the Judgment Gate in Jerusalem known as the *Russkie raskopki* (Russian excavations) with a hospice building above it.

This last place served as the administrative center of the Russian Orthodox Palestinian Society, and following the establishment of the State of Israel in Palestine, it became the residence of the chief of the Russian Ecclesiastical Mission. Its marble floors, deep red draperies, and life-size portraits of tsars on the walls were reminiscent of the imperial pilgrims who at one time occupied these quarters when they arrived in Jerusalem. Other Russian properties including the original headquarters of the Mission outside the ancient walls of Jerusalem became inaccessible to Russians living in communities located in the territory that after 1948 began to be administered by the Hashemite Kingdom of Trans-Jordan.

As I was growing up among those Russians, I learned a lot about village life in the different regions of imperial Russia, as well as city life throughout its European and Asiatic regions. I recognized differences in the various nuns' Russian speech depending on the regions they came from and was fascinated by their descriptions of Russia's vastness and its varied natural beauties. I had a hard time visualizing the never-ending forests or the tall grass in the steppe while living in the barren, rocky regions of Palestine. Their life revolved around the Christian calendar of feasts and saints' days, whose names some of the clergy, monks, and nuns bore and whose lives they tried to emulate. The day began and ended in church, which was the unifying focal point of monastic life.

A typical day started early as the Mission chief and an assistant went to officiate in one of the communities depending on the feast day particular to the place. After church services, a meal was usually shared in the community refectory where pilgrims and visitors were invited. Afterwards the various workshops were visited: one community specialized in the ancient art of egg-based painting of Byzantine icons; another community excelled in silver and gold thread embroidery used for Eastern Rite church vestments and also weaved yarn prayer ropes and made beeswax candles for use in church. Nuns from those communities were also teachers in the Bethany Girls School for Christian Arabs.

In the Holy Land, many days of the year were holy days as the faithful attempted to live in tune with the events in the Bible, particularly the New Testament. The year began with the nativity of Christ in the town of Bethlehem and continued in other holy places such as the Holy Sepulchre in Jerusalem on Easter. Hundreds of pilgrims of all nationalities and creeds filled the ancient temples constructed centuries ago. Such an accumulation of dress and color, language and race, such an elation of spirit and universal feeling of brotherhood could be seen on major Christian feasts perhaps nowhere else as in the Holy Land.

Bethany Boarding School

Archimandrite Antony (Sinkevich), chief of the Mission, arranged for my mother to work as a nurse in Bethany Boarding School for Christian Arab girls, where I was enrolled as a boarder. The school was run by two British women, who in the early 1930s came to Palestine on their way to India, where they planned to be Anglican missionaries. During their temporary stay, they rented a small house near Jerusalem in the biblical Garden of Gethsemane, which was on Russian property acquired in the nineteenth century and inhabited by a small religious community. Here they attended services in the Russian Orthodox Church of Mary Magdalene and met Sister Valentina (Tsvetkova), a Moscovite, appointed by Archbishop Anastasy (Gribanovsky) to organize monastic communities in Jerusalem and Bethany.

This multilingual Russian nun convinced the two Anglican missionaries to convert to Orthodoxy and be missionaries in Palestine instead of going to India as they had initially planned. Following her advice, they remained in Palestine and become Russian Orthodox nuns. Marion Robinson, who was

English, was renamed Mother Mary and assigned to be head of Gethsemane Community, and former Scottish Lady Ellir Isabella Sprott was renamed Mother Martha and became director of Bethany School. Both nuns became most dedicated to their difficult jobs. Between Arab and Russian cultures, they preserved their British decorum, an almost impossible task. We boarders learned to be devoted to them and knew that Mother Mary loved us but had unpredictable moments of mixed emotions, whereas Mother Martha was always the same: a strict but very fair leader of the school. She was tall and slim, wore small spectacles, and in Bethany School was frequently visited by the British High Commissioner.

On Christmas Day in the morning, we were usually taken by bus to Gethsemane for Christmas liturgy at the church, where we had communion and at breakfast the older girls led a small choir of the younger ones with good voices in singing Russian Christmas carols. Afterwards the officiating priest and several nuns with the novices and older girls went by bus to Bethlehem to worship at the Holy Manger. The rest of us younger boarders returned to Bethany School, where in the late afternoon on that day a division of English soldiers were invited to our school for a Christmas party. We sang Christmas carols all together in English and ate English Christmas pudding prepared at our school, and the soldiers played games with us and distributed gifts, toys, and boxes of candy, for which we children adored them.

Year by year, growing up as boarders we learned much about dealing with the necessities of daily life. This was in addition to getting an education that followed the curriculum of regular day schools. Here we were taught what we needed to know about housekeeping for life in general by rotating job assignments. Keeping cleanliness on the school grounds was the responsibility of older boarders under the direction of teachers on duty. Our life was strictly structured, always starting with morning prayer and ending with evening prayer.

After breakfast the older girls with the help of younger ones had duties to perform before the school day started. One of the most unpopular jobs was cleaning the toilets. Every day toilets were cleaned by an assigned team that rotated every two weeks. Water had to be brought in one bucket at a time and splashed on the squat-type toilets and the stone floor, which then was washed down with brooms. This had to be done within the time allotted for this duty, as girls would line up to use the toilets hurriedly before the bell rang for classes. It was as difficult for them to wait as for us workers to quickly get the place ready. Most of the other jobs were less unpleasant, and favorite jobs were cleaning the dorms, the dining rooms, and classrooms, but everyone got their share of the bad and the good jobs, and it was all done in spite of the fact that in those days there was no running water and no electricity where we were living.

In spring and summer on Saturdays everybody had to carry out their bedding to the school yard. Mattresses were laid on low stone fences in the hot sun. An Arab villager came to our bedrooms with a lit torch with which he burned out the bed bugs hiding in the corners of our metal beds. That took a few hours, after which we carried the mattresses back and made our beds. The big girls had to help the little ones—good training for future motherhood. The villagers on the outside usually did not have a bed bug problem. They slept on thin mattresses on stone floors, and every morning they neatly stacked their bedding for the day at one end of the room, as the same room often was used throughout the day for other functions such as a living room and dining room. In this regard it was good that they usually had little or no furniture and one big room for everybody in the family to sleep in. One Palestinian boy brought to America as a guest felt unloved in the beautiful guest room he was put in to sleep. He said he wanted to sleep in the room where everybody else slept.

I became accustomed to boarding school life and learned to enjoy playing only during recess. At other times we were doing useful things that I also learned to like. But, of course, there were days of punishment and misery, sometimes deserved, at other times seemingly unfair, and at such times I thought that only my mother was fair. I would wait for her to pick me up for holidays to spend together. Upon arriving home, at first I missed my friends and school life. Mother would shower me with hugs and kisses and would ask me if I liked school. The rule of going to bed on time did not apply here, so in the evenings Mother allowed me to stay up late so she could enjoy my company longer while I was home with her. But I was accustomed to discipline, study hall, dinner, prayer, bath time, and bedtime for everyone with complete silence. I would appear gloomy to Mother and she would ask me if I did not love her anymore. Such an emotional question would make me burst into tears, to my poor mother's consternation. Next day, however, I would get used to not being at school, and life would look all right again. At breakfast, I talked more than I ate and looked forward to all the things we would do together during my holidays.

In Bethany School at that time there were only two Russian boarders, Katia Romensky and myself; as a result, occasionally we were granted a few privileges such as special private lessons in Russian culture. As we were novices, when we went for the weekend to Gethsemane Convent with the other novices who were Arab, we got to sleep in the private room of Mother Tamara (née Grand Duchess Tatiana Romanov), a relative of the Russian imperial family. She would tell us about her family life in Russia when she lived there with her parents and brothers and sisters. They were all grand princes and princesses who, except for herself and her younger sister, perished in the revolution. She read to us the famous poem her father, poet Konstantin Romanov, wrote, titled "The Gospel," and told us about their pious life in tsarist Russia. She was a soft-spoken person and treated us like family, often telling us that even though she might never see Russia again, we would surely one day return there to help restore it to its past glory.

At school our food was usually cooked by Arab cooks and was generally made of locally grown or produced ingredients such as olives, feta cheese with bread similar to pita bread, green *za'atar* (thyme) powder with sesame seeds eaten with bread dipped in olive oil, and dates and other dried fruit for breakfast. On special occasions, for dinner we were served lamb and rice, and our favorite dinners were zucchini or eggplant stuffed with rice and meat called *mahshi* or rice and meat wrapped in grape leaves, called *waraq dawali*. Our English superiors thought we should sometimes have an English breakfast such as porridge. Regardless of nationality most of the boarders detested porridge, and often there were tears shed over a bowl of porridge at the younger girls' tables, but we had to learn to like it or go hungry. Something English we did like to eat during Christmas holidays was the famous special Christmas pudding, which some of us helped make ahead of time in the school kitchen. Mother Martha took a few girls at a time to the kitchen, where we got to help mix the ingredients in a huge container several days before Christmas, when it was finally ready to eat.

Sometimes Mother Mary with her Russian assistant Mother Barbara took Katia and me to the new sector of Jerusalem for us to learn to interact with European families. We visited British families who often resided in the King David Hotel when their stay in Palestine was temporary. They served in the British army, or taught in schools like St George's English school for boys near the American Colony in Jerusalem. Other British citizens worked in government buildings or on archaeological projects bringing their families with them to Palestine. We enjoyed those special privilege trips and learned from them about the lifestyle of the British ruling class and their cultural behavior.

When there were holidays from school and I would accompany my mother on a shopping trip in Jerusalem, she always wore the yellow and black striped ribbon of the St George's Medal on her Red Cross nurse's uniform,

which she had resumed wearing when we lived in Palestine. British officers often saluted her upon noticing the ribbon on her uniform because they
knew its significance. Once when Mother and I were shopping at the British
grocery in the new sector of Jerusalem, an elderly British officer gallantly
saluted her. He then said, "Allow me to present you with a box of chocolates," and he handed her a box of "Black Magic." This was considered to be
the best quality chocolate at that time. Inside the black box beside chocolates
in fancy wrapping there was a silver teaspoon and a cake fork, which Mother
later gave me and which I still treasure.

It would be inaccurate to dwell only on the positive memories of my
childhood. There were times of fear and want when adults around us and
our teachers spoke of the dangers of war. It was during the World War II
years that we heard much talk about the Germans and enemy attacks. They
said that the war may reach Egypt, and if that happened, there would be air
raids on Palestine. Our British Mandate government issued various safety
regulations, one of which was the "blackout" rule at night. This meant our
windows had to appear black on the outside in case of an air raid by the
enemy. Thick black curtains were hung on all the windows and lights were
turned off earlier than before, but as we were living in just a small unimpor-
tant Arab village, we wondered why anyone would want to bomb our school.

We were far from the raging war in Europe, yet we knew that in Egypt
stood divisions of South African and Australian troops, whom we saw sometimes visiting Jerusalem in small groups and recognized them by their differing uniforms. In general there was much tension in the air at that time.
However, we were reminded that we lived in the Holy Land, that according
to the Gospel, two thousand years ago Jesus Christ spent time at the home of
Lazarus, and his two sisters, Mary and Martha. According to tradition, the
Arab village of Azarye that surrounded Bethany School was the site of Lazarus's home, which is why Mother pronounced the village name as "Lazarye."
We accepted this as historical fact, as well as that before He was betrayed and
put to death on the cross, Christ raised Lazarus from death, saying he was not
dead but asleep, and that it happened here in Azarye.

We children lived through the commemoration of those events one week
before Pascha (Hebrew *Pesach*) or Easter, the feast of Christ's own resurrection, whereas the Saturday of Lazarus's resurrection was our school's feast
day. This was because we had on our school grounds an ancient rectangular
rock with an old Greek inscription on it that said "Here sat Christ on his way
to Jerusalem." Over this rock, Russian missionaries built a tiny white chapel
open to us children for prayer. We were told that perhaps here stood the

home of Mary, Martha, and Lazarus. As if by coincidence these were also the names of the two British missionary nuns who ran our school with spiritual guidance given by an Orthodox monk priest, Father Lazarus (Moore), also English. Two life-size colorful murals in the school's dining room portrayed two events: Christ visiting Mary and Martha and Christ resurrecting Lazarus. These paintings had details reminiscent of local village life. The house in the background looked like the stone village houses around us. The boy crossing the yard with a pitcher of water, the chickens, and the grapevines as well as clothes worn by those portrayed were so much like what we saw around us worn by the Arab villagers that it all made those bygone days very real to us.

On our school feast day, we were transported to that long ago time even more vividly when we walked in procession through the village on our way to Lazarus's tomb hewn in a rock at the side of a hill outside the village. There we descended the steep narrow steps into the tomb, a few of us at a time, our way lit only with the candles in our hands. We experienced both fear and excited anticipation in this transition place to the unknown life beyond the grave, which, of course, we somewhat misunderstood. This was here and now, a mysterious adventure we looked forward to, and a special event in our regimented school life.

On our return to the school grounds, a vegetarian dinner awaited guests along with our parents and teachers and then us children. Food was something we greatly cherished at that time of frequent hunger. The war created food shortages; the poverty of the region and of the Mission aggravated the situation. Now before Pascha there was Lent, which further sharpened our hunger pangs. Most meals consisted of cooked vegetables and fruit with hardy dark bread baked in the boarding school's own bakery. The older girls helped bake it, cut it, served it, and used it to barter with each other between meals. They often bribed the younger girls with a heel of bread produced from their pockets when help was needed to do chores around the school. Such a small piece of bread could be a precious commodity during the long boarding school day with occasionally a few dry dates or figs for a snack between meals.

Thursday evening before Easter, novices and other older girls would be on their way to the other side of the Mount of Olives, the one facing Jerusalem, to the Garden of Gethsemane Convent. After the Russian Revolution, this convent became the resting place of the body of Empress Alexandra's sister, the martyred Grand Duchess Elizabeth. On this day in the evening,

Father Antony, chief of the Mission, read twelve pertinent passages of the Gospels during the church service. These passages told us about the events leading to Christ's death and resurrection. It was a moving ceremony, after which, with lit candles in our hands, singing in Slavonic, we walked up the hill from Gethsemane toward the Old City of Jerusalem. A severe-looking Muslim Arab gatekeeper, with an immense iron key in his hands, unlocked the ancient gate that was already locked for the night and let us inside old Jerusalem. It was surrounded by an ancient wall, which had witnessed many wars whenever possession of this city changed hands.

As we entered the narrow medieval streets, our chanting resonated against the massive two-story stone walls of the tightly packed old buildings. In the windows up above the streets of the Via Dolorosa, also known as the Way of the Cross, we could see faces of Arab Muslim onlookers. They were used to this yearly devotion of Russian Christians and looked forward to this diversion. Three powerful faiths occupied this city, each with its own mysterious ceremonies, as witnessed during ordinary funeral processions to three different cemeteries located almost side by side outside the city walls, on the way up to the Mount of Olives. During daylight of the same week another Christian procession took place, which was the reenactment of Christ's Way of the Cross by various groups of pilgrims from Christian countries. They carried a heavy wooden cross, the kind, they believed, Christ carried on the same path to Golgotha, an elevated place where He was crucified.

Outside the city walls, beyond the Mosque of Omar plaza, Muslims bought and sold live sheep in preparation for the fast of Ramadan. There was no open conflict yet between the Arabs and the Jews while they lived apart, each in his own customary area in the Old City of Jerusalem and its outskirts, so life was relatively peaceful. With the arrival of more and more enterprising European Jews to Palestine, there started to be more and more trouble in different areas of the country. In our location the reason for unrest was the weekly passing of Jewish truck convoys through Azarye, the Arab Bethany village. Our school faced the road to Jericho, where those trucks were passing on their way to the Dead Sea to pick up loads of salt. Bethany School was surrounded by the village and got the brunt of the cross fire between the two groups. The Arab villagers considered the Jews to be trespassing on their land. This usually happened very early in the morning, when all the boarders were still asleep. The teacher on duty would rush into our dorm and order everybody quickly to get under our beds and lie there until the cross fire stopped. Around 6:00 p.m. those same trucks would be returning past our school, their trucks loaded with bags of salt. The cross fire would start again, but at that time we were usually in our cave chapel at evening prayer. We stayed at prayer with our teachers sheltered by the cave as long as it was necessary.

My mother was the school nurse when I was a boarder and was also the Bethany village nurse or healer, *al tabiba,* as the villagers called her in Arabic. British funds as well as the personal assistance of Abbess Mary (Robinson) maintained the clinic for the local Palestinian villagers, and Bedouin tribes. The latter spread their black goatskin tents in the distance as they moved around grazing their sheep and goats on the rocky hills surrounding my school. Mother received the ill and later on the wounded in a two-room clinic, where she administered medicine, bandaged wounds, and gave shots and immunizations. On occasion when school was out, including summer vacations, I accompanied Mother to the clinic. The place was full of flies and screaming babies in their mothers' arms.

One particular day stuck in my memory when a tall, skinny Bedouin brought his camel to be treated at the clinic. On the camel's forehead near its right eye was a boil, which mother had lanced a week earlier. Now the camel was sitting beside the entrance to the clinic, where his owner tied his head to the railing of the porch so Mother could reach the painful wound. The camel was quiet, but every time she gently reached with pincers into the wound to remove the already forming maggots there, the camel emitted a terrifying scream that made me shudder. Yet Mother continued to work and eventually healed the camel. In the same manner she cared for the villagers and their offspring. Patients with sundry problems came hoping to get help. They often had a skin problem or internal pain that would not go away, or they had beginning trachoma in their eyes, a particularly feared eye disease that led to blindness. Day in and day out they came to Mother always hoping to get better, and she encouraged them, never allowing anyone to give up on life. For this, everyone in the village knew and loved her.

After the end of the British Mandate, Mother's work at the Bethany village clinic ended, and she began to work as night nurse at the Augusta Victoria Hospital near the Hadassah Hebrew Medical School on the road to Jerusalem. During the day she cared for the elderly nuns and monks in and around Jerusalem, who were Greek, Russian, and Romanian. She was given a room in the Mount of Olives Convent, which became my home as well. Here I spent summer vacations from school in our one room on the second floor of the guest house. It had a beautiful view of the church, the belfry, and the wide, unpaved walk leading to the church, which was surrounded by tall fir trees full of singing birds.

Back in Bethany School the curriculum stressed spiritual education. Besides morning and evening prayers, there were daily religious studies classes as well as attendance at Sunday and feast day church services at Gethsemane Convent. Our general education besides three languages included mathematics, world history, and geography as well as some music and art. In spring and summer the sun was up at 5:00 a.m. and continued shining full blast until 6:00 p.m., giving us no mercy from the heat. The large cave in the school yard, which was converted into a chapel for daily morning and evening prayer, housed an icon of the Mother of God given to the school by the Orthodox Bishop Elias of Aleppo, Syria, whose niece attended our school. This was our favorite icon in front of which the older girls read the daily prayers, and here was the place, where in the heat of summer, we were given pleasant relief from the extreme heat outside and a shelter from stray bullets during the Arab–Israeli conflict.

When I was about thirteen years old, after the church service in Gethsemane on the feast of the Epiphany commemorating Christ's baptism, our school went by bus on a trip to the River Jordan. When we arrived there, after the appropriate prayers we put on long white gowns in which, according to custom, Orthodox Christians immerse themselves in the river three times commemorating the Trinity. Most of us girls were never taught to swim and knew little about the dangers of a fast-moving river. Five of us older girls merrily clasped each other's hands making a semicircle and together walked into the river. We were trying to immerse ourselves in the water when two girls who reached the center of the river suddenly slipped and their hands let go of us who were nearer the shore.

The current was stronger in the center, and they screamed, being unable to hold themselves up above the water. I don't remember what we shouted in their direction, but I saw their heads bobbing a couple of times, until the current carried them away, leaving only circles in the water, which soon disappeared. At that time the river was high, not as today when it is overexploited by modern enterprises. We quickly climbed on shore and ran to the teachers explaining what happened. At first they thought we were playfully joking, but soon realized the tragic truth of the fact that two of the schoolgirls drowned. There was a frantic search down the shores of the river until dusk, but it was to no avail. Only in a day or two did the bodies of our friends surface on the shore of the Dead Sea into which the River Jordan flows. After this incident for a long time the whole school grieved together with the parents of the girls. It was especially hard on us, the classmates of the drowned girls. We felt it was somewhat unfair that they drowned and we did not. The teachers explained that this was God's will and that we will all meet again in God's kingdom of heaven and will then understand the reason for it. But we continued to talk about it during recess and compared it to other disasters, the reasons for which we thought we could never understand.

Father Lazarus (Moore): Spiritual Father and Friend

Father Lazarus (Moore) was our spiritual guide and at one time religious studies instructor at Bethany School. He was one of those rare Englishmen in Palestine who mastered the Russian language. During his life in the Holy Land as well as in other countries in which he later lived, he translated spiritual books from Russian into English. My mother often helped Father Lazarus with his translations by obtaining the necessary materials for his projects. I remember the two of them discussing passages from volumes written by Bishop Ignatius (Brianchaninov), who lived in nineteenth-century Russia. Those spiritual books were highly regarded in prerevolutionary Russia, and Mother tried hard to obtain them for him, which was not easy as they were out of print and banned in the atheistic Soviet Union. Mother's hope rested on a Russian monastery on Mount Athos in Greece, from where she finally was able to get them.

Father Lazarus was overjoyed and spent every spare moment on translating. They enjoyed a certain kinship of souls as they worked together and discussed nuances of how best to express Russian words in English. It was not always easy for him to find the right words in available lexicons, and Mother's well-read literary background would come in handy with selecting appropriate terms fitting various parts of the English translation. As he was born in 1903, the same year as my father, and was often asked by Mother to pray for my father's health and safety, Father Lazarus played a big role in my upbringing. He helped my mother with his spiritual advice when needed, and helped me with my growing-up problems as only a father could. Not having a father or older brother in a country where the culture was male dominated was difficult for me, and he became my spiritual father, remaining as such many years into my adult life. He continued to guide me with his wonderful letters, where I felt he understood my needs and therefore was able to give me spiritual strength and a positive outlook on life. Even when it became necessary for him to leave Jerusalem, his letters continued to guide me. The following is an example of our correspondence:

Illustrations - Chapter 1

1.1 Anya and her mother, Maria Alexandrovna Berezina, in Belgrade, 1937.

1.2 Anya Berezina Derrick in 1937.

1.3 Anya's father, Sergius Dubrova, in 1920 as a cadet in the Military Academy–Crimea Corps.

1.4 Anya's paternal grandmother, Anna von Kazenkanph.

1.5 Anya's grandfather, Major General Nikolai N. Dubrova, who died at the hands of Bolshevik Revolutionaries.

1.6 Anya's mother and father met through involvement with this choir photographed in 1928. Her mother is in the second row on the far left.

1.7 General Vrangel in Yugoslavia, 1922.

1.9 Anya's father circa 1942.

1.8 The White Army medical staff of the Red Cross in 1922. Anya's mother is in the middle.

1.10 Anya's maternal grandmother, Anna, in Moscow. She died during the Siege of Leningrad.

1.11 The gravestone of Anya's father in the Russian military cemetery in Vienna.

1.12 Peter II Karadordevic circa 1946. He was the heir to the throne of King Alexander of Yugoslavia.

1.13 Queen Maria of Yugoslavia arrives at the Russian Church.

Illustrations - Chapter 2

2.1 Archimandrite Antony (Sinkevich), who was chief of the Russian Ecclesiastical Mission in Jerusalem for seventeen years.

2.2 The Church of St Mary Magdalen on the grounds of the Gethsemane Convent.

2.3 Mother Martha (Lady Ellir Isabella Sprott), director of Bethany School, with the British High Commissioner.

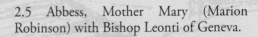

2.4 Mother Barbara (Sister Valentina (Tsvetkova)) with Archimandrite Anthony (Grabbe).

2.5 Abbess, Mother Mary (Marion Robinson) with Bishop Leonti of Geneva.

2.6 In front of Bethany School in 1946.

2.7 Ekaterina Borisovna, the head mistress of Bethany School, with her husband Georgi Alexandrovich Aleéff, a former White Army officer and artist.

2.8 Anya (on the right) with fellow Russian boarder Katia Romensky.

2.9 Mother Elizabeth, a teacher at Bethany School and later abbess of the Russian Gornia Convent.

2.10 Anya (on the left) with Nastya, a Russian friend, on vacation by the Sea of Galilee.

2.11 Sister Olga (Mechnikov), teacher of Russian language and Church Slavonic, with novices.

REPORT

BETHANY SCHOOL OF ST. MARY AND ST. NICOLAS

Report for term ending **oh: 29ᵗʰ December** 1944.

Name : **Annia Berezina**   Class: **R. IV** Age: **14** Average age of Class: **12.3**

SUBJECTS	GRADES Term.	REMARKS
Religion		
Holy Scripture		Отлично.
Liturgics	H	Большое усердіе, вниманіе къ предмету
Church History		С. Гемянса.
Catechism		
Apologetics		
Methodies		
ARABIC Grammar		
„ Syntax		
„ Literature		
ENGLISH Grammar		V. Good. C.B.
„ Literature	B	V. Good C.B.
RUSSIAN Grammar		
„ Literat. & Comp.	A	Очень хорошо
French	C	Travaille très consciencieusement et fait des progrès. C. Aleff
Arithmetic	A	Very good and shows lively interest A.R.
Algebra		
Geometry		
History	A	Has worked well & is interested M Martha
Geography	A	Очень хорошо
Domestic Science		
Botany	H	Прекрасно
General Science		
Hygiene		
Drill & Games	B	good
~~Music~~		
Class Mistress		Поведеніе было бы отличнымъ если бы самолюбіе не мѣшало ой.
Head Mistress		Tries hard in everything C. Aleff
Superior		Very serious, Tajgi. A.M.

2.12 Anya's 1944 report card from Bethany School.

2.13 Anya with her mother who was a nurse at Bethany school, 1939.

London

12/25 June 1950

Dear Anya,

Your blue letter came today, so now I owe you two, only the paper is blue; in spirit it is much less blue than the first one! I'll try to answer the first one first. I have just prayed about it, and this is the message for you. Never feel that you are at the mercy of the elements, or the circumstances, or even of your moods or passions. You are in your Father's hands, and His care and love for you is that of all fathers and mothers multiplied by infinity. He says, "Be still and know that I am your God." At any moment we only have to be still enough to turn our attention to Him and He begins to speak peace, confidence, trust, faith, hope, joy. When you are torn by conflicting desires, remember that we cannot possibly save ourselves, but Jesus is standing at the door of your heart and knocking. He is waiting only for the tiniest invitation to come in and be King, and reign and rule, and make your soul a house of prayer. So invite Him, and then thank Him that He has come and is answering your prayers. You may not feel anything special, but you thank Him in faith out of obedience.

He will let you feel and see the results later. And this is His message. Soon a most wonderful opportunity is going to come to you, so that you will be able to live the happiest and holiest and highest kind of life. So live like a faithful slave who is expecting his master to come quite soon and make a wonderful new offer to him. Every evening THINK and THANK, review the day and think of all God has helped you to say and do and be, and thank Him from your heart. At the same time confess all the sins of the day and ask God to forgive you, not for any worthiness in you, but for the worthiness of Jesus Christ our only hope and Savior. In the morning thank God for your little resurrection to a new day and new life and new opportunities, and then say the prayer of the Optina Elders I sent you. Say it slowly as an offering of love, thinking how God is watching you and loving you.

Morning Prayer of the Optina Elders

O Lord, grant me to meet everything that this day may bring me with spiritual peace. Grant me to surrender myself gladly to Thy holy will. In every hour of this day lead me and support me. Teach me to accept whatever news I may receive in the course of the day with peace of mind and with the firm conviction that Thy holy will is in all things. In all my words and actions direct my thoughts, feelings and senses. In all unforeseen events grant me not to forget that everything is sent by Thee. Teach me to act frankly and wisely with everyone I meet that no one may be hurt or embittered. O Lord, give me the strength to bear the fatigue of the coming day and all that may happen in the course of the day. Guide my will and teach me to pray, to believe, to hope, to suffer, to forgive and to love.

Now I will explain the difference between human and divine love. Human love is a natural power planted in us by God; for He is the maker and lord of nature as well as of heaven. But divine love is so different from human love that we must understand the difference very clearly. Human love is not a gospel; it can and it does exist alongside sin: pride, selfishness, jealously. It seeks to possess the object of its love. It says: "I like this person (or thing) and want him (her or it) for myself. It requires no effort of the will for such love is natural. Animals have the same kind of love and for the same reason. But Divine love is the gospel of God for every creature. It is a spiritual gift that unites us with God. It requires a definite effort of the will to love in union with God. It is the life of love with God and one another, begun here, to be continued forever hereafter. Divine love does not show partiality; that is, it does not express itself toward some and not toward others. It is the same toward all. It seeks to give rather than to get, to help rather than be helped, to understand rather than to be understood, to love rather than to be loved. It is the greatest force in the world. In fact, love never fails.

I was overjoyed to read in your letter that came today that you are beginning to find what a wonder-working power love is, and how the more you give, the more you get; it comes back to you in waves of love and happiness. I am also delighted that you are trying to be "properly dressed" that is, to wear your smile! If you sometimes smile in the wrong place, that is a peccadillo.

Let me know what is needed for your last term at school if no one comes to the rescue. Never worry. God has made us in such a way that we can only bear the burden one day at a time. If we tried to carry the past and future, it breaks our back! I send Greetings to all.

Ever yours in Christ,
Archimandrite Lazarus

Life was becoming difficult in Jerusalem as troubles between the Arabs and the Jews increased and both sides seemed to disregard the British authorities. At that time Mother Elizabeth (Ampenoff), born and educated in St Petersburg, a teacher at Bethany School became abbess of the Russian

Gornia Convent in Ein Karem, an Arab village. Some Bethany School grad-
uates, upon completing their studies, joined her as novices in Gornia Convent. Father Lazarus at that time was appointed officiating priest there. Arab
novices in Russian convents felt vulnerable as their native villages became
targets of the ongoing conflict. It was hard for them at such a time to remain
totally detached from the world, and they needed more guidance and help
than before. Some of the novices were blood sisters, a year or two older than I
was, and we studied together at one time in Bethany. On weekends we were
taken to the Convent in Gethsemane for monastic training such as reading
psalms in Slavonic during church services and singing in the church choir.
We were expected to be good students, show leadership in the classrooms,
and volunteer to be teachers' helpers.

Two novices, whose family name was Janhu, were very good looking
with features resembling European young women, so one could easily wonder if their ancestors may have been part of the historic Crusaders. Their
two younger sisters got married, while their two brothers became business-
men. The younger brother had an opportunity to study in Germany, where
he married a German classmate and remained there. The older, Abdul-Nur
Khalil Janhu, who was born in Jerusalem, married a local Christian Arab
woman and remained in Jerusalem. Later he went into business for himself
and opened a grocery shop in Ramallah, a West Bank town. I met this family again many years later during my first visit back to the Holy Land with
my older son who was almost sixteen. We visited them at their large home,
which they managed to build in spite of the Israeli occupation. The house
had a territorial view, was well furnished, and one noticed archeological treasures displayed here and there.

As we sat with his wife for a cup of coffee, she praised my son's looks and
spoke about her oldest daughter as if this was a match-making event. She
told me that a young man for her daughter would have to be not only handsome, but also rich and well educated. Whether her wish materialized or
not I never found out, but several years after this visit, I read in the obituary
section of the *Jerusalem Post* the following: "Some 1,500 persons attended the
funeral of Abdul-Nur Khalil Janhu, the prominent Ramallah businessman,
who was slain by an unidentified gunman near his home last Wednesday.
The funeral cortege passed through the Old City of Jerusalem to the Christian cemetery on Mount Zion. There were no incidents." Aboud, as he was
called when he was growing up, was one of six children living in the Old City
of Jerusalem, raised by their widowed mother, Sit Lydia. She supported her
large family with her work as a very popular midwife and visiting nurse. She

worked among Christians and Muslims alike at a time when Arabs of both faiths often attended one another's weddings and funerals and visited each other's homes.

Holy Week and Pascha

On Saturday before Easter, Christians and some Muslims came to the ancient Church of the Holy Sepulchre in Jerusalem to receive the holy fire, believed to be miraculously sent by God on this day. They walked in a procession around the Kuvuklia,[1] a small chapel built over Christ's burial place, prayerfully calling out to God to show His benevolence by sending the holy fire. Sometimes this form of supplication lasted for a long time before the Greek patriarch, who entered the Kuvuklia earlier, would finally exit with the holy fire burning bundles of thirty-three candles in each of his hands, to match Christ's age at the time of His crucifixion. The patriarch would then pass it on to the surrounding people, clergy, monks, nuns, local inhabitants, and a multitude of pilgrims from all corners of the world. Everybody present carried lanterns or candles in their hands and reached out to light them with the holy fire from their neighbors as it was passed on from the patriarch. This was a moment of universal joy expressed by some with tears as they touched the fire with their bare hands, applying it to exposed parts of their bodies for a few seconds, without getting burned, a miraculous event, never to be forgotten.

The week after Palm Sunday, Jerusalem was full of Christian Arabs from Egypt, Syria, and Lebanon, all renting space in a home or monastery for the whole week. The Greek patriarchate was full of pilgrims from Greece, the Armenian patriarchate with Armenians, and the Ethiopian monastery next to the Russian Raskopky[2] was full of Abyssinians. Buildings for guests in the Russian convents were filled with Russian pilgrims from Eastern Europe and some Western countries. However, there were no Russians from the Soviet Union for what felt like a very long time. This was something my mother often shed tears about, and I would try to console her as I was growing up in Jerusalem. She was grieving about religious repression in Russia and that her relatives there were not allowed to celebrate Pascha the way we could in Jerusalem. During this whole week, people prayed at the holy places, where there were daily long services culminating with the greatest one of all—the midnight service on the day of Christ's resurrection.

On the feast of the ascension, Christians as well as Muslims visited the small shrine on the Mount of Olives built over the spot from which it was believed Christ rose to heaven. Historically at one time this was a Christian shrine; however, during the Ottoman Empire it became Muslim but remained open to everyone. It was customary on that feast day for neighboring Arab villagers and their families to go to the Mount of Olives Russian Convent, where the gates were open wide that day, and people could visit the church and then picnic under the olive trees for the rest of the day. I remember hearing that at one time Muslims were believed to be just another Christian sect, who considered Christ to be one of God's prophets. Even prostration during prayers in the mosques some believed to have been taken from what is still practiced by Orthodox Christians, especially during Lent.

Favorite Teachers

My mother was my first Russian language teacher. She not only was the first to talk to me in Russian, but also from early childhood she read aloud to me. As I was growing up without a radio or television, books played a big role in the formation of my reasoning, and, before going to school, I learned a lot from Mother. Even after my school years started, her influence on me continued. During summer vacations spent with her, while I knitted or embroidered, she read aloud to me. I think she had a special talent for reading aloud to listeners. She was a favorite reader in church where she was occasionally asked to read the Psalms in Old Slavonic. This language was difficult to understand, but she seemed to have an innate quality of diction in her speech that helped the listener to catch every word. Through the years during summer vacations with Mother, we read and experienced together some of the best-written Russian short stories and novels. This was especially true of Ivan Turgenev's and Leo Tolstoy's fascinating works. Feodor Dostoyevsky was left for me to tackle later in my adult life.

My mother's best friend and my favorite nun was Mother Antonia. Her marriage early in life to a young general soon ended when he lost his life in battle. After this tragedy, she decided to dedicate her life to God. Fleeing Russia through Finland she reached Yugoslavia, where she entered the Khopovo Convent and became a nun. Later from here she was sent to Palestine to head the Mount of Olives Russian Convent. I was too young to understand her high position; all I knew was that Mother was her nurse. When she was not well we often visited her together in her always neat and tidy cell, as nuns' and monks' rooms were expected to be. The icon corner always had a *lampada* votive light burning. She noticed if my hair was tidy and my braids were nicely braided, and for this she complimented me, as I sat quietly while she and mother discussed her medical condition.

One day she called me into her room through the open window of her cell, as I was passing by absentmindedly munching an apple. When I entered she said it was not ladylike to eat while walking: "You should first sit down on a bench in the garden and then calmly eat. This is healthier for you and looks better." This made me start to watch what I did, especially when I walked on the convent grounds or any other place. With time I realized how concerned she was about my upbringing, and I watched and admired how she did things with grace and self-assurance and I started to copy her. She gave me little gifts for my name days that she made herself, little booklets with examples of ideal behavior handwritten in them, surrounded by attractive designs that she drew. Often she would ask Mother to come over and help her open a parcel from abroad filled with gifts from some friend in a faraway country. She would end up sharing them with us: useful things like bars of soap or pretty towels or simply chocolate bars. All this left me with a good feeling toward her, a much older person who was not even a relative. However, as I grew up it was her wisdom that truly enlightened me, and continued to do so in her letters to me after my mother's death.

Among my favorite teachers at Bethany School was Sister Olga (Mechnikov), who taught Russian language and, to the novices, Church Slavonic for reading aloud during church services. Good students were encouraged to do so on special occasions. Sister Olga was a niece of the famous Russian scientist-biologist Mechnikov who together with Pasteur, also a scientist in Paris, France, did research and discovered bacteria and what makes milk turn into yogurt. Sister Olga loved us children and spent a lot of free time between classes with us. She showed us how to make pretty decorations for the Christmas tree, and how to make useful items to give as gifts on birthdays and name days. She was also the artistic director of plays we sometimes performed in Russian, which required special costumes and stage sets.

Mother was her nurse when old age set in and Sister Olga started to suffer from heart problems. I watched Mother place leeches on her neck. They held on to the skin so tightly it was difficult to take them off when enough blood was withdrawn. At that time, this method of relief from high blood pressure was standard in this part of the world. Once when we traveled together along the winding road to Jericho, Sister Olga panicked when through the bus window she looked down the deep ravine on the side of the narrow road and her heart started racing. She was probably already suffering from atrial fibrillation and Mother tried to help her with smelling salts, but she was so agitated that the kind bus driver had to stop the bus several times. That same year the doctor suggested Sister Olga spend Christmas vacation in the hospital; she thanked him for his concern but refused. She said she wanted to spend Christmas Eve in Bethany School with the orphaned boarders who had no home to go to. So that Christmas night she spent with the girls in Bethany School and later that night died peacefully in her sleep.

Miss Anna Vasilievna Kutuzov was another favorite teacher when I was older. She taught us math and impressed me with her beautiful handwriting and mellow personality. I was not one of the brightest in class when it came to solving mathematical problems, but I had the kindest teacher one could wish for. With great patience she would explain a rule that we were supposed to have understood and memorized. However, if the class for some reason became noisy and inattentive, she would turn her back to us and stand quietly praying while facing the bare wall until we became quiet. Miss Kutuzov, as we addressed her, was related to the famous Russian military leader Field Marshall Mikhail Kutuzov, thanks to whom Napoleon was defeated during the 1812 invasion of Russia and capture of Moscow by French troops. Students enjoyed listening to her when she brought up stories of incidents from her own school days in Russia. Later she became a nun with the name of Mother Arsenia and was Abbess Mary's assistant in Gethsemane Convent. On one of my trips to Russia in the late 1990s, I visited Kazansky Sobor (Kazan Cathedral) near Nevsky Prospect in St Petersburg, which was built in memory of Russia's victory under Field Marshall Kutuzov's leadership. In front of the Kazan Cathedral stands a large statue of Kutuzov. It is in a very picturesque area of the city not far from the Hermitage and across the canal from the beautiful church named the "Church of Our Savior on Spilled Blood."

Ekaterina Borisovna Aleéff, the head mistress of the school, taught Russian and French literature in the last two classes of my days at Bethany School. From her I acquired my Russian national awareness, as she often spoke of our great and noble Russian origin. She reminded us of our duty to study the Russian language and culture in preparation for our future return to Russia. Someday, she would say, Russia will rise again like the "phoenix from the ashes." She strongly believed in the fall of communism and the end of our exile. She wrote poetry on this subject both in Russian and in French, which was most impressive to her students. She sounded quite dramatic as she read aloud to the class some great piece of poetry. I never forgot her rendition in French of the famous French writer Victor Hugo's poem "The Cracked Vase." "Do not touch the cracked vase" was the impassioned refrain, meaning be gentle to people with a broken heart, she explained, saying this was the intended message of the poem. Her husband, former Russian White Army colonel Georgi Alexandrovich Aleéff, was our art teacher. He gave us watercolor painting lessons, the products of which still hang on the walls of my home. The exit from Russia of this refined couple occurred at about the same time as my parents' departure, except that their flight was to Turkey, from where they eventually immigrated to Palestine with their three infants.

All these wonderful old teachers were the remains of the Russian intelligentsia who fled Russia after the revolution. Most were living somewhere in exile in the Balkan countries, in Europe, or in the Near East. One of our teachers in Bethany School was Miss Imsellam, a Christian Arab from Damascus, Syria, who in her childhood studied in a Russian mission school there and thus spoke good Russian. There were such schools for boys and girls in Syria and Palestine, built by missionaries from tsarist Russia for Christian Arabs. Miss Imsellam also lived at Bethany School, where she had a room on the first floor of our dorm building. She tended to have a particularly benevolent attitude toward the older students, although in general, she was fair with everyone. Before morning prayers and breakfast, she allowed the thirteen- to fifteen-year-old novices to come to her room for a tiny cup of black coffee. It was brewed in one of those small brass coffeepots one sees in Arab or former Ottoman Empire–occupied countries as in Serbia, Bulgaria, and Greece. The small pot was usually filled with water, brought to a boil, and a tablespoon of finely ground coffee was put in it. This foamed to a golden light-brown color on top and its aroma filled the air. They drank this coffee in a ceremonial way, in special small cups for Turkish coffee, which felt like a rite of passage into adulthood. These girls were teachers' helpers and were assigned special duties, so the morning coffee gave them extra energy and worked as a unifying element between teacher and student.

Another special privilege for older girls was a weeklong absence from school when we were allowed to accompany Sister Elena (a Palestinian) to make jam in her native village, Bait Jalah. In its vicinity there were hillsides covered with vineyards, which belonged to her parents' large family. I believe it was in early fall that they would allow grapes to be collected for making jam for use by Bethany School. When we arrived there, we put together a small shed in which to sleep and rest from the sun at midday. Early in the mornings, two of us walked down the hill from where we were making the jam to the opposite hill. We were leading a donkey with large, empty baskets attached to his sides and descended to the village square at the bottom of the hill with various shops and a noisy coffeehouse. Here the radio blared the news and Arab music played, making it at our age the interesting part of the walk. We then would start to climb up the vineyard hill, picking and tasting the grapes as we went, and gathering them into the baskets on the donkey's back. Upon our return to our outdoor jam-making area, we washed the grapes with well water from a nearby deep well, pulling the water out with a bucket attached to a long rope. A round pit was formed with large stones for a fire on which we placed a huge metal cauldron. Then we filled it with washed grapes and some sugar and in turns, day and night, continuously mixed the jam with a large wooden paddle, removing seeds that came to the top. We continued to add grapes to the cauldron, where they slowly cooked, turning eventually into jam. We spent days that way in the hot sun, and then in the evenings, which seemed to suddenly turn very dark and pitch black before bedtime, we sat and talked around the boiling cauldron with the only light coming from the fire below and the millions of stars in the sky above. We always ended the day with a prayer just as we started it at sunrise that same morning.

Pleasant memories of school life also included the season of gathering olives at the Mount of Olives Convent. Some of the olives we picked were turned into olive oil for use throughout the year in the convents and in Bethany School. I remember long spring walks that our teachers would lead, one class at a time, over the rocky hills of Palestine. Everything that managed to grow between the endless rocks turned green and colorful for a very brief time, before the hot sun burned it or the grazing sheep and goats ate it. We collected dandelion greens for salad that was served the same evening for supper and was quite tasty with lemon juice and olive oil. Later in life when I became a married woman and returned to this area with my jokester husband, he would say, "Look at the sheep, they graze on rocks—there is nothing else on those hills!" Yet we children, like the sheep and goats, knew how to find the smallest, daintiest clusters of edible weeds growing among the rocks, some of which, like *za'atar*, had a pungent smell that drew us toward them on those country walks in Palestine.

At the Mount of Olives Convent, I often accompanied Mother on her rounds to see ailing elderly nuns who needed medicines administered, temperatures taken, or dressings changed. I looked on with interest at the work Mother did, and I loved her and her patients. This was a much bigger place than the boarding school in Bethany. It was purchased by the Russian Mission during Turkish rule in Palestine. The considerably large compound originally was planned to be a monastery for more than two hundred monks. But there were many more women than men willing to join the monastic way of life, and so it became a convent.

Besides the buildings where the nuns lived, there was a house for the abbess where she hosted monastery guests. It had its own reception room, dining room, kitchen, and bedroom. Farther away there was the house for the clergy and special guests. It was built over a sizable museum of artifacts found on the grounds during construction periods. The windows opened to a view of olive groves as well as pine and fir woods that had grown from saplings brought from Russia in the late 1850s. These woods provided a cool place for children to play in the fresh air. The nuns who worked in the kitchen claimed that at a certain time of the year they were able to collect enough mushrooms in the woods for the community dinner soups! Beyond the convent walls, the rocky desert stretched out into the distance.

There was a building used as an infirmary, a small library building, and a large refectory. A chapel with an ancient mosaic floor contained an indentation at the place where St John the Baptist's severed head was found. In the center of all this stood the large Byzantine-style church and the tall belfry, while near the entry gate to the property was a large two-story guest house, where Mother had a room that I called home.

When I was a little girl, one of my favorite buildings was the *prosphora* bakery; whenever I passed by, the scent of the *prosphora* baking would entice me to knock at the door and go in to watch. The kind sisters would give me a freshly baked *prosphoron* before sending me on my way.

When I became a teenager, the belfry became my favorite place; it was sixty-four meters high and had three floors with bells of all sizes brought from old Russia. I was allowed to watch the art of ringing bells until I acquired the skill needed to be able to help ring the bells for church services. To escape from all distractions during exam periods, I climbed what seemed an innumerable number of steps to the very top floor, the highest point in the territory, and studied there for hours at a time in total seclusion and with a fantastic view of Jerusalem.

There were two cemeteries at the convent. The upper one, situated next to the belfry and the church, was where clergy, abbesses, and outstanding donors were buried. In the lower cemetery were buried the rest of the sisters including Orthodox lay helpers of the convent such as the convent nurse. During my visits home from boarding school in Bethany, Mother and I liked to sit on a bench in the lower cemetery and admire the Dead Sea far away in the distance. We thought of the sisters and the men and women we knew at one time who were now buried here. Among them was a Russian soldier who was stationed in Egypt during World War II, where he became ill with a rare ailment and was brought to Augusta Victoria Hospital for special care, but soon died and was brought here to be buried on Russian soil. I remember mother saying that when she dies, she would like to be buried next to the

Russian soldier as it reminded her of her youthful days as a Red Cross nurse for wounded soldiers.

In addition to all these places, there were other small buildings spread around the compound. These were built by the private funds of Russian women who were allowed to live in them on convent grounds because of the wartime situation that had made it impossible for them to return to where they came from or legally live elsewhere than on Russian property. These women sometimes worked outside the convent in the homes of British officials or in hospitals as aides, something that was done with the superior's permission as their abodes would eventually be left to the convent. As I was growing up, I observed that they dressed modestly but not in a nun's habit, and their living style seemed more independent; so was the interior decor of their rooms.

One of these elderly women, I was told by the nuns, was once a beautiful young lady who arrived on a ship from Eastern Europe and was unable ever to return home. Because her blond curls were always slipping out from under the kerchief on her head, they called her Duniasha Lakhmataya, meaning "the tousled hair Dunia." The ending *-sha* was added to her name as an endearment, thus, "dear Dunia with the tousled hair." Like everyone else, she was assigned a duty in the convent that over the years probably changed many times. At the time that I remember her, it was her duty to collect food waste in a bucket and spread it on the soil in the kitchen garden as a fertilizer. She lived in one of those small buildings near the woods, actually shared her living quarters with her chickens. It looked and smelled like a chicken coop with roosting places and cubicles for hens to lay eggs. Duniasha was considered a little odd, but was gentle and kind, often smiled, and I was told that she was perhaps a *yurodivaya* or fool for Christ. This was a form of voluntary virtuous living in Old Russia, a form of self-sacrifice. Often as I wandered around this large walled religious community, where life was so different from the Arab village surrounding it on the outside, I imagined myself in a Russian village with a monastery in it. Later in life when I finally got to see Russia with my own eyes, I found out that my imagination had not led me too far from reality.

I remembered one snowy winter, a rare occurrence in Palestine, when I suffered from an abscessed front tooth. My face became swollen, a disaster, I thought at age fourteen. I cried from the aching for a couple of days and nights. Mother said I needed medical help, which she, although a nurse, was unable to give me. I needed to have my infected tooth pulled out, she said, but what could we do about it in this deep snow? The buses to Jerusalem were not running, and there was, of course, no other transportation, not even a donkey to ride, whose owner would not risk letting it out in such a snow-storm. On the way to Jerusalem from the Mount of Olives Russian Convent and beyond the Augusta Victoria Hospital, on what was called Mount Sco-pus, there was a Jewish Hadassah hospital and a university dental school. Mother bundled herself with all the clothes she owned and told me to do the same and said that with God's help we would make it on foot to the hospital. Thus we trudged through the snow in shoes as light as sneakers, until we walked into what seemed the most important place for me at that moment in time.

Dr Mankovsky, one of the kindest doctors around, was born to parents who were Russian Jews, but married a Lutheran German wife he met in medical school in Berlin. He had two children, and sometimes during sum-mer vacations the family spent time living in the Russian convent on the Mount of Olives. Abbess Antonia reserved for them a nice big room on the second floor of the museum building with a view toward the Dead Sea. While on vacation with my mother, I often helped with the Mankovsky kids, whom the nuns enjoyed and even spoiled; after all, Dr Mankovsky was the convent's favorite doctor.

Fortunately Dr Mankovsky was on duty at the hospital that day when, teary eyed, my face looking crooked from the swelling, we walked into his office and asked for help. He quickly arranged for my tooth to be extracted as it was the only recourse left to relieve me of my pain and put a stop to the infection. The excruciating pain of extracting the tooth without an anesthetic passed so quickly that the several days' aching afterward was relatively bear-able, although perhaps today things would have been done differently. It was one of my front teeth, and I had to live a long time with a missing tooth. Only after living a while in America was the tooth finally replaced, and so I was freed from my self-consciousness about the gap in my front teeth.

Just as there were different kinds of people in Russia's vast territories, the sisters in this convent were all different and came from different back-grounds. There were even some nuns who were not Russian and spoke Romanian or Bessarabian or were Moldavian. The non-Russians were reputed to be very tidy and good cooks in the convent kitchen. Some older nuns lived with young novices, who as Arab orphans were brought to be raised in the convent. In a short time, they learned to speak good Russian and usually became quite attached to the nun raising them.

Abbess Antonia and her faithful assistant Mother Taissia were well educated and spoke several languages. They were once citizens of Russia's greatest cities and were from well-to-do families, but their rooms were simple monastic cells like those of the rest of the sisters. They did the necessary administrative work as well as dealing with the governments, be it the British Mandate or later the Kingdom of Trans-Jordan.

Christian Arab parents were eager to send their daughters to live and learn skills in the convent. Often girls became so attached to the nuns and the orderly life in the convent that they became nuns themselves. Abbess Antonia was a close friend of my mother and took great interest in my upbringing. I learned from her how to be organized, to always be polite, and to dress neatly. For my birthdays she would put together little booklets with colorful designs, and using calligraphy she wrote in them ideals for me to follow. She made the booklets small enough so that I was able to put them in my pocket for daily use, and whenever I looked at them, their words encouraged me to be good and hard working. I have kept these booklets to this day to remind me of the youthful zeal for virtue that Abbess Antonia tried to instill in me during my life in Jerusalem.

Her assistant Mother Taissia fled from Russia to Turkey with other intelligentsia as well as her sister's family, the Aleevs. From there she traveled to Yugoslavia, where she decided to enter the Khopovo Convent and where she met the future Abbess Antonia, whom she later followed to Palestine. Mother Taissia was an artist and icon painter. She painted the icon murals in the Mount of Olives church and taught young novices to paint. When she was in her early eighties, she fearlessly climbed up the wooden scaffolding and did most of the restoration work of the interior of the church. In the evenings, she worked by the light of a kerosene lamp in order to finish the work on time.

Besides French and German she spoke English and thus was able to manage the economic and business side of convent life and was official helper of the abbess. Mother Taissia became a good friend of my mother as they both were educated in similar Russian institutes of higher education and therefore had a lot in common. Mother Taissia liked to share with my mother the news she could read in English newspapers. Times were not peaceful and news tended to be depressing, so mother would try to stop her from reading aloud the bad news, saying, "I don't believe in newspapers, they are full of lies. I stopped reading them during the Russian Revolution." But to this Mother Taissia would simply respond that some of the news reminded her of the apocalyptic predictions in Revelation about the end of times for which we should be prepared. She remained a faithful friend of my mother's and was with her near the end of Mother's life.

At the Sea of Galilee

Mother and I sometimes spent summer vacations on the shores of the Sea of Galilee, also called Lake Tiberias. We stayed in a house with a big garden that belonged to the Russian Mission. At different times of the year its use was permitted for members of Russian Orthodox communities. The water in this lake was amazingly translucent. Before sunrise in the morning it looked grayish, at midday it was blue, and in the evening it became dark green. We swam daily in its waters and in the adjoining springs that formed shallow pools. On these waters Christ walked, and He preached on its shores. Close by was Magdala, where Mary Magdalene lived.

At night, we slept on the flat roof of a stone house in the open air under what seemed a low sky, full of bright stars at which we gazed while falling asleep. Once we had a Russian girl named Nastya (short for Anastasia) staying with us. She was also twelve years old like me and was spending the summer with us away from her home in Tel Aviv, where she lived with a Jewish father and two brothers. Her mother was a Russian Orthodox Christian and hoped her daughter would get at least a little bit of exposure to our faith while staying with us. I enjoyed Nastya's company and pretended she was my sister, which I always wished I had.

Father Antony and his much younger brother Misha, who was a teenager, sometimes spent a few days here with us. Misha mostly swam and teased us, but Father Antony conversed with Mother and us girls explaining spiritual concepts from the Gospel. To lighten the atmosphere, he amused us with simple mathematical puzzles, or tricks such as making us write and draw while looking not at our hands but in a mirror that he placed on the table in front of us. We quickly discovered how difficult this was, so we giggled and wiggled and tried and tried again, but our efforts produced nothing more than ridiculous scribbles.

This was during the British Mandate, so the borders between Palestine and what later became Israel were still open, and visits from both sides were possible. We would awake quite early in the morning, and as we watched the sun rise in the sky we could not help exclaiming: "Look, look at the sky, it is so beautiful!" A bright yellow sphere would slowly rise from behind the low mountains until its reflection was in the sea. From the distance we could hear the echo of the clicking typewriter of an English journalist, who did his writing early in the cool morning, while he sat in a small boat in the lake. The fresh morning breeze was pleasant, and we hurried to take a dip in a nearby spring that formed a warm pool of water that eventually ran into the lake. We rushed down the incline slipping on the stony path, not listening to Mother's warnings to be careful lest we fall down. First we'd say a short prayer, then my brave friend Nastya would be first to jump into the water.

She was my age, but much more assertive than I was. She swam and screamed with such abandon that Mother would call to us and try to slow us down. Mother often reminded us that this was where Christ Himself at one time walked on the waves and that the water was therefore holy and we should not be so loud. By the time we came out of the water the sun was already quite hot. With our wet towels around our shoulders we climbed back up the hill toward the house, where Mother was waiting for us in the shady garden with breakfast. From here looking down toward the Sea of Galilee, we could spot the white sails of fishermen's boats. The tropical heat and humidity rapidly intensified. We took quinine pills every day to prevent us from catching malaria.

Before lunch we went swimming again, while in the heat of the afternoon we rested indoors and Mother read something to us from Ivan Shmelev's book *Leto Gospodne* (*Year of the Lord*). It was full of colorful detailed descriptions of how the main holidays of the year were celebrated in Russian tradition. Only toward late afternoon could we go out to the surrounding garden filled with orange and lemon trees and a banana grove. Before bedtime we read evening prayers on the flat-top roof, where we spread our bedding for the night. The mosquitoes were less bloodthirsty here.

We watched the stars and listened to the noises of conflict in the distance as the times were not peaceful and occasional shooting far away could be heard. An intense search light sometimes pointed in our direction, and terrified dogs barked at it in the neighborhood. Once in a while we could hear the echoes of night fishermen's conversations in their boats on the lake. Mother told us that the housekeeper warned her to be on guard because the main road was quite close and there were both wild Bedouins and trigger-happy Zionists passing by. It was never totally safe on the road, she said, and we were protected by no one else but the "Heavenly Dwellers."

Gethsemane Convent and Royal Patrons

Gethsemane Russian Convent, located on the side of the Mount of Olives facing the Golden Gate of Jerusalem, also faces the Mosque of Omar, sometimes called the Dome of the Rock. In the Garden of Gethsemane, Christ spent with his disciples His last evening on the way to His crucifixion. Amid the fir and cypress trees planted by Russian missionaries before the revolution stands the church of St Mary Magdalene built during the reign of Tsar

Alexander III (1845–1894), in Muscovite style with five onion-shaped golden domes. Grand Duke Serge (1857–1905), uncle of Tsar Nicholas II, and his wife Grand Duchess Elizabeth presided at the consecration of the church in 1888 as representatives of the tsar. Following the assassination of Grand Duke Serge in 1905, the widowed Grand Duchess chose monasticism as a way of life and founded in Moscow a convent named after the Gospel sisters of Lazarus, Mary and Martha. Shortly after the Russian imperial family was martyred, the grand duchess and others with her were also martyred. Her remains were transferred later to the Holy Land and were entombed under the church of St Mary Magdalene in Gethsemane.

Various members of European royalty who were related to the Romanov family made occasional visits to Gethsemane. The first one that comes to mind is Prince Philip Mountbatten, future consort of Queen Elizabeth of England. His mother, a member of the Greek royal family, after becoming a widow came on an extended visit to Gethsemane Russian Convent so as to be close to the burial place of her relative, the Grand Duchess Elizabeth. Prince Peter, the eldest son of King Alexander of Yugoslavia, visited the royal grave site as he too was related. During his visit, Mother and I talked to him in Serbian, and he gave us his latest photograph, which I still keep. This was after communism engulfed his country, resulting in his exile to the United States, where he spent the rest of his life. At the time, Abbess Tamara, daughter of Grand Prince Konstantin Romanov, lived in the Holy Land, and she too was occasionally visited by European royalty.

During World War II, Emperor Haile Selassie of Abyssinia (Ethiopia) with his two daughters visited the Mount of Olives Russian Convent. The older daughter's name was Yorkuha, the younger was Elizabeth. One Sunday they attended the convent's long church service, after which my mother walked up to them and invited them for tea. Of course, I was delighted to meet the girls, one of whom was close to my age. Later both princesses were placed in Bethany School as boarders, and we shared a dorm. This was done for the safety of the girls because at that time their homeland was at war with Italy. Their regal family had an ancient residence in Jerusalem, above which at the entrance door there was a colorful mosaic of the "Lion of Judea," which was their national symbol.

The Ethiopian Coptic Church shared general characteristics of Eastern Orthodox churches. There were theological seminaries in the capital, Addis Ababa, and students would be sent to Alexandria or Greece for further studies in theology. Church services were conducted in Amharic, the dominant language of the Abyssinian people. They were also known as the Habesh tribes on the Arabian coast where they came from. According to their tradition, they were the descendants of a son of King Solomon and the queen of Sheba, who fled to Sheba with the Ark of the Covenant and other trophies. As early as 1890, imperial Russia sent a mission to Abyssinia and maintained a warm relationship ever after.

Portraits of royalty, whether they were Russian or British, hung on our walls in the monasteries as well as in Bethany School. I remember looking at these portraits of royal families and thinking about what our English superiors, Mothers Mary and Martha, told us about them in school. We knew that Princess Elizabeth, the older daughter of King George VI, who was a cousin of the late Russian tsar, someday would be queen of England. Later when I was grown up, the pending marriage of Prince Philip to Princess Elizabeth was announced, and the date was set and publicized across British domains, one of which was Palestine.

When it was announced that the royal wedding would be broadcast on the radio, Mother and I eagerly accepted an invitation by a Circassian family, living within walking distance of the Mount of Olives Convent, to come and listen with them on their radio to a broadcast of this wedding ceremony. This family was rather well to do, as two of their sons owned the local bus company, which serviced round-trips to Jerusalem in old buses they purchased while they were studying at a university in the United States.

The convent, of course, did not have a radio, and while our mothers were visiting with each other, the sister, the brothers, and I were enjoying the royal wedding on the radio. It was incredibly exciting listening to every word of the reporter's colorfully expressed descriptions of the marriage ceremony. Every word and inflection in the tone of the reporter brought to each one of us, in differing colors, an image of something more spectacular than we had ever seen. We sighed with wonder, laughed, and clapped our hands with joy as our imaginations ran off with us in different directions. It left even stronger and more colorful images on our minds than if we saw it all in reality or as we do today in virtual reality on television.

From the stone walls of Gethsemane Convent facing the Mosque of Omar in Jerusalem, we watched a yearly Christian procession. It started from Bait Faje at the bottom of the Mount of Olives along which the road to Jericho passed. Walking to Jerusalem in this procession, all in their distinctive uniforms, were students from various Christian schools, Boy Scouts, Catholic monks and nuns, as well as pilgrims from all over the world. In their hands they carried palm branches and chanted in Latin and Arabic "Hosanna!" as they relived Christ's own entry into Jerusalem before His crucifixion.

From the same wall at different times, we could watch ceremonial burials performed in the surrounding Muslim and Jewish cemeteries.

After Stalin allowed the reinstatement of a patriarch and the partial opening of churches in the Soviet Union, the Church of St Mary Magdalene at the Gethsemane Convent was visited by the new patriarch himself. He was surrounded by young KGB agents as they marched together into the church. Nobody as much as even turned their heads in the patriarch's direction; we were given strict instructions by the convent abbess to totally ignore this visit, as this was Stalin's appointee. The Russian Orthodox Church Abroad did not trust guests from the Soviet Union. However, after the group exited, I walked out of the church and stood by the door for a long time watching the group's disappearance into the distance. I was raised fearing the Soviet government and their ruthless ways, yet longed to know the Russian people who lived behind the Iron Curtain.

✠✠✠

CHAPTER 3

Coming of Age

Russian Jerusalem

Before there was the State of Israel, the Russian Compound in Jerusalem occupied the equivalent of several blocks in the new sector of Jerusalem, outside the ancient walls of the Old City. It consisted of the beautiful Trinity Cathedral, a Pilgrims Center with a large library, and buildings for the clergy as well as a general hospital, which to the present day retains in the Cyrillic alphabet above its entrance door the inscription "Russian Hospital." This compound evokes memories of Father Antony (Sinkevich) and several other mission residents. He was also from Belgrade, where he had arrived as a White Army cadet. Father Antony later espoused monasticism and then the priesthood; he was our greatest protector, as my mother used to tell me. During the British Mandate in Palestine, he was appointed chief of the Russian Mission and carried the responsibility of managing all Mission properties with their occupants. He received foreign dignitaries in the Mission headquarters as well as the British High Commissioner and other visitors.

On Holy Days, the Greek Orthodox patriarch and the chief of the Russian Mission exchanged greetings and mutual visits. There were Christian missionaries from European countries such as England, France, Italy, Germany, and others. Many of them had missionary schools of their own for the local population which accepted both Christian and Muslim children and maintained cordial relationships with each other. Indeed Jerusalem was a multilingual city, a reality from which young people growing there benefitted just like I did; many of us grew up speaking several languages from first grade on. German Lutherans, French Carmelite nuns and other monastic orders, Franciscan brothers, and Anglican clergy all exchanged greetings with the Greek, Armenian, Coptic, and Russian Orthodox communities.

Father Antony's mother was the Russian community's dentist and had her own practice in Jerusalem. Anesthetics were not available, so a trip to the dentist was an especially frightening experience. When she did my fillings and pulled my teeth, I screamed at the top of my lungs. During the procedure, poor Mother probably suffered just as much as I did when she tried to hold on to me. Those two loving women were trying their best for my own good and that of others in my situation. However, this pain was the direct outcome of the greatest problem in this part of the world at that time: namely, poverty. We were always somewhat hungry, somewhat dirty, and in winter very cold inside the stone buildings we lived in without central heating.

The British authorities rented some Russian Mission–owned buildings for use as their government offices. The Mission allowed the monasteries and convents to house Russian nationals who were homeless and jobless and in return worked in those places. Mother and I were in that category and like the majority of such people had few personal possessions. There was a lack of clothes, shoes, and comfort items such as toothpaste, soap, and medicines. During World War II and for a long time afterwards, South African nurses who were serving with the British troops stationed in Egypt sent us parcels or, whenever they visited, brought us gifts such as hand soaps, towels, and other toiletries not otherwise available to us.

Palestinian villagers did menial work in various Mission communities. Arab women were hired to do the big cleaning tasks and laundry by hand. The men did outside hard work, and all were paid the best we could afford. Over the years, feelings of mutual trust and interdependence developed. Russian nannies were held in high esteem, for instance, and some elderly Russian women became very attached to children of the more affluent Arabs or Jews in whose homes they worked. During the British Mandate when troubles between the Arabs and Jews had not yet escalated, an already very old nanny (in Russian *nyanya Katya*) faithfully visited the little boy she cared for and loved, now grown up and in prison. He was a member of the well-known affluent Palestinian family the Husseinis and was jailed for leading insurrection activities.

Another such Russian *nyanya* worked in the Jewish sector of Jerusalem, raising children of a well-to-do Jewish family, who later moved to New York City. At the time, I was getting ready to leave Jerusalem for America, so she packed a parcel for them that she gave to me with their address. She asked me to make sure to find them and give it to them, telling them how much she missed and worried about them in distant America. When I finally did find them in Brooklyn, they remembered their loving *nyanya* with great fondness and wished her well.

As I learned to speak Arabic, it put the women working for us at ease, and when I asked questions they willingly answered and often tried to explain to me the facts of life. When I was nearing teenage years and stood around them, watching them do the laundry and cleaning the floors, those women were my best confidants. I heard a lot from them about their customs in general, but particularly about girls' preparation for weddings. I remember the horror that overcame me when one such woman told me that all she remembered of her wedding night was how she experienced her first conjugal relations in a less than appealing way. Virginity was highly regarded; in fact, it was a must before marriage and without it there might never be a marriage for a young woman. I swore to her at that time that I'd never want to experience a man, to which she responded ominously, "A man will hold you, bewitch you, and so you'll give in."

One frightening experience happened to me when I was still very young. Mother was taking care of an elderly patient, a member of the clergy, in his room at the Mission headquarters. I was on vacation from boarding school, so she took me along. Her patient was suffering from epileptic seizures as a result of a stroke. Of course, I knew nothing about such things but soon found out more than my young mind could accept. Mother left me alone with her patient for a few minutes. I was sitting on a chair beside the bed when suddenly a deafening scream from the patient startled me and I saw him turn crimson and start to contort all over his body. It sounded and looked so dreadful to me that it took a long time afterwards for me to get over what I saw. Long after the patient died, I shuddered every time I passed the door of his room and avoided that corridor ever after. Yet this was just the beginning of my education about human suffering, and shortly after the British left Palestine, I often saw violence and death on the streets of Jerusalem.

The Arab–Israeli Conflict

I was seventeen years old when the first Arab–Israeli War (1948) began. But already much earlier there were instances of conflict that made an impact on my growing-up years. We were living surrounded by Palestinians, who had no organized leadership and were no match for the trained, well-armed Zionist fighters with their jeeps and telephones. It was the beginning of the sad fate that in 1948 befell the Palestinians as they were driven out from their homes and to this day can still see their ruined villages from a distance but can never return to them. They referred to Russians as *Muscob* or "Muscovites" and Mission properties to them were *al Muscobiyeh*. When the State of Israel was established, Russian property on the Sea of Galilee, communities in Haifa and Jaffa with an Orthodox school for Christian Arab girls, and the expansive Russian Mission property in the new sector of Jerusalem, as well as the lovely Gornia Convent in Ein Karem, all fell into Israeli hands, thus becoming inaccessible to us living in what was left of Palestine.

Zionist terrorist groups, such as the Hagana, terrorized Arab villages, ordering everyone to leave. One of those villages was Deir Yasseen, not far from Ein Karem where Gornia Convent was located. According to reports by the fleeing villagers, those who did not leave their village were summarily killed. Horrified by such reports, whoever was able fled. Christian Palestinians came to monasteries and convents in and near Jerusalem, to the Greek and Armenian patriarchates, and to other Christian communities where they sought shelter. As such incidents became frequent, Palestinian villagers were compelled to flee through Jericho to Trans-Jordan, Lebanon, or Syria. They were considered Palestinian refugees in those countries, and later when benevolent organizations donated tents to shelter them, refugee camps were formed like the one in Jericho, which remains to this day.

When a group of armed Zionists similar to those who were victimizing Arab villagers reached the Russian Mission buildings in Jerusalem, among them were some who wore the Soviet red star on their caps. They made it clear to the residents that they were at their mercy. The fighters, some of whom spoke Russian, admitted that among them there were extremist elements. When in mid-May 1948 the British Mandate ended and was replaced by the State of Israel, the Russian Mission was occupied by armed Israeli soldiers. The resident monks, clergy, chief of the Mission Father Antony (including his mother), and a few laymen were placed under house arrest, and on the following day began the official Arab–Israeli War.

For many days, the Mission and its surrounding buildings were under fire. Outside its windows unending explosions were heard. Some residents of the Mission hid in the basement; others stayed in their rooms, and as a result one monk was wounded through the window and died. It became necessary to request permission from the new authorities to bury him, and the remaining monks were allowed to dig a grave in the yard for their deceased brother. He had to be buried without a coffin in the small garden adjoining the cathedral. Many sleepless nights and nerve-racking days ensued before the explosions and cross fire finally ended. Then early in July, under the auspices of the International Red Cross, the Mission's chief and its residents withdrew from the Russian Mission property. A wounded monk and his caretaker were allowed to remain temporarily in the Mission until property ownership papers were settled by the occupying forces.

Former Mission residents were given haven in various Russian monasteries that became part of the Hashemite Kingdom of Trans-Jordan. Father Antony was temporarily staying in the building designated for clergy at the Mount of Olives Convent. Mother and I already had a room on the second floor of the two-story guest house near the convent entrance gate, where occasionally Father Antony visited us and drank tea with bread and jam; sugar was scarce, so usually friends brought their own sugar for tea. The conversation centered on old memories of life in Belgrade, or on the current state of affairs in the Holy Land and its questionable future. We liked to walk Father Antony to his residence through the quiet, moonlit convent garden. Late in 1951, he departed to the United States, where he was ordained the Russian Orthodox bishop of Los Angeles.

Many years later, while travelling in Europe, I met several young Palestinian Orthodox nuns who were my friends in Bethany School, now living together as a religious community in London. They fled from Gornia Convent with Abbess Elizabeth and Father Lazarus the day Israeli armed forces took over the Arab village of Ein Karem, where the convent was located. Palestinians living in the village fled from the ruthless occupying forces, and so these Christian Arab nuns felt compelled to flee. The following letter from 1948 describes how those young nuns and their abbess fled with the help of Father Lazarus. When I met them in their convent in London, they had opened a small school for children and converted part of their large home into a beautiful chapel, with regular church services on Sundays and holidays.

The way this building was designated for their community was remarkable. After they fled from Ein Karem, they spent time in a Christian Arab village called Al Salt in Trans-Jordan, where my mother and I visited them and where they were living in dire poverty like many Palestinian refugees. Abbess Elizabeth had a blood sister in England, a physician who they hoped might be able to help them relocate to London. After this became a reality, they searched for a home in London, looking at various real estate possibilities within their benefactors' means. Eventually they found an old mansion that appeared to be a suitable place for a convent. When they climbed into the attic to check out the condition of the roof, they found a couple of spots in it repaired by rectangular pieces of planking that they decided to remove. Upon looking on the back side of those planks, they noticed paintings of ancient Russian icons: one was an icon of the Mother of God. They interpreted this as an indication from above for them to make this place their convent, and they asked Bishop John (Maximovich), who was in Europe at the time, to bless their undertaking. With the hierarch's prayerful help, they were able to purchase and remain in this place for the rest of their lives, surrounded by a rose garden with a picturesque summer cottage in its center, for use by officiating clergy and by overnight guests on weekends and holidays.

The following letter from Father Lazarus (Moore) written in 1948 fills in the gap between the years of our childhood at Bethany School and my old school friends' life in England:

C.M.S. School, Amman, Trans-Jordan
St Stephen's Day 1948

Dear Anna Vasilievna,

I was delighted to get your letter yesterday, your triumphant letter which is yet another proof that all is for the best to those who love the Holy and Glorious Trinity. I don't know what news you have, so I'll try to tell you our story in brief.

The Mission was occupied by Hagana, but extreme groups (Irgun and Stern) were occupying nearby buildings, and their members sometimes appeared in the Mission. It was particularly unpleasant when Father Antony met a soldier in the Mission with the Soviet red star and hammer and sickle on his helmet, who gave him a piercing look. Once men shouted in Russian, "Your blood is going to flow!" Bolsheviks made several attempts to abduct Father Antony. One occasion is characteristic. A well-known Soviet agent appeared (Babitch from Haifa), introduced himself and said that he was called a Bolshevik, but that it was not true that he had never been a member of the Party, that he considered that in such times, we all should unite around the Church, that even unbelievers when shells explode involuntarily make the sign of the cross (and he waved his hand vaguely in front of his face, proving that he himself never made the sign of the cross). "You are under home arrest," he said. "Your life is in danger. There are extreme elements here. You have made mistakes in the past: it is known that you have issued certificates to the Arab Committee. I want to introduce you to certain influential people. A car will be sent for you tomorrow." But Father Antony refused his offer, saying that it would be better to talk when the guns stopped talking. It was clear that this might have been simply a repetition of the recent assassination of the Polish Consul in Jerusalem by the same method.

On the day Father Antony left the Mission, Mother Elizabeth and Sister Suzanna walked from Ein Karem to Bethlehem, and then took the car which went by the new desert road past St Saba's Monastery to Jerusalem. Miraculously they met him as he was leaving the Old City in the ambulance! Having learned by bitter experience what to expect, Father Antony gave orders not to wait till Ein Karem was taken, but if after the truce it was attacked, we were to leave at once. Next day Mother Elizabeth was back in Ein Karem. The very first day after the truce Ein Karem was again attacked. On Saturday July 10th a breathless messenger told us that there was no one left in the village, all had fled. So we took in our hands and round our neck and on our backs what we could, and staggered up the mountain towards Miss Carey's house at about 10 pm. We spent the night beside that half-finished bell tower, practically without sleep, ready to go on to the village of Bait Jalah. But the Jews did not attack, though there was some shooting, and even shelling.

At dawn we went down to the convent, I read the rule and then served as if nothing had happened; and almost no one knew that twelve of us had spent the night on the mountain! But that was the last service in Gornia Convent in Ein Karem. It was Sunday, July 11th. That morning the attack began in earnest, and we left. A camel took the heavier baggage, and my typewriter which we have left in the bell tower on the mountain with a guard. And we walked the other way up the mountain where God had put the truck, which took us to Bethlehem. There, Mother Elizabeth and sisters lived in Janho's one room, sleeping on the floor, while I went to stay with the Loossi family.

On July 15, hearing that it was quiet in Ein Karem, I and four others went to Ein Karem on foot with eight donkeys. It was about two hours walk in the scorching sun. We spent about two hours in the convent (with intermittent shooting) loading the donkeys with sacred vessels and vestments, books, oil, flour, clothing, etc.; and even then we only took the most necessary things. We were only just in time and had to return to Bethlehem under fire. Arab troops had retreated right onto our path, and they shouted to me and Sister Fadwa who were with the last donkey, "If you see a tank on your way, send it to us because we must have help." But we never saw a tank!

On July 18th the Jews took Ein Karem and are now occupying Mother Elizabeth's house and Miss Cary's I understand. Apparently Samarsky opened the church, and now the Soviet group is using it. I will not repeat other reports as they are uncertain, and perhaps you know more than we do. We then got a truck, loaded it with our stuff and ourselves, and went through the desert to Jericho, where we found Father Antony. We spent one night in a hotel, and then moved on to Amman, Trans-Jordan, where we stayed another night in a hotel, and since then we have been living in this school which is full of refugees.

Ever yours in Christ,
Archimandrite Lazarus

During various periods of time in my early childhood in Palestine, painful experiences were etched in my memory as a result of the beginning phases of the struggle for this country. Often while a boarder at Bethany School, other girls and I in my dorm would wake up at night from hearing shots fired. Outside on the road to Jericho early morning convoys of Jewish salt-transporting trucks passing the Arab village of Bethany would often evoke cross fire between the two adversaries. Later in the morning we'd often go to the low stone wall around the school yard to look down the winding Jericho road. We would see on the road, here and there, corpses clad in a black Bedouins' *abbaya* (overcoat). They were lying in puddles of blood, victims of Jewish or Arab sniper bullets. At other times when staying with my mother for the weekend, I would open my eyes and see Mother on her knees praying before the lit *lampada* in front of the icon of Christ. It was a very old icon painted in the typical Greek iconographic style, which traveled with us from Athens, where Mother bought it on our way to Palestine. Mother often mentioned that it was thanks to this icon we remained safe and away from the war in Europe.

Those were difficult times of our life in Palestine as we were neither Arabs nor Jews yet caught in their struggle. A sniper's bullet once killed a deaf nun, who sat next to a window of the bus we were riding on our way from Jerusalem to the Mount of Olives. As we were passing the Jewish Hadassah Medical School and Hospital, the Arab bus driver shouted for everyone to duck: "Get down!" the bus driver screamed. The deaf sister Alexandra could not hear his warning and was instantly killed by a sniper's bullet that came in through her window. No one ever knew if a trip to Jerusalem might cost them their life. Going to town was most often a necessity either to buy food or go to the doctor, but whether the bus would bring them back home alive was a constant question. In their purses Mother and other people carried with them their valuables, and old letters and photos were with them at all times; everyone always had a bag packed and ready. Mother wondered where we would be refugees again perhaps for the third time in our lives. She was a refugee from Russia to Belgrade, Yugoslavia, and then to Palestine. "Not again," she would exclaim at a moment of anxious uncertainty.

Nursing in Bethany

It was a known fact that someday the British Mandate in Palestine was bound to come to an end and adults around us mentioned it in passing, but it seemed as if the last straw that forced the British to leave was the bombing of the King David Hotel in the new sector of Jerusalem. It was accomplished by Zionist terrorists. On the eve of the explosion, Mother Mary and Mother Barbara took me and my friend Katia to pay a visit to a British family who was staying at the King David Hotel in Jerusalem. As we conversed and enjoyed English tea with cake none of us suspected the fate that was in store for our English friends.

Early the next morning when the Jewish milk truck brought its usual delivery to the King David Hotel, the big steel containers were full of explosives instead of milk. A huge explosion occurred and the hotel with its guests was blown up. Moshe Dayan, who masterminded this event, later became a general and president of Israel. Next morning when we heard the explosion and then the shocking news, we were all speechless with horror, and yet this was only the beginning. A bloody war ensued, and it engulfed all residents of the region regardless of their faith or nationality.

Shortly after all the boarders were sent home for summer vacation, Bethany School was officially converted into a hospital. There were two other European volunteer nurses besides myself and a Christian Arab young woman as well as Mother Martha who did her best to help wherever she was needed. We were saving lives by helping the war wounded and sick villagers. Dr Majaj, a Christian Arab, and his wife, a nurse, both studied medicine at the American University in Beirut, Lebanon. They led our small staff as we struggled day and night to keep up with the truckloads of wounded Trans-Jordanian soldiers and Palestinian villagers brought to the high iron gates of our school now functioning as a hospital. I was only seventeen at the time, one of the few untrained volunteer nurses who stayed behind to help save lives. I administered medicines, bandaged wounds, and was even called to assist at brain surgery!

Internal organ surgeries, amputations, and suturing of wounds were all done with great difficulty and sometimes in the middle of the night without the help of adequate light. I assisted at a brain surgery of a thirteen-year-old Palestinian village boy, blond, blue-eyed, perhaps traits left over from the times of the Crusades in Palestine centuries ago. This innocent boy died a couple of weeks later. A beautiful twelve-year-old girl also died not long afterwards, and I still remember how her chest heaved at the end of her young life. A black African Arab man, father of a large family, who lived nearby and worked occasionally in our school was wounded and died in our hospital at the time I was administering medicines in his ward.

One night a military truck loaded with wounded soldiers arrived. We did not know where to start, whom to help first. I approached a very young soldier who was holding his right hand with his left hand. I noticed it was attached to his arm by a thin strip of skin, while his whole elbow was missing—blown up. He beckoned to me, turning his eyes on his comrade lying on the floor. He told me first to help his friend who screamed with pain, as he lifted his leg, which was bleeding profusely from a wound in the groin. The attending physician was overwhelmed; he complained about the poor lighting and got irritated at us young, inexperienced nurses. There was no time for relieving fatigue, hunger, or thirst, no excuse for ignorance, only on all sides were lives needing to be saved and excruciating pain to be relieved with few or no painkillers available.

Another time when a truckload of wounded was brought, it was a family of refugees who were packed into a pickup truck fleeing to the Kingdom of Trans-Jordan. While driving down the steep, winding road to Jericho, the truck overturned and rolled down into a deep ravine, so the question was how anyone managed to be rescued and brought to us alive. That night, the unconscious mother and her fifteen- and ten-year-old daughters lay in our hospital dying. I remember seeing large, intestinal worms making their way out of the girls' bodies through the anal passage. By next morning the girls were dead, the father frothed at the mouth and also died, while the mother quietly stopped breathing. Miraculously only the grandmother, who held the youngest member of the family in her arms, a baby boy, survived. Several days later grandmother and the baby were able to leave the hospital.

When the Jewish military forces reached the walls of Jerusalem wounded Trans-Jordanian soldiers were brought into our hospital. They wore their national military uniform with heads covered with red checkered *kaffya* kerchiefs, so their features were not readily distinguishable. The first few days they lay listlessly, suffering excruciating pain, while we continued to have very few pain relieving medicines available. Later, as the wounded soldiers got better, they became livelier and took off the head covering, so we were able to recognize among them occasional British soldiers dressed in Trans-Jordanian uniforms, the way "Glubb Pasha's Arab Legion" stationed in Trans-Jordan might have dressed.

We volunteer nurses were soon joined by a Polish young woman who also volunteered to nurse the wounded. At night sometimes she suffered break-downs from all the work, lack of sleep, and no relief from seeing suffering day and night. She already had her share of suffering as a little girl during World War II in Poland. Sometimes at night she would explode with violent sobbing and simply repeat the words, "I cannot take it anymore—I cannot take it anymore!" After the war, when we all went our different ways, I was told that this transplanted young woman married an Arab man in Lebanon. I always hoped she would get the relief she deserved and prayed for.

One remarkable volunteer nurse with a very unusual spiritual gift was a Christian Arab young woman, Hilane Nicola. Muslim women were not allowed to be close to men who were not directly related to them, so they could not volunteer as nurses. Hilane was from Abu Snan, a Christian village near Gaza, and was for a few years a boarder at Bethany School. When she was about eleven or twelve years old, she was well known throughout Palestine as St Hilane of Abu Snan, and Arab newspapers wrote about her. Pilgrims came to this village and prayed in the village Orthodox church, where Hilane with her family prayed. It was then that my mother, having heard about this unusual child, decided to see it all for herself.

So we took an old, rickety Arab bus to Gaza and arrived at Abu Snan. It was Sunday morning; in the village church, the liturgy was being served in Arabic. As we entered, we saw Hilane standing on the right side dressed in a white dress and head covering. Toward the end of the service, when the officiating priest usually gives the blessed bread to the congregation, Hilane held the tray with the holy bread for the people to take. When we approached her, I noticed the fingers on her right hand were crossed over as if in a knot so she could hold the big tray with only her left hand, something that appeared odd.

After the service, guests were invited together with the priest for a cup of coffee in the family courtyard where stood a wooden table with benches. Next to Hilane sat her father and the village priest and guests; Mother and I sat across from them. During the meal, Hilane's face suddenly became very pale and dark circles formed around her eyes, which she closed. She was helped to stretch out on the bench on which she was sitting, and then something most unusual happened. Little Hilane, who never went to school and was illiterate because at that time very few villages had schools for girls, began to speak in classical Arabic. She related how while she was tending to her parents' small sheep herd on the rocky hillside, she saw a young man come from around the hill riding a white horse. "It was St George," she said, and that he told her all about the forthcoming war (this was before the start of the 1948 Arab–Israeli War). He said there would be much suffering and that people needed to be prepared to bear it all; thus she continued on and on in classical Arabic. Then suddenly she stopped, sat up, smiled as if embarrassed, and ran off to play with the rest of the children her age—as if unaware of what had just happened. People tried to touch her and to give her gifts, but she quietly withdrew.

When she became a teenager, Hilane stopped having such episodes of prophetic predictions. Because of her notoriety, her parents wanted to protect her, so they brought her to be a boarder at our school in Bethany. She was a poor student and reading and writing were difficult for her, but she became a superb nurse while practicing in Bethany School Hospital during the Arab–Israeli War. Wounded soldiers called to her, asked for her, and wanted only her to change the dressings on their wounds. They claimed her touch relieved their pain and they insisted that she could heal them. I saw their ardent belief in her special gift of healing touch, whether they were Muslim or Christian patients. I was jealous of her, but soon realized that she was simply an unusual human being. After the war, Hilane asked to go back to her village near Gaza, by then on Israeli territory, so as to reunite with her family, and I never saw her after that.

Once, a sniper's bullet affected the lives of twin brothers, who were dressed as Franciscan order monks and were from a nearby Catholic monastery. They wore brown cloaks with an image of Christ's heart on their chest. The unwounded brother brought his wounded twin to us for help. A bullet was lodged in his chest near the heart. He was bleeding to death while we nurses did all we could to save him. I'll never forget the healthy twin's desperate pleas for us to save his brother, and his uncontrollable sobbing over his dying brother's body.

Into the Trans-Jordanian Desert

After the establishment of the State of Israel, the remaining territory of Palestine was ruled by Abdullah, King of Trans-Jordan. Transportation from Jerusalem to the capital Amman and to towns further into the desert was difficult to find. Fortunately a Palestinian acquaintance, who owned a car for his business and whose wife was Mother's patient, offered to take us to Amman or even further to Zarqua, a tiny Circassian village in an oasis in the Trans-Jordanian desert. These Circassians at one time fled from the Soviet Union and settled here. Our Arab driver brought us and left us there, assuming someone would turn up to drive us back to Jerusalem.

In Zarqua we had friends from Jerusalem, a middle-aged Russian couple, who after the Arab–Israeli War came here to open a European bakery serving British military personnel. The Royal Air Force in Trans-Jordan was located reasonably close by, and British military vacationers liked to spend time in this oasis. There was no electricity or running water in this village as was the case in most rural Trans-Jordan, but kerosene lamps at night and water from watering holes near the tiny lake kept life going. We had no common language with the local Circassian country folk from the Russian Caucasus, but they were positively predisposed to Russians, who they knew also at one time fled from the Soviet Union. They supplied all our food, water, and lodging in a small stone house for a fee we could afford.

I wanted to meet some local young people, and in a few days I was able to join a group of Circassian girls about my age, on their way to the lake past our house. They were intrigued by my different looks and clothes, were very friendly, and we swam together in the small lake. According to their Muslim faith, girls could swim only with other girls with no males around. Some of them understood English, which they learned from British families vacationing in their village. During our stay in this remote settlement, no one came from anywhere, not even a truck with supplies, yet the time was fast approaching for us to return to Jerusalem. We were told that no transportation was expected to be available for quite some time, but they also encouraged us to hope and wait patiently while watching the horizon for passing small caravans or vehicles to flag them to stop with a white cloth.

Then one day we noticed on the horizon a truck approaching, so we frantically waved a white sheet in their direction until they stopped and started to drive toward us. My Arabic helped us to understand that they were transporting salt bags to the market in Jerusalem. We begged them to give us a ride for a small fee, and agreeing, they helped Mother and me to climb on top of the salt bags in the truck. There were already several Bedouin men sitting on the hard, sackcloth bags. After the usual greeting "Al Salamu Aleikum" ("Peace to you all"), we sat quietly in the opposite corner.

It was already evening in the desert, and most travelling in summer was done on moonlit nights. The extremely hot sun during the day made it unbearable to travel in the intense heat. There was no road across the desert sands yet the driver knew the way from past experience. The moon shone brightly above us, and on occasion we saw desert rabbits run across in front of the truck. We were completely at the mercy of the driver and a companion sitting next to him. The three Bedouins on top of the truck occasionally sneaked a curious glance at Mother and me, a pretty teenage girl. Mother quietly warned me not to look in their direction and that my eyes should never meet theirs. We sat quietly with olive wood prayer beads in our hands silently repeating the Jesus prayer: "Lord Jesus Christ, Son of God, have mercy on me a sinner." This was a prayer I was taught from early childhood to repeat at moments of anxiety and difficulty. Bedouins also carried strings of beads but different from ours. Their bead strings had no small wooden cross attached and we did not know whether theirs were for prayer or for counting the beads just to while away the time. Thus we traveled all night with our bottoms getting sore from the hard salt bags. Finally toward morning the winding Jericho road became visible in the distance, and we were relieved by the knowledge that there would be a bus available to take us back home to Jerusalem. We were two women in the company of several Bedouin men safely arriving in Jericho after a night together in the desert. Later I often wondered if we would have fared as well in the Western world, but here in the desert, honor still existed as a cultural manifestation, so we were safe with those desert dwellers.

Our Russian Choir Goes to Amman

Russian nationals, especially the young ones, who didn't leave the country at the onset of the war had no jobs, no money, and no residency status. Father Antony, displaced as Russian Mission chief, was waiting for a new assignment from his bishop in New York City, a result of the confiscation of the Mission headquarters by the new government authorities. In the meantime, he got us together and formed a Russian music choir. Being musical himself and a good conductor capable of preparing us for a concert trip to Amman, most of us gladly joined him. In Amman there were international embassies and enough educated well-to-do people to be interested in our concert, we hoped.

Arrangements were made for us to stay in various homes while giving concerts in the city. I was assigned to stay with the Christian Arab family of the finance minister. One evening, my host and several other ministers had a meeting at his home, and his wife, wanting to show me off to the guests, sent me instead of the maid to serve them the customary Turkish coffee. My host introduced me to his guests, who started to ask me questions about the makeup of our choir, about my life in Jerusalem, and what I wanted to do with my life. Our conversation was in Arabic, and my fluency impressed them when they found out that I was Russian by birth. I said I would like to be a teacher one day, but that probably I would have to become a nun in a convent, because my mother had no financial means to help me complete my education.

The next morning at breakfast, my host announced that he had a surprise for me. He said that after I walked out of the room the previous evening, the ministers had quite a discussion about the fact that I was considering becoming a nun. They thought of another possible future for me: each pledged personally to help me complete high school so I would be able to pursue studies at a university to become a teacher, because the Kingdom of Trans-Jordan was very much in need of teachers. His wife suggested I finish high school at the French boarding school of Notre Dame de Sion in Jerusalem, as she attended such a school in Alexandria, Egypt. The ministers lived up to their promise; they financed my high school studies in one of the best private schools in the region. This enabled me to graduate and pass my Oxford and Cambridge examination board administered tests and then matriculate for entrance to the University of London.

At this crucial period in my life, although my mother was pleased with my ambitious outlook and hard work, I also needed Father Lazarus to give me spiritual support at least by correspondence. I was breaking away from my formative years in the security of a Russian Orthodox community and entering adulthood in a different environment. This is how he encouraged me:

10/23 August 1951

Dear Anya!

I was delighted to get your interesting letter and hear your wonderful news, and I said to myself that I must write at once and congratulate you. And here is the reality! But even this is quick for me, and many people never get answers. Now I do heartily congratulate you for passing the London matriculation, that is really a great achievement. One has to work to pass any matriculation. When I was in my twenties I passed the Durham matriculation, which was supposed to be easier than the London. So I can imagine that you are feeling exhausted, and it is also good news to hear that you will be able to teach and get a respectable salary. I have just received a two-page descriptive pamphlet of Jordanville, which ends with the words, "The members of our Brotherhood praise God for His countless blessings and they never forget what a great joy they have in being able to spend their lives in work and prayer." I suppose that is more or less what you feel too.

After leaving you I spent five days in Al Salt in Trans-Jordan and then three days in Beirut, Lebanon, eight days on a Greek ship, and two days travelling from Marseilles to London. It was a difficult voyage on the ship because it was overcrowded. I slept as often as possible on the hatches, but when there were storms I had to sleep in a bunk. We went through two thunderstorms and the waves splashed onto the decks, and it was difficult to keep our baggage dry. Most of the people were seasick, and very few appeared for meals on those days. I was quite well all the time, but I had to suffer in many other ways. The food was very good even in the fourth class and plenty of it, but the waiters were skunks! Only one asked me if I was Orthodox and was a little kinder than the rest. Every one complained of their bad manners as they almost threw the food at us!

Owing to the crowds at Port Said, my box of books was put off there. But your book (Brianchaninoff) is with me safely, as I had it in my bag. I have cabled and written to Port Said, and God can return the books if it is His will that we should have them. If you have any questions, write and ask me, and let me know your news. God bless and guide you.

Your servant in Christ,
Abbot Lazarus

After a short stay in London, Father Lazarus was assigned by the Synod to India where he was to establish an Orthodox Mission. He was to continue his work translating Orthodox Church service books with the help of secretary-typist Mary Mitchell, who was originally from England but who also lived and worked at the Russian Mission properties in Jerusalem, where she became an ardent Orthodox Christian and a close friend of my mother.

Notre Dame de Sion School

From the terraces of Notre Dame de Sion School we could see the Mosque of Omar, which was within walking distance. The school was built over excavations named "Ecce Homo," Latin for "Here is the man," because they were believed to be the remains of Pilate's palace, where the Roman ruler presented Christ, a prisoner, to His Hebrew accusers. Our school stood amid two-story buildings in which lived Jerusalem's Arab population with narrow ancient streets between us.

Sister Gabriel was my most important teacher, as she was our class monitor in charge of preparing about ten upper-class young women between eighteen and twenty years old to pass London matriculation examinations. In addition to an English exam, we needed to pass exams in two more languages, one of which had to be a "classical" language. The Arab girls took English, French, and classical Arabic. Armenian girls took classical Armenian, English, and French. I took English, Russian, and Latin as my classical language, because Russian was not considered a classical language.

Other than the required languages, we had to pass general mathematics, world history, British colonial history, the Bible as literature, and English literature. All this took very hard studying, and most of us passed, thanks to Sister Gabriel's dedication to lead us to a successful future. At first I disliked her insistence on perfection, but with time I understood that she was my mentor, and I began to admire her dedication to hard work. She was born in Berlin of a well-to-do German-Jewish family that immigrated to Palestine. In Tel Aviv, her father became owner of a successful business; her brother, whose ambition was to become a millionaire by age forty, became a builder of high-rise condominiums in that city. He achieved his goal in his early forties, but alas, soon after, he died of a heart attack. Through her brother's marriage, Sister Gabriel was related to Abba Eban, a renowned Israeli politician.

When she came to Notre Dame de Sion French School in the Old City of Jerusalem, she became interested in converting to Catholicism and became a nun and an excellent teacher. Unfortunately, her father, in his great displeasure at her independent choice of lifestyle, laid a curse upon her. Many years later on his deathbed, he removed his curse and died at peace with his daughter. Other than teaching, she assisted the convent's mother superior, who was a well-known French archeologist and scholar who worked on excavating passages under the school building. Here were found rooms in which Roman soldiers may have spent time playing chess on chessboards engraved in the stone floors.

Father Arnold, a priest from St Benedict's Abbey in Atchison, Kansas, and professor at St Benedict's College[1] there, became my Latin instructor. He was temporarily staying in Jerusalem at the French Peres Blanc Abbey, where he was studying classical Hebrew and was preparing himself to pass biblical studies exams in Rome. Three times a week we met to read together Caesar's *De Bello Gallico* (*The Gallic Wars*), to study Latin grammar, and for me to do translations from and into Latin. Thus I was able to pass my classical language requirements for entrance into London University.

The local British Council administered exams for entry into British universities in London as well as to Oxford and Cambridge, for which I preregistered. Exams were offered twice a year, summer and winter. I sat for my exams in winter, an unfortunate choice of time because buildings in Jerusalem had no central heating. We were allowed to bring hot water bottles and wool plaid blankets to stay warm during the five-hour daily written exam on the subjects we were required to pass. Monitors constantly walked around the tables at which we sat writing, lest there be any attempt at cheating. We were practically searched for cheat notes.

During this final phase of my school years, a memorable historic event took place across the street from Notre Dame de Sion School on Via Dolorosa. King Abdullah, ruler of Palestine and the Kingdom of Trans-Jordan, came from Amman to Jerusalem on Fridays to pray at the Mosque of Omar. He was known to give alms to the poor on the streets, as taught by the Quar'an. This mosque was built on the site of the Jewish Temple that was destroyed by the Romans a few decades after Christ's prediction. One Friday[2] we heard gunshots coming from that direction, and from our terraces witnessed the great confusion of the crowds and heard screams echoing throughout the narrow streets: "The king was shot! The king was killed! The king is dead!" Later we found out that the killer was a Palestinian Arab, and his people wanted a Palestinian ruler.

My Latin instructor was planning to leave Jerusalem shortly after I sat for my exams. He would go to Rome for his own PhD exam and then return to his abbey in Atchison, Kansas. Previously, we discussed my future and what possibilities existed for me to complete my higher education. From a financial point of view, it seemed there were no options because my mother's salary from Augusta Victoria Hospital was small and she was already sixty-two years old. I knew it was time I took care of her—not the other way around. Being aware of my scholastic aptitude and hard work, Father Arnold suggested I apply for a scholarship to the Benedictine women's college of St Scholastica. He and my other instructors sent recommendations for me, and eventually I was granted a four-year scholarship to study in the United States.

At this time I was residing at Notre Dame de Sion and working as a teacher in the lower grades. My salary was five pounds monthly for room and board, but I knew this was temporary. Sister Gabriel helped me with advice and later prepared me in various ways for the possibility of receiving a scholarship and leaving Jerusalem. My boarding school girl friends were also starting new lives. One, whose father was the minister of education, soon married a physician in Amman. Another one, whose father was the prime minister, was engaged to a Syrian banker but kept in touch with me. Later with her father's help, because I lived most of my life in Palestine and spoke Arabic like a native, I was granted Jordanian citizenship and a passport for travel. Now I could travel abroad and study to become a professional teacher. I planned to return to Jerusalem and find a good teaching position.

European employees who worked in British establishments also were trying to leave for other lands to find employment. By that time, Israel was getting established and was preparing young people to teach Ivrit, the simplified Hebrew language for Jewish immigrants. These classes were free and made teaching positions much easier to get for speakers of Ivrit. We who grew up in Palestine had no such opportunity as we lived in Jordan, and a barbed wire fence with a no-man's-land was between us and the new state of Israel. I was in a minority group living in a country at war, and all around were snipers and barbed wire. Local inhabitants had almost no future, much less financial means for any hope of getting away from it all into peaceful, prosperous lands of opportunity. Such was the sad state of affairs in the early 1950s in Jerusalem.

One particular evening comes to mind. I dropped by the room of my neighbor, a tourist who was staying for a day or two at our school. We were sitting wrapped in our coarse, gray blankets, dreaming of a blazing fireplace. On the table in front of us was a tinsel-covered pine twig, a reminder of the Christmas season. Outside, the rain pattered loudly against the yards and roof terraces. The chilly dampness was creeping through the cracks around the doors and windows. It penetrated our clothes and settled in our joints, aching from the cold. A hot fire to snuggle in front of and a warm cup of tea to warm one's hands around were visions of luxury filling our thoughts. I was almost twenty years old, a former student, now teaching first grade. I was here because there was no other place to go to work or do further studies, whereas my neighbor from America was staying here for a short time of her own free will. As soon as her visa to the Israeli side of Jerusalem was ready, she would say thank you and good bye, probably forever. That alone made our attitudes toward life quite different.

For her, living inside the walls of a convent in the Old City of Jerusalem at Via Dolorosa over the remains of Pilate's palace had an exotic fascination to it: to wake up at the tolling of bells and fall asleep to the chanting of Latin hymns, to grope on the way up and down the dark winding stairways, to get lost in never-ending hallways, and to live in the constant whisper of prayers that accompanied all chores. The sound of prayers echoed in the colonnades and over the long rows of beds, where student boarders got dressed and tidied up their beds while rattling off Latin verses in chorus. All this gave the sensation of living in a different century than the twentieth century; perhaps it was more like the age of the Crusades.

The smell of beeswax candles and incense, the rustle of long skirts, veil-covered figures in black and white always moving but never rushing, often silent but with friendly smiles on their faces as glances met. Never a raised voice, never a harsh word (or thus it would seem to an outsider), but, of course, this was not always true. Nevertheless, this was a way of life, perhaps not of our times, yet a life one could still find here in this broken-up, torn-asunder, and tourist-hungry Jerusalem. "I have tried the world, I know its temptations and suffering; but only here have I found a haven." These were words I heard from both Russian Orthodox nuns and French Catholic nuns living in convents who were there by personal choice and devotion to Christ as His brides.

In an atmosphere of hatred and threats and political intrigues, the desperation of impoverished Arab refugees and the boredom of UN officials drinking at the city bars in the evenings, the convictions expressed by those sisters seemed especially valid to me. To stay in one place, to avoid taking a stand on political issues, to quit seeking distant horizons that always recede farther and farther away from the seeker: is this the true meaning of peace, and is it the real meaning of happiness?

These were my thoughts and questions at that time, but they were sporadically carried away by the whirlwind of youthful desires. To live now, fully, freely, whatever the consequences, whatever realizations and disappointments may ensue. Now, today, perhaps tomorrow, my own experiences, not those of others, were all that mattered. My visiting neighbor spoke to me of a different life, different values; she was my window into the outside world and its mysteries, rewards, and punishments. "You are brave and strong," she told me. "You broke away from your surroundings before and went your own way. You will do it again when the time comes. I don't know what life holds in store for you, but I believe you will find your own horizons."

Courting

By this time I had already experienced a couple of romantic friendships. My first romantic friend—with whom, of course, I never was alone—was my own age, the son of the owner of the first Shell gas stations in Amman. He owned a flaming red American car in which he drove from Amman to Jerusalem to see me. This was a mark of affluence at that time in this part of the world. I met him in Amman when the Russian choir in which I sang was giving concerts there. At that time, parties were given in various well-to-do Arab and European households to which we were invited. I was discrete and simply dressed, which seemed to fascinate him. He said I was not like the rest of them at the party or in Amman, and he liked this about me and wanted us to be friends. That was how we met, and after my return to Jerusalem he continued to want to see me.

On Sundays he drove his red car to Jerusalem, usually with his friend, future King Hussein's youngest uncle, who was about our age. This was a good thing, providing us with a chaperon, as was the custom for courtships in Palestine. They came to the Mount of Olives guest house by the convent gate, where I was staying on weekends. As they drove through the Arab village that surrounded the convent, the car sounded its siren to announce the arrival of the king's uncle who was considered a Jordanian official. This brought excitement to the lives of the villagers, because it meant that someone important was driving through their village square. Adults would look up from their work, and children would run outside to see what was happening.

Our courtship soon became the talk of the village. Everybody on the Mount of Olives knew my mother, "Um-Anya al tabiba"—Anya's mother the healer, they called her. Our hired help such as the milkmaid, women who washed our clothes and helped with house cleaning, the village bus driver, and Salim the gatekeeper and night guard of the convent all talked about me as if they were experts about my life. These simple but well-intentioned people wished for a big Arab wedding for me, once a little girl at her mother's side but now old enough to be a bride.

In the Muslim village that surrounded the convent, weddings and funerals usually lasted a whole week. Their various noises carried into the convent as well as through the village square. Throughout the week, we could hear wailing after funerals, but when there was a wedding, there was loud music and clapping of hands, and women emitted in unison a special high-pitched noise. The smell of roasted lamb filled the air, and it was difficult to get a quiet night's sleep. Practically everyone was expected to visit at such occasions so as to admire the bride and to bring gifts. She was seated high on a chair in the center of the room, beautifully dressed and wearing in a showy manner golden jewelry bestowed on her by the groom.

Among favorite topics of the villagers was a wedding for me. Mother found this annoying, but she knew that they said it out of kindness to her, and the idea of a big wedding to them was appealing as such events were their main source of entertainment. They told her what an excellent match it would make—pretty blue-eyed Anya marrying a rich man from Amman where the king lived. Their enthusiasm indirectly suggested that they all would be richer and happier if this happened, and my mother kept repeating, "It would never work; he is Muslim while Anya is Christian." I knew that all this talk was more than unpleasant for Mother; after all, we lived in a convent and sometimes I thought that her true wish for me was that after my education was completed, I would choose monasticism and become a good abbess like some of her closest friends were.

One Sunday afternoon my friend and his companion arrived as usual. After a short visit, they suggested I ask my mother to allow me to go for a ride with them to the American Colony tea room, which was considered to be the most sophisticated place around. Of course, Mother advised against it, but I continued to beg her to let me go, promising we would return before dark. Finally, Mother gave in and we took off through the village square, siren and all, to the new sector of Jerusalem.

Our little tea party turned into a long drive almost to Amman and back. My friend wanted me to meet his mother in Amman. I said, "Not without my mother's knowledge" and that I promised to be home before dark. I knew Mother was anxiously waiting as this was the first time I had gone out alone with the young men. Seeing my anxiety, my friend understood my concern and turned back on to the road to the convent, driving as fast as he could; it was already getting dark and becoming a windy evening.

When we arrived at the convent gate and knocked there was no response, so we knocked again and again; the wind was howling through the tall fir and cypress trees that had been planted around the church a long time ago by Russian missionaries. Salim, an eighty-year-old Arab man faithfully guarded the convent as night gatekeeper. Rain or shine, he made his nightly rounds with a kerosene lantern as was his job for the past fifty years. Earlier he would have been at the gate in a little booth, but now he was away checking the high stone wall around the convent and could not hear us.

No one in the convent heard us knock, and after a while we decided to return to Jerusalem to the American Colony. Across from it a barbed wire fence divided the Arab land from a no-man's-land beyond which was Israel. We were on the Arab side where from time immemorial lived the well-known old Nuseibeh family, and next to their house was the family home of their son, a popular Palestinian lawyer. Those two stone houses miraculously survived many cross fires in that area between Arabs and Jews. The daughters, who also graduated from Notre Dame de Sion School, were my friends. I knocked at their door with the small hand-shaped brass knocker, and they let me in. I told them my problem, and they allowed me to spend the night with them so my friends from Amman could return home.

Early the next morning, I thanked the family for their kind hospitality and took the first bus back to the Mount of Olives. Salim was on duty at the gate and let me in so I could hurry to our room in the guest house. When I entered I saw my mother, teary-eyed sitting at the table with an exhausted look on her face. I hugged her warmly, as she sadly said, "I never went to bed last night. I sat waiting and worrying about you, my dear and only daughter." Then she added, "One day your actions will kill me." Those words cut deep into my heart, and I burst out crying and cried bitterly for a long time. My mother wanted to discuss my future and what was right or wrong about what I was doing in light of my background and upbringing. By the end of that day, we decided that this would be the last time I saw my friend.

Several months later, Mother and I took a trip to Amman where we visited our Russian friends my old teachers at Bethany School: Georgi Alexandrovich Aleéff, my art teacher, and his wife, Ekaterina Borisovna. Their daughters were my school friends, but their only son at age fifteen died from sunstroke after running in a school marathon near Jerusalem. His sudden death was a tremendous shock for the family and the Russian community, and the parents were still grieving. Their younger daughter had married an English policeman and moved to England with him at the end of the British Mandate. The parents were living with their older daughter, a tall, good-looking young woman, fluent in several languages and popular at bridge-playing parties.

Bridge was played in Amman diplomatic circles as well as among well-to-do Arabs, providing an opportunity to mingle. Our friends took us along to such a party where we met several young German engineers who were building a new cement factory near Amman. Some of those engineers once belonged to an elite German youth group and still wore its emblem on the back side of their lapels. My mother was fluent in German, so she carried on a conversation with them. One of them expressed an interest in coming to Jerusalem to visit the Russian convent on the Mount of Olives and hoped to see us there. So he started visiting us because young Europeans were scarce after the end of the British Mandate, and there were not many places where one could speak German.

With our new German friend we often walked with my mother to her work at Augusta Victoria Hospital, the former summer residence of Germany's last king and queen. He was always polite and respectful, but his English was poor and my German nonexistent, so most of the communication was between him and my mother. We did sightseeing together, and when I introduced him to friends he made a good impression on them. Then a couple of months later, our German friend told us that his contract at the cement factory was coming to an end, that soon he would be returning to Germany, and that he would like us to get engaged so he could bring me home to his parents as his bride. They lived in Bavaria, and he had already written to them about me, "his Russian friend," and they answered that they would start to make preparations in their home for our arrival. He slipped a gold ring on my finger asking me to wear it. It was all like a dream, and I somehow did not realize things were moving forward so rapidly. So far we both had acted with the proper restraint expected of young people in that part of the world, and I was simply enjoying his company, mostly in my mother's presence.

I struggled with the thought that soon I would have to part with my mother, but I also knew that it was she who encouraged me to study hard so I would be accepted to a university. To live in Germany without knowing the language did not make sense to me. In broken English, my friend expressed his feelings for me as well as his concern about my mother in a country at war. But he was able to converse much better with her than with me. I hated to lead him on and knew I needed to make a decision. I liked him, but I was already also committed to the idea of going to study in America if I were to receive a scholarship. What was I to do?

It was a painful conversation for both of us, when I tried to explain to him that I must first get an education and only afterwards marry. He was a proud German, and for me to be thinking of going to America when he earnestly wanted me to be his wife was unacceptable. He said, "You will not be the same after America. I want you the way you are now." I attempted to explain that I would remain faithful to him, but he knew life in the Western world, whereas for me there was plenty to learn about it. We stood there together with teary eyes; then both of us silently walked away from each other, never to meet again.

I was young, lacking wisdom and practical knowledge about life in the world. I did, however, know that we had no means to pay my passage abroad to college even if I got a scholarship. I would need to have some type of citizenship and a passport to get an entry visa to a foreign country. All these considerations also preoccupied my mother's thoughts, which she shared with me. We were Russian, and there was no Russia; the Soviet Union had taken its place, and we had no Soviet passports. The British Mandate was humane enough to allow us a yearly renewal of our temporary visas for living in Palestine, as long as we were attached to a Christian mission. Therefore my mother pointed out that I had only two choices: to become a nun and stay in the monastery for life, or to marry, but not, of course, to a non-Christian.

Mother had good friends in Damascus, Syria, a Russian Orthodox family, who owned a small business in that city. On great feasts, they sometimes came to Jerusalem and got in touch with us. They had a son about my age, whose future also was unsettled, and they too had no citizenship of any kind, but were pleased with life in Damascus. They had learned to speak Arabic, and the local authorities allowed them to live there along with others like them. After one such feast-day visit to Jerusalem, they invited us to spend a couple of weeks with them at their home in Damascus, do some sightseeing together, and get acquainted with job opportunities and life in general there.

Not much later we had an opportunity to travel to Damascus. We enjoyed this historic city and enjoyed being with our hosts, who were delightful people with a background similar to ours and whose son was a polite and fairly good-looking young man not much older than me. The parents hinted that their dream for their only son was that he would marry a Russian Orthodox girl but that they were scarce in the Middle East. One evening at supper, they addressed us two young people, saying that we would make a perfect match, being of the same religion and nationality. "These days," the mother pointed out, "one has to take advantage of such opportunities when they arise"; to this, my mother added that she totally agreed. Then, the father turned to his son and said, "We are having such a good time with our guests, why don't you two, who seem to like each other, get engaged, start to see each other regularly, and perhaps God would show His mercy by joining your hearts?"

The next morning we all went to the fascinating Damascus bazaar. Here amid all the noise and distractions we saw a jewelry store with a beautifully arranged display window. The young man's mother asked to go in and look around, so we did. In the store she noticed a pretty ring and asked if I liked it, adding that it would look nice on my hand, and then she turned to her son and said, "Come on, son, offer Anya this ring, and let's find a similar one made for young men." That day without much thinking, we were carried away by the moment and became engaged to please both our parents. However, upon my return home with Mother to Jerusalem, I suddenly woke up to reality and panicked. I told mother that I had no feelings for the young man, that I hardly knew him, and that I still wanted first of all to study and acquire a profession. Meanwhile the parents of the young man informed close friends of our engagement and plans for a wedding. In my confused state of mind, I wrote about it all to Father Lazarus, telling him I was returning the ring by next mail and was not going to go through with the wedding.

Soon after this I received the following letter from Sister Mary (Mitchell), secretary of Father Lazarus in India:

Martha Maryam Mandiram,[3] Tiruvala, India

6–3–54

My dear Anya,

Father Lazarus tells me that you didn't get married after all! We were all thinking of you and praying for you on that day, but I was feeling very unhappy about it. I can't tell you how much I am relieved that you have changed your mind, or rather that God has made it clear to you that it wasn't the way for you. How near we can be to each other through prayer, even though we are hundreds of miles away in the flesh. I am sure that something much better is going to come to you.

We are still in this Mandiram as boarders and I am swamped with work as always. Typing, typing all the time. Father Lazarus comes to the Mandiram Chapel twice a day to serve our English services at which I do practically all the reading. This is quite a big job and takes time to prepare well. For every service Father Lazarus retranslates little bits of it so that gradually the English services are getting into good order. This compound is very beautiful, full of trees, lots of fruit and heavenly birds. In the mornings and evenings I climb the little hill in the compound and especially in the evening it is wonderful when the sun is setting behind the vast forest in front of me and the moon is coming up behind surrounded by twinkling diamonds. I stay up there in the moon light in an ecstasy of song and prayer. The sisters are hoping to build a convent up there one day; they have all been blessed to take vows. They are such gentle, patient, loving young women and inspire me very much. We are still hoping and praying that God will let us go to our own place some day; where it will be we do not know.

Give my warm love and a big hug for your dear Mother and much love and prayer for your future, dear Anya.

Ever yours in our Lord,
Mary Mitchell

Parting from Mother

At the end of that same month, I received a letter from America informing me that I was being granted a four-year scholarship to St Scholastica's College in Atchison, Kansas. My emotions were so overwhelmed at reading this news that it left a blank space in my memory. I hurried to inform Father Lazarus of my good fortune and received this response:

Peruvazhi P.O. Travancore, India
March 1953

Dear Anya!

I was delighted to get your letter in response to mine and heartily congratulate you on achieving a scholarship for the Benedictine College in Atchison. I quite understand that you are working at white-hot speed to pass the Intermediate! It is all very exciting and engrossing and it is good to be busy. I shall certainly pray that you may discover God's will in the matter. If your mother can't go with you in September, probably quite soon it will be possible for her to follow you. Short partings of that kind aren't bad; in fact, they are often quite useful in the spiritual life, and God deliberately plans them. Of course, if we were quite free and unattached there would be no need of them. But He is willing to go to all lengths to help us to love Him with all our hearts, that we may be attached solely and only to our One Beloved Creator.

It is a true sign that we see God in all things when we love Him equally in all things. The unevenness of our tempers and our love can only stem from the consideration of something that is not God. As Saint Augustine says, "So long as there is in me ought that is not wholly Thine, O God, sorrow and suffering will be my lot. But when I shall be Thine alone, then I shall be filled with Thee and wholly set at liberty." Certainly this applies equally to your mother. It takes two to make detachment and freedom in love, and it takes two to make a quarrel!

In this part of India life is very primitive as we are about twenty miles from the station and twelve from Adur, a sizable village. Windows have no glass, so when the wind blows not only the cradle will rock, but papers fly, lamps go out, calendars fall from the wall, etc. As there are no ceilings, not only lights and inspirations come from above but also dirt, dead rats, squirrels, etc., are apt to drop! Rats, ants of various kinds, and large flying cockroaches are our chief pests. Our food is mostly rice, and wheat and bread are not used in these parts (we get a little wheat with some difficulty for "prosfora" (*sacramental bread*). No time for more now. God bless you and guide you to the haven of His will.

Yours in His service,
Abbot Lazarus

On a bright day in June 1954, I woke up early to watch the sun rise over Jerusalem for the last time. A pale orange ball appeared from behind the bell tower of the Russian convent on the Mount of Olives. In the distance, the Dead Sea sparkled like bright silver as it lay silent and forever dead. I turned in the direction of Jerusalem and the early morning slant of the sun's rays made this ancient city look golden. I tried to imprint this image in my mind as I wondered whether I would ever see such beauty again; there was something uniquely celestial about Jerusalem.

A chorus of birds chanting their jubilant morning songs turned my attention away from the ancient walls of Jerusalem, and I moved toward the green tops of the Russian church. I entered the church and could hear the weak, low voice of the already very old priest I had known since early childhood. He was serving the Liturgy with the aid of the angelic singing of the old sisters who helped raise me and whose soft voices were now like an echo of their past beauty. Then some very keen sorrow gripped at my heart. I was going away from them, perhaps never to see them again. What would the future and distant America bring?

I was sorry to leave, but happy to begin new adventures. At the airport stood many of my friends, a small banister separating them from the passengers. Only then did I realize how dear every one of them was to me. In a few minutes my hands were full of gifts, books whose titles fit the idea of my departure: *Gone with the Wind* and *Over the Hills and Mountains;* there were hankies to cry into and souvenirs from Jerusalem. There was a special gift that I was asked to open right away and use. It was my first tube of lipstick, and having applied it on my trembling lips I opened my handbag to put it away. To my great alarm, I discovered that neither my wallet nor my plane ticket were there.

The plane was to leave the airport in a few minutes. In a panic I stood wondering what to do and suddenly remembered that I had not taken them out of my drawer at home and I never put them in my bag. Like a meteor the taxi rushed me homeward. At the convent gate, someone said that this was a sign that I'll return home someday! Fortunately, it all happened in Palestine, where distances were not so great. As I finally climbed the metal steps leading to the plane's door, those who did not know the real cause of the delay must have mistaken me for someone of special importance; snapshots were taken of me from all sides. The plane waited for me, leaving the airport forty-five minutes after the scheduled time.

Mother accompanied me to my first stop, Beirut, Lebanon. The city looked very modern and beautiful. A special sea odor filled its air, attracting me to the seashore. In the bay stood the majestic *Esperia* that was to transport me to Italy. I spent the night with Mother at a local hotel close to the seaport. The night was beautiful; I admired the view from the balcony of our room. The city looked splendid with myriads of lights. Soft notes of music could be heard coming from somewhere not far away, and a melancholy flute on which a Middle Eastern tune was playing made me wonder if I would ever hear that kind of music where I was going. I turned to Mother and hugged her as tightly as I could; I hated the thought of parting with her the next day, and I broke down and cried on her shoulder as I never had before.

Such was my last night in the Middle East, the night that put an end to one beautiful chapter of my life: my childhood in Jerusalem, Palestine. In the morning, Mother said we might never see each other again; this is how it happened when she left Russia and never saw her family again. When we left Belgrade, we never saw my father again, and now for the first time Mother and I were separating. Standing together before the entrance to the ship, I wished she too would be boarding with me. But it was time for her to leave me. I boarded the ship and stood on the deck, wishing I could give her just one more hug. Watching the receding lights of the city where Mother was, still so close to me yet already out of reach, I sailed away wondering when I would see her again.

CHAPTER 4

✠✠✠

Settling in America

Journey to America

It is remarkable how one's memory more readily singles out emotional experiences; thus, my parting with Mother bothered me for a long time. More than the stress of uncertainty while hoping to receive a scholarship to a college in America, or worrying about getting citizenship and a passport to get out of the country should I get a scholarship, or the distress of turning down possibilities of marriage that I was simply not ready for—breaking my physical ties to Mother seemed to be worse of all.

Nevertheless, I persevered through the mental and emotional agony; I received the hoped-for scholarship, the greatest impediment was cleared when I was granted Jordanian citizenship and a passport, and when financing transportation to America became another problem, a mysterious American benefactress solved it. It was the dawn of my independence, and I looked forward to new adventures where the Italian ship *Esperia* was going to take me. After crossing the Mediterranean Sea, my first stop was in Italy at Brindisi, a seaport town full of helpful young sailors all trying to assist me with my luggage to the train station. The train took me to Rome, where I stopped for several days at a branch of Notre Dame de Sion School. From here I took tours to enjoy magnificent sights of what remained of the Roman Empire's past greatness. My eyes opened upon scenes I had tried to imagine when I studied Latin with Father Arnold. Remains of ancient Roman catacombs and an amphitheater where early Christians gave up their lives for their faith in Christ were spectacular sights just as was St Peter's Basilica and the whole center of the Catholic Church with its beautiful interiors and the papal residence making a lasting impression on me.

Toward the end of my stay in Rome I needed to pay a visit of a personal nature. It was a special request from my dear mother that I should have tea with her old acquaintance from Moscow: Princess Contacusen, now living in

Rome. Mother corresponded with her and knew that she had also raised her only child by herself, who was now a young man. I took the bus as instructed and arrived at the address at the appointed time. The elevator of the elegant building was made of glass. It brought me to the fifth floor where I needed to go, but the door did not open, and no matter how hard I tried to open it or figure out how to do so, it remained closed. I waited for someone to use the elevator who would show me how to get out but no one came.

I panicked and pushed the door so hard that some of the glass shattered, leaving an opening big enough for me to squeeze out. Seeing a stairway across from the elevator, I quickly stepped over the broken glass and, forgetting everything else but my sudden fear of wrongdoing, dashed out and down the five floors of stairs to the exit of the building. I was frightened about what I had done to the elevator: breaking someone else's property in a foreign land. In Jerusalem I never saw or used an elevator, but the worst of it was that I did not think to get in touch with my mother's friend afterwards to let her know what stopped me from visiting her. Much later I read in a letter from my mother how her friend waited for me for tea that day and did not know what happened to me or how to get in touch with me. Both mother and her friend were disappointed that I missed the tea and did not get to meet her or her son.

After my misadventure in Rome, I took the overnight train to Paris. It was not easy to sit on a hard wood bench all night with no accommodation for resting. Next to me sat a young black African Franciscan monk, who, while sound asleep, kept sliding toward me every time the train jolted. I was glad to finally arrive in Paris and promptly took a taxi to the Narishkins' apartment. These were Russians my age, a brother and sister whom I had met a couple of years before while they were on a pilgrimage in Jerusalem. At that time we exchanged addresses, and they invited me to visit them in Paris.

When I arrived and knocked at their door, I was met by teary-eyed Natasha, the sister. She led me to the bedroom where in one corner on the floor was a mattress on which lay her brother. "My brother is dying," she said. His sunken cheeks were crimson, and his deep-set eyes had a strange glow in them. She explained that this was the last stage of the disease and that she too had the rapidly advancing tuberculosis and that I would get it if I were to stay with them. Then she took the telephone and proceeded to make arrangements for me to stay in the home of an elderly gentleman who lived with his little granddaughter at a villa not far from the Narishkins.

The elderly gentleman picked me up, and we arrived in his small black car to his two-story elegant villa in the center of Paris. He was a businessman, formerly a German national who remained in Parish after World War II and became a French citizen. While his granddaughter Nicole was in school, her grandfather showed me around Paris. What a magnificent city it was! He took me for the day to the Louvre and other museums, which were walking distance from his home. Here he left me to wander around till he returned later with Nicole, whom he would pick up from school. Nicole and I enjoyed evenings together speaking French; I listening to French jokes she loved to tell me and that I didn't quite understand. One evening we went to the famous Folies Bergère, with its somewhat risqué entertainment. Beautiful young men and women danced and did acrobatics in skimpy attire; it was a shock to me at that time but today would be totally acceptable by most people.

One morning, very early, we went to the famous Paris produce market to watch how French country folk sold their wares from the countryside. They set up their stalls while making lots of noise and filling the air with chatter in various French dialects. What a marvelous experience this was for me, a French student. Mother spoke French, and I heard it from early childhood, but not that kind.

On Sunday I took the train to Furque outside Paris, where on the grounds of an old mansion was located Lesninskaya Russian Orthodox Convent, which had been moved from Russia during the revolution to Yugoslavia and then to France. I arrived in time for the Sunday morning Liturgy served by Bishop John (Maximovich), later of Shanghai and San Francisco. Afterwards the friendly sisters invited me to the monastic refectory for the midday meal. A young nun read the life of the saint of the day and everyone listened while eating. On leaving the refectory, I was introduced to Bishop John, who offered a nearby bench in the beautiful garden for us to sit and visit. He was an acquaintance of my mother from their days as refugees in Belgrade and wanted to know all about our life in Palestine.

Hearing that I was on my way to college in America, he gave me a warm blessing, promised to pray for me and my mother, and wished me success in college and happiness in life. I could not foresee that many years later I would meet him again in Seattle in what became my parish church on the last day of his life! When I returned to Paris that evening, I hastened to write my mother the following short letter that I found among her books and old letters, which she saved and I read after her death.

Paris, France, 1954

Dearest Mother,

   I returned to Paris from the convent in Furque with a feeling of such joy as I never felt before. Bishop John blessed me and promised to pray for you and me. In our conversation as we sat on a bench in the garden, he convinced me that my future was in God's hands. During the church service I watched him pray with such fervor as if he was addressing God in person here and now. Something in his eyes when he looked at me and the words he said were so inspiring that I thought I was looking and speaking to a saint.

Your loving daughter,

Anya

Little did I know that in 1994 in America, Bishop John (Maximovich) would be sanctified for a life full of kindness and love for all those he met and especially for saving the lives of Russian refugees from the Communists in Manchuria (now China). After helping them relocate to the United States, he organized orphanages for children without parents and gave refuge to elderly Russians and anyone who was lonely.

Later that month, after a memorable fortnight in Paris, I boarded a French ship called *La Flandre* for a week on the Atlantic Ocean sailing to New York City. There were two classes on this ship, first class and second class. Being in second class placed me in a cabin with two other young women of whom I remember very little. It was my dining table companions who made a lasting impression on me, and perhaps, one could say, sealed my destiny in America.

My dining table was set for six people, three couples. There were two elderly couples, a professor and his wife from Chicago and a couple from New York City. The latter were Jews and took particular interest in me, a Serbian Russian from Palestine. They treated me with exceptional care and explained things to me, giving me advice that would be helpful in my life in America. Then there was me and a young man, both single, both quiet, and assigned places next to each other. When I asked him his name, he said I could call him Mac.

I was not only homesick, but also very seasick the first few days on the ship. Often during dinner just looking at food made me rush upstairs to the deck for a breath of fresh air. Mac would ask whether he could eat my food if I didn't come back. I watched him on the deck playing chess and noticed that he smoked Soviet-made cigarettes. Then I discovered a pleasant surprise: while I was standing on the deck reading Turgenev's short novel *On the Eve,* Mac stopped beside me and started to read in Russian over my shoulder. This kindled my interest in him, and I wondered what he may have had to do with Russia. He explained that he worked in the United States embassy in Vienna,

Austria, where he met Soviet citizens at diplomatic parties, and wanting to be able to communicate better with them, he studied the language. He said he would like to practice speaking Russian with me, and that of course was enough for us to start a friendship.

As we neared America's shores, the Statue of Liberty became visible in the distance. Life on the ship became noisily hurried. One could feel excitement in the air and see it on people's faces. Tourists, immigrants, students like me—everyone tried to get a glimpse of the Statue of Liberty. Some people smiled, and others shed tears of joy. Soon I realized I was parting with my new friend to whom in a week's time I became somewhat attached. Yet all I knew about him was that he worked in the State Department and would return to Washington, D.C., after a briefing in New York City. He told me that after Vienna he had worked in Paris for the past two years but that now he would be reassigned to another foreign embassy. Bidding me farewell, he encouraged me by saying, "You will have a good time at the college in Atchison, Kansas." When we arrived at the Port of New York, he disappeared into the crowd leaving the ship, and I thought we would never meet again.

However, when I was finally allowed to come down the steps of the ship, I saw Mac standing beside a middle-aged couple who were looking at me. They approached me smiling, and I noticed that in their hands they had my photograph. At this point Mac said, "Now I can leave; you will be in good hands as those are friends of your Latin teacher." Then with a reassuring smile and a hand wave, he walked out of the crowded halls of the port. After a lengthy screening at the immigration checkpoint, where the officers on duty were impressed with my knowledge of English, the nice couple drove me to their home in Elizabeth, New Jersey.

Among my first impressions of America were the comfortable lodgings and the tasty chocolate cake with glasses of cold milk I was offered and drank continuously at the home of the kind couple. They had a daughter a few years older than me, were of Slovak origin, were friends of Father Arnold, and they would help me reach my destination. I spent a few days with them, and then their daughter drove me to the station and helped me board a train to Kansas. I left my hosts' hometown impressed with its clean streets and the tidy one-story ramblers that seemed to me to be built in what looked like parks. I was charmed by the local inhabitants, by their neat homes with manicured lawns and gardens as well as by the sidewalks next to wide streets, by attractive store windows, and by the overall law and order among friendly, smiling people. It was all such a contrast to war-torn life in Jerusalem.

At the Benedictine College of St Scholastica

Upon arrival at the Benedictine college in Kansas, I was placed in the women's dorm on Mount St Scholastica, where I met the sister in charge and liked her right away. Some of the other boarders offered help settling me in my new home, and a few I noticed by their accents were also foreign students. I was accustomed to institutional life, having always been a boarder in the schools I attended in Jerusalem, yet I wondered how different it would be living at an American college. The course work I was offered toward a major in English language and literature with a minor in biology sounded appealing, and the size and beauty of the college campus impressed me. However, there was one thought that again began to bother me: "My dear mother alone and far away: is she well? Does she have all she needs? How can I help her at such a distance? Oh, God, what have I done abandoning her this way!" However, soon my new life's tempo began to distract me and at least during the day dissipated my sad thoughts about my past and the loving people I left behind.

I was comfortable, sharing a good room with a friendly roommate from San Antonio, Texas. She was a heavy smoker and had a boyfriend who was a football player at the Benedictine college campus. The food was the best I have ever eaten, and my studies left enough time for recreation. Nevertheless there were times of occasional homesickness and I felt guilty when I thought about the poverty and political instability in Palestine while I was living in peace and comfort in the hometown of the renowned aviator Amelia Earhart.

As my English professor, Sister Scholastica was my principal instructor. Her mellow personality made her approachable anytime one needed extra help. I remember her smiling when I approached her office, saying, "I knew it was Anya coming," to which I would ask her how she knew, and she would answer, "By the sound of your special footsteps." Her lectures on Willa Cather's stories such as "Neighbour Rosicky" or Walt Whitman's poetry about himself fascinated me. I knew Sister had a heart condition; her lips were often blue, but she was always cheerful and well prepared for class, so her lectures were most interesting.

Sister Dunstan, house mother of our dorm, showed strength of character although she never raised her voice, even when we deserved a reprimand. It was enough for her to rest her glance on us to make us understand that we were doing something we should not. On weekends after a ball game on the boys' campus, girls often stood for a long time in an embrace with their escorts on the dorm porch. A hug or a kiss tended to last a bit too long, although it was time to go to our rooms. Later Sister would tell us that it was unfair of us to excite the boys by holding on to them too long, and that it would actually be unkind to them, under the circumstances.

Sister Imogene (Baker) had been the Dean of Students for many years and understood foreign students' psyche. She knew that being homesick for many of us was inevitable. Even students coming from the poorest and most dangerous circumstances still could not help but feel homesick now and then. There were students from Korea, Taiwan, Vietnam, Puerto Rico, Germany, and me, a Russian-Palestinian from Trans-Jordan. Just the fact that she took time to listen to me and understood my problems made me remain forever thankful to her.

In college I continued my correspondence with Father Lazarus, who was doing missionary work now in Pankajam, South India. This is what he wrote:

Kotagiri, South India

25/11 1954

Dear Anya!

I was overjoyed to get your two letters, one written en route. I thank God that you had such a wonderful voyage and that now you are happily settled in college. I moved into this house alone in July, and have taken it for a year. I was joined about a month later by a Canadian, Joseph, whom I first met as a pilgrim to Jerusalem. He is about thirty, of Ukrainian origin, and a very good soul. The other novice is teaching in a school in Travan-core. We are about six hundred feet above sea level here. It is never very hot or really cold. The mountains are green to the summit and the chief scenery is eucalyptus forests, tea and coffee plantations, interspersed with green fields growing various crops, such as potatoes which won't grow on plains; we have a little garden with all kinds of flowers which go on and on. When I came in July there were violets, and now there are still violets filling the air with fragrance. There are also two cherry trees.

Our chief food is no longer rice; we can buy whole wheat bread here and vegetables and fruits. Best of all for our work we have electric lighting. I am up to my eyes in translation work. I have nearly finished the Oktoich (the eight tones of Sunday services), in fact it should be ready at the end of next week. Then the Ladder of Paradise is going on well, perhaps two-thirds already done, and the church calendar is in its third month. All these things involve a lot of research, so you can imagine how little time I have for correspondence.

I am sure you will like America with all its modern conveniences and resultant cleanliness, its clean cities and towns, its beautiful scenery and vast open spaces. I must away. Write again. I promise you I will answer any spiritual questions you want, as I will make time for that. God bless and keep you and fill you with His spirit. With love and prayer,

Abbot Lazarus

An Unexpected Christmas Card

My last Christmas vacation during college was in December 1954, and I was invited to spend it in Erie, Pennsylvania. That cold and snowy winter was one of my worst. I was spending time with Russian immigrants, DPs (displaced persons) from a refugee camp in post-World War II Germany. They invited me sight unseen, by mail, and paid my round-trip train passage, taking into consideration my impoverished foreign student status. I was to spend Christmas with them and their single son in his twenties. This was the result of my answering an advertisement in a Russian newspaper published in New York City, *Novoe Russkoe Slovo* (*The New Russian Word*): "Young man wants to meet young woman, has honorable intentions." The advertisement was placed by the parents of the young man. Foreign students, I was told, who have no parents or homes in this country were known to spend vacations this way, quite safely, away from college. I received flowers and gift parcels at first; later the invitation and train passage ticket arrived.

Thus I traveled to Erie and was met by a young man, who drove me to his parents' home. The family was nice but had scarred souls from life in a wartime postwar refugee camp. When they went to work the next morning, they locked me in their house without telling me. I discovered this when the mailman knocked at the door to deliver some special delivery mail for my hosts, which I was unable to take from him because the door was locked. I was surprised that they did not trust me, but in those days I was naive and inexperienced. When my college forwarded my mail to their house and the mother handed it to me, I remember her penetrating gaze into my eyes.

Opening my bundle of mail, I found one envelope addressed to me in a strange handwriting and with stamps on it from Hanoi, Indo-China (now called Vietnam). It a Christmas card from Mac at the American consulate[1] in Hanoi, where he was working. It read as follows:

Dear Anya,

All I can think about is our trip together across the Atlantic Ocean, how pleasant it was especially in comparison with life here. Please write about your life in college. Perhaps someday we will meet again.

Sincerely, Mac

I was by the fireplace surrounded by the family with their son sitting next to me. In happy surprise I exclaimed, "This is from Mac, I met him on the ship when I was sailing to America." This definitely was not a happy moment for my hosts; the mother retorted, "Why didn't you tell us you already had a boyfriend? We would not have invited you to meet our son. Our poor son, this is another disappointing experience for him. We shall call the railroad station at once, and tomorrow you should return to college," and so I did.

They did not believe me when I said I hardly knew the man and I didn't even know his real name other than "Mac." My sad departure was followed by a letter from the family. In it the mother wrote that I was an adventurer, not a serious person, and I took advantage of their hospitality, when my heart belonged elsewhere. I cried about the unintended hurt I caused this kind family, and tried to explain in a long letter back to the mother that my primary concern in life at the moment was my student life and studies, but to no avail; neither the young man nor his father ever wrote.

Several years later, while working at the Tolstoy Foundation in New York City, I understood much more about this family and many others like them whom this benevolent organization helped relocate to America. Unjustly abused as they were in the refugee camp, people saw abuse everywhere even where it did not exist. I started to realize how fortunate I was by comparison to them. No wonder my mother often exclaimed during our life in the Holy Land, "How lucky we are to be here! Just in time God lifted us from the middle of World War II in Europe and placed us here as if into the safety of His bosom." Consequently I did not have to grow up in a refugee camp, as so many of my young friends from Belgrade did after they were relocated with their parents.

Going to New York
The following year was my last at college, so I had to devote all my time left to intensive study. I planned to spend summer vacation on my own before returning for final examinations prior to graduation. I was aware that in addition I must be prepared to return to Jerusalem afterwards. Believing that I would soon be back with my mother lessened the anxiety I felt for her welfare whenever I thought about her. But now there was a new feeling of attachment I felt for America that grew stronger every day. I realized how accustomed I had become to the common comforts of the American way of life and especially the absence of conflict that so intensely aggravated the discomforts of life in Palestine.

I imagined myself back on the Mount of Olives in Mother's modest room with all its inconveniences. No electricity, so I would have to read at night by candlelight and fill the kerosene lamp with the pungent-smelling oil that required daily washing of the soot from around its burning light. There would be no running water or a warm shower. I would have to carry the water in a bucket from the closest well and heat the water on the small kerosene stove one kettle-full at a time. I would wash first the top part of my body then the bottom in the same water in a large bowl as water was precious. In America, every function in life deemed necessary or unavoidable was simplified and made convenient to the point of being pleasurable, a condition much easier to get used to than the other way around.

Enumerating all the discomforts of life on the Mount of Olives or in Bethany School would be a very long list. After just a few years in America, I dreaded to think about returning to them. Nevertheless, as I mused about the past in what I regarded as my true homeland of Palestine, despite all its difficulties and inconveniencies, it still evoked strong sentimental feelings about both its people and places.

Then one day in the spring of 1955 I found in my mailbox (every student had her own locked box) a surprise letter from "Mac," now signed "Wayne Derrick" and with a return address in New York City. I read the following:

My dear Anya,

Let me first tell you how happy I was that you have not forgotten me. Your small flowers from your homeland were beautiful, Anya, I thank you so much for your thoughts. I have been back from Indo-China for a while now and I am going to stay in New York for some time. When you will finish the school year and perhaps will be looking for work in Kansas City, why don't you come instead to New York City and work here? I am sorry that I have not written more often, Anya, but I was never certain if my letters would ever leave Indo-China. Please write to me again and I will write back. Do you think you can come to New York?

Best wishes,
Wayne

I wondered about Hanoi, Indo-China, a place I did not know existed, and why he thought his letters might never reach me. After receiving his Christmas card, I had sent him a short note at the address in Hanoi, enclosing pressed dried flowers from Jerusalem but had heard nothing from him since. Only much later was the situation clarified for me by the following

newspaper story from the *Seattle Times* published in 1954 under the headline
"Former University of Washington Student on Duty in Hanoi":

Wayne Derrick of Tacoma, a former student of the University of Washington, is a member of the United States consular staff in Hanoi Vietnam.

A communist government took over the city October 10th. However,
the United States government takes the position that, since it did not sign
the Geneva Treaty and does not recognize the partition of Vietnam, it can
retain its Hanoi consulate.

Derrick and six other consular officials continue to occupy the consular
quarters. Among the six is Donald Barrett, formerly of Redmond.

The consulate is in a state of virtual siege although its officials are in no
immediate danger, according to reports from correspondents.

The consulate has food for months. The windows are double-barred in
case of demonstrations. Officials do not go out much because the government will not issue them identity cards.

Derrick is the son of Mr. and Mrs. Derrick of Tacoma. He was born in
Puyallup. He was graduated from Hoquiam High School and attended
the University of Washington two years after spending two years in the
Air Corps.

Derrick worked for the United States consulate in Paris and attended
the Sorbonne. He also attended the University of Vienna and was in the
consular service there.

Derrick, 31, was sent to Hanoi in September, according to his parents.
He has written them twice since, reporting that he was "getting along
fine," but adding that in his opinion all United States citizens will have to
leave the country.

The seven consular officials and a freelance correspondent, Ernest L.
Zaugg, now are the only Americans in Hanoi. Zaugg is a cousin of Mrs.
Earl Lasher, wife of a Seattle physician.

Derrick went from Vienna to Hanoi, with a two-week stopover in
Washington D.C. for briefing in his new assignment.

This explained what was happening when we met on the ship as I was
travelling to America. Reading Wayne's letter from New York, I thought to
myself that my life was full of miracles and this was one more of them. What
an exciting idea, to work in New York City and again be with Wayne. This
was just what I needed to do before graduating from college and returning
home to Jerusalem. I wrote Mother about this new idea, and she seemed

to favor it because Metropolitan Anastasy, who she knew from her days in Moscow and Belgrade, resided there, which gave her some reassurance about my security. She even discussed it with Abbess Tamara, her superior after Abbess Antonia's retirement, who suggested I write a letter to her son, Prince Teymouraz K. Bagration Mukhransky, who was employed at the Tolstoy Foundation in New York City.

I followed this advice and received an offer of a job at the Tolstoy Foundation in New York City for the three months of summer. Wayne wrote that he would meet me at the airport and, of course, help me in any way he could. I started to feel as if a heavy load was being lifted off my shoulders. My classmates and instructors said they were pleased for me as I would have a chance to get to know the biggest city in the United States of America.

When I arrived at the airport in New York and tried to remember how Wayne looked, I realized it was his pleasant personality I remembered clearly; the rest was vague. But as I carried my suitcase toward the exit, I glanced at the crowd awaiting the passengers. I immediately recognized him and experienced what is called love at first sight. I liked the English tweed suit he had on, which much later he told me was tailored for him in Europe. I liked his smile and deep voice, but best of all was his soft and at the same time sure manner. He made me feel secure and comfortable although I knew him very little.

We went to the hotel I reserved at the time of purchasing the ticket. Wayne said he would return the next day to help me with further arrangements for my life and work that summer. That same evening I telephoned the local Russian church, and they directed me to an elderly Russian lady who was able to rent me a room in her large apartment. The next day when Wayne came over, he helped me locate the place and move in. The lady of the house introduced me to her other tenants, two elderly Russian gentlemen. We were not allowed to receive guests in our rooms, but could entertain them in her drawing room.

The Tolstoy Foundation

To get to my job at the Tolstoy Foundation headquarters, I took the subway to Columbus Circle. I was given a pile of letters, primarily in Russian, that I was supposed to read and decide where to file. There were hundreds of case files for letters, and many new letters arrived each day for which I had to create a file depending on the type of case it was. This was usually determined by the various department heads who handled new cases. Most letters were either an appeal for help to immigrate to America, or a thank you letter with a check enclosed to repay passage money loaned by the Tolstoy Foundation. Repayment letters were generally from those who had arrived and were living and working somewhere in one of the states.

Prior to their arrival, many of the letter writers had lived in World War II concentration camps in Europe. Now those immigrants were living wherever the Tolstoy Foundation was able to help find work for them. The happier ones lived in cities where there were Russian immigrants and churches where they could meet others like themselves. But I read letters from many who were most unhappy in their new homeland. This was primarily because they were unable to communicate with their employers and did not have the right skills or experience to do the work required of them. Some worked on distant farms alone with no family and no language in common with those around them. They begged for help finding other employment. Some wrote that the climate was unbearable, that they were ill, or they were so depressed that they were contemplating suicide.

I worked under the direction of a nice older lady, Elizabeth Tomashevsky, who took interest in me, asked me personal questions, and helped me with my work. At lunchtime I was sometimes accompanied by a lovely couple, the Olsufievs, who came to work daily by train from Sea Cliff, Long Island, a small town where some of the older Russian intelligentsia preferred to live and where there were two Russian Orthodox churches with social life connected to them. Miss Alexandra L'vovna Tolstoy, the president and founder of the Tolstoy Foundation—a nonprofit, international philanthropic organization without political or religious affiliation—was the youngest daughter of Leo Tolstoy. On occasion she would pass through my office and ask how I liked my work. Then she would tell me something about herself. Once she told me that she enjoyed her work on the Tolstoy farm best of all.

The farm was on seventy acres of land in Valley Cottage, New York, acquired by the Tolstoy Foundation in 1941. World War II refugees who were new arrivals to this country would sometimes stay there while waiting to be placed in a permanent location where there was work for them. There were also orphans there of whom she was a guardian. She often spoke of how much she enjoyed working with them and showing them how to plant potatoes and raise chickens. There was a church on the premises where she sang in the choir with the youngsters. The Farm in Valley Cottage became the TF Center, and continues to offer a home to many people seeking care in their old age in a secure Russian-speaking environment.

In 1956, her father's famous novel *War and Peace* was made into a film. Alexandra Tolstoy and the employees of the Tolstoy Foundation were invited to the premiere of the film, which of course thrilled most of us. We especially enjoyed the time afterwards, when we could discuss with the writer's daughter herself the quality of acting in the film and what was good or bad in it. Miss Tolstoy was the personification of the words her father wrote in 1886, expressing his belief that "The vocation of every man and woman is to serve other people," and this is what she did most of her life.

Teymuraz K. Bagration Mukhransky was Miss Tolstoy's closest associate and later became president of the Tolstoy Foundation. He was born in 1912 in Pavlovsk, St Petersburg. On his father's side, his ancestors were from the ruling Bagrationi dynasty of Georgia. In 1801, Georgia asked Russia to protect it from the onslaughts of the Turks and Persians by making it part of the Russian Empire. Since that time, members of the Bagration royal family married into the Russian imperial family, sharing with them Russia's destiny. During the 1812 war with Napoleon, Prince Pyotr Bagration was an outstanding general in the Russian army.

On his mother's side, Teymouraz was grandson of Grand Prince Konstantin K. Romanov, the talented poet who signed his poetry "K.R." It was expected that little Teymouraz and his younger sister Natasha would grow up to lead a privileged life. However, in 1914 World War I began, and in 1915 their father, Prince Constantine Bagration, lost his life serving their country. Two years later the Bolshevik Revolution erupted, and the children's mother, Tatiana K. Romanov, a young widow with two infants, faced unimaginable difficulties and exile. They ended up in Geneva, Switzerland, where the children went to local schools. Upon finishing school, Teymouraz was admitted to a military academy in Yugoslavia, where his sister attended an institute of higher learning.

Yugoslavia was occupied within days of the start of World War II. Miraculously Teymouraz was not taken as a prisoner of war and eventually was able to relocate to America where he married. His sister went to England and there became the wife of a future ambassador to India. In New York, Teymouraz met Alexandra Tolstoy, who soon recognized his moral and business attributes. Indeed, he had a marvelous personality; between his natural mellowness and polished mannerisms, he was a joy to be around. I felt blessed that he later became my first child's godfather.

After both her son and daughter were happily married, Tatiana Romanov went to the Holy Land where she entered Gethsemane Convent. Later she moved to the Mount of Olives Convent, where she became Abbess Tamara (she took the monastic name of a Georgian saint). In 1958 she directed the celebration of the hundredth anniversary of the founding of the Russian Mission in the Holy Land. A personal representative of the King of Jordan participated in the festivities. During the Six Day War of 1967, she and the sisters survived the bitter exchange of fire between the Arabs and the Jews.

Besides time spent in the company of my Russian co-workers at the Tolstoy Foundation, I also attended church services at the headquarters of the Russian Orthodox Church Abroad and visited its chief hierarch, Metropolitan Anastasy, who knew me as a child in Belgrade and later in Jerusalem. He also was once on the examining board in Moscow when my mother was finishing her studies at the Mariinsky Institute. Two other priests in New York, a father and his son, were also special friends who knew mother and me in Belgrade. They were Father George Grabbe and his son Father Antony, who was also born in Belgrade and graduated from Holy Trinity Monastery Seminary in Jordanville, New York. As a young man in St Petersburg, Father George was a page at the tsar's court, and the Grabbe family bore the honorable title of Count before their family name.

A Deepening Friendship

At the end of my workday, Wayne often came to pick me up and thus met some of my friends at the Tolstoy Foundation. He would take me out to dinner or to some party where I would meet his friends. They were mostly bachelors, former U.S. State Department employees. They worked in Europe after World War II at the same time Wayne did and therefore had a lot in common to converse about. They struck me with how self-assured they were, how freely they discussed and sometimes criticized their government, and how little interest they showed in religion. No one prayed before meals or talked about feast days or fasting days or even church on Sundays. Religion had always played an important role in my life, as it did for many I met on my life's paths, but here no one seemed to care about it. They talked about their work, living quarters, and entertainment. Most of the time I spent in the company of this group of young men and women was of little interest to me, other than the fact of being in Wayne's company.

I could feel that every time we saw each other we became closer and understood each other better. He was thirty-two years old and so far led an almost bohemian lifestyle with frequent changes of job assignments in different countries. His last assignment turned out to be the shortest, as with the coming of communism to Indo-China, the staff of the American embassy in Hanoi were put under house arrest and later returned to the United States earlier than originally planned.

My landlady once asked me who he was and what I liked about him. I could not tell her who he was because I myself did not know; I just knew he had a job. Then she asked me what religion he was, I said I did not know that either. She was not satisfied with my short answers and said, "You better ask him those questions before you get too involved, after all you are in New York City where anything goes." I was not very pleased with her inquisitiveness and unsolicited advice. I was raised to trust people, and Mother always said it was in poor taste to ask personal questions. Nevertheless, even though I was a grown woman, it did make me think.

I reflected on my previous encounters with young men. The first suitor I gave up on account of our differing religious beliefs. The second one I gave up because we did not speak a language in common and I wanted to finish my education. Now some three years later, I wasn't as open with Mother in my letters to her as I had been when I was younger. Also I tried to avoid causing her anxiety about my welfare.

The following Sunday I asked Wayne to go with me to church. It was the first time he entered a church not as a tourist but during an actual service. Afterwards we stayed for a cup of coffee in the parish hall, where we met other young people from whom I found out about a weekend pilgrimage to Holy Trinity Monastery in Jordanville, which was being planned for the Fourth of July holiday. It was too early in Wayne's spiritual awakening to be interested in such a trip, but I wanted to go. He understood, saying it was part of my native culture. On this trip I met other young Russian Orthodox women and men with whom I kept in touch and spent time even after the trip.

Pilgrimage to Jordanville

Holy Trinity Monastery impressed me with the magnitude of the territory surrounding the church and the seminary. The beauty of the church service was enhanced by the choir made up of monks and seminarians, who also farmed the land belonging to the monastery. They served meals with pitchers of fresh warm milk from their own cows. Male pilgrims ate with the monks in the monastic refectory, while the women ate in another room.

From conversations with the monks, I understood that there were different Russian Orthodox churches in the United States. There were those that were under the leadership of the Russian patriarchy reinstated by Stalin in the Soviet Union, as well as the independent American Metropolia and the Russian Orthodox Church Abroad to which this monastery belonged. I was told that the latter was the true Russian Orthodox Church transported abroad from prerevolutionary Russia. When the atheistic Bolshevik government outlawed religion, the incarcerated former Patriarch Tikhon instructed his bishops to flee abroad in order to preserve the traditional church of Russia.

I was also told that when, God willing, the atheistic rule of the Soviet Union would fall and Holy Russia would be reborn, the true Russian Orthodox Church would return to the motherland.

Hearing talk about these matters reminded me of my life in Jerusalem. Upon returning to New York City, I wrote a long letter to my spiritual father and friend, Father Lazarus (Moore). I felt I could write to him about my thoughts and doubts more openly than to my mother. There were too many questions I needed answered about churches and the American philosophy of life I was discovering in New York, and I wondered how to live with them without losing my old self. This is how Father Lazarus answered:

Pankajam, Kotagiri
2/1/1955

Dear Anya!

Thank you for your letter and prayers. I have two Josephs with me at the moment, one American and one Canadian, both about 30. We have daily services. I am writing from Pankajam, Kotagiri in India.

You ask me to help you to get some questions straight, so although I am up to my eyes with work, I will try to answer you.

Why the frictions and separations? These are not confined to us Orthodox. The Roman Catholics and Protestants all have them too. If you pick up the New Testament you will see that we were warned that in the world you will have tribulations, trouble, sorrow, suffering (John 16:53). But Jesus told us all His secrets so that we might have peace in the midst of the world and its troubles, because He has overcome the world. As a great Indian Christian said, "Hope and experience will teach the unbeliever that joy follows pain, but that joy does not endure. But Christ gives ease in pain, and perfect happiness and peace." Mostly others try us from without only because we lack peace within. You know that the oyster accepts the grain of sand that gets into its shell and would otherwise irritate it and turns it into a pearl. Love of God in our hearts will enable us to turn into pearls those troubles and trials which would otherwise annoy and distress us.

It is the cross that lifts us to heaven and unites us with Christ. In fact, the cross is the gift that God gives to His friends. We are also told that our struggle is not against flesh and blood, that is, not against a physical enemy, but against the potentates and powers of evil, against the unseen rulers of this dark world, against wicked spirits in the regions of the sky (Ephesians 6:12). Regions of the sky could be translated as the heavenly or spiritual realms. That means that the greater the treasure you carry, the more that thieves will try to wreck and rob you. If the Orthodox people are harried more than others, there is the reason.

You will be just what you allow in your mind. You must seek the Kingdom everywhere, seek Christ in everyone. But if you look at bodies instead of souls, you will find it next to impossible for Christ to reign in you. And remember Christ is Victory, Joy, Purity, and Peace. The hills that have to be leveled are pride, self-will, vanity, conceit, and all selfishness. And it is easy to see that what is crooked in us must be made honest and straight if Christ is to be born in the cave of our heart, for He is Light and in Him there is no darkness at all.

The spirit gets control of the body if we feed the spirit with constant reading of the word of God and prayer, while fasting physically. If temptation is felt, you can always go without a meal and use the time for prayer or spiritual reading. Or you can go a whole day without food. That helps a lot. All the saints did that sort of thing. If you want supernatural help you must live the supernatural life. Also keep your eyes off what tempts you. If you have looked once, don't look a second time. You must know that if you allow people to touch you in certain parts of the body (e.g. breasts, lips) your passions will be aroused and you will lose control and will become a slave of anyone and any devil. But if you are watchful and prayerful, you should not find life difficult. Christ's yoke is easy and His burden light to those who love Him. But I don't know exactly what your trials are. So perhaps I've said enough. No time for more. God bless and guide you and fill you with his Spirit.

Ever yours in Christ,
Archimandrite Lazarus

Time was flying that summer faster than ever before, or so it seemed. I wrote my mother every week, and told her about my work and that Prince Teymouraz always asked me how I was doing and that Father Antony called and offered any help I needed. But most of all I told her I was grateful for Wayne's friendship. I described to her how we spent weekends together going to museums and the city's beautiful parks and commented positively on his personality. I pointed out his good traits, because I think that was all I noticed at that time. I admired the fact that he had traveled a lot, studied both at the Sorbonne University in Paris and at the University of Vienna, and that I enjoyed his sense of humor, which made him bring cheer to any party.

In my letters to Mother I did not mention that Wayne and his friends enjoyed having alcoholic drinks, that they liked to meet at the German pub

Illustrations - Chapter 3

3.1 Abbess Antonia of the Mount of Olives Convent.

3.2 The bell tower of the Mount of Olives Convent.

3.3 The Church of the Ascension of Our Lord, Mount of Olives.

3.4 Archmandrite Antony and Mother Mary in Gethsemane.

3.5 The view of the Mount of Olives Convent church from the belfry.

3.6 Father Lazarus and Abbess Elizabeth with Palestinian nuns of Gornia Convent who were fleeing the occupation of Ain Karem by Israeli troops in 1948.

3.7 Father Lazarus in India.

3.8 Anya with four of the Palestinian nuns from Gornia Convent in London.

3.9 Bishop John Maximovich with Abbesss Elizabeth of the Russian Gornia Convent.

3.10 Anya with Nyanya Katia, the Husseini family nanny.

3.11 This Arab woman was one of Anya's helpers and a confidant.

3.12 Anya in her nurse's uniform at Bethany Hospital, 1948.

3.13 Hilane Nicola, known throughout Palestine as St Hilane of Abu Snan, with the Greek Patriarch Timotheus, 1948.

3.14 Via Dolorosa (the Way of the Cross), ran next to Notre Dame de Sion High School.

3.15 Anya's graduating class at Notre Dame de Sion High School.

3.16 Anya teaching the Cyrillic alphabet to novices.

3.17 Anya's German suitor and her mother on the Mount of Olives.

3.18 This is the last picture taken of Anya and her mother on the Mount of Olives.

Illustrations - Chapter 4

4.1 Anya is pictured here speaking to a Benedictine alumna, a former administrative secretary to President Harry S. Truman, at Benedictine College, Atchison, Kansas.

4.2 Father Arnold, a professor at Benedictine College and Anya's Latin teacher at Notre Dame de Sion High School in Jerusalem.

4.3 Anya with classmate Alice at Benedictine College.

4.4 Anya pictured in an interview conducted by a local TV station in Atchison, Kansas.

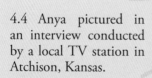

4.5 Anya at her 50th college reunion. She is pictured here with then college president Stephen Minnis.

4.6 Anya in front of the Benedictine College the weekend of her the 50th class reunion.

4.7 Anya (third from the left), Wayne (fourth from the left), and friends pictured in front of the City Hall in New York.

4.8 Anya and Wayne in front of the New York City Court House. after registering to be married.

4.9 Wayne Derrick with his three sons.

4.10 Danish nurse Sister Ulrica de Mylius (on the right) is pictured with her friend the Grand Duchess Olga Romanov (the sister of Tsar Nicholas II), 1948.

4.11 Sister Ulrica is pictured here with Sister Dunia and Father Seraphim (a former White Army officer).

4.12 Mother Taisia, the icon painter, is pictured here, age of 93, with her caretakers at the convent on the Mount of Olives.

on Fridays after work and this seemed to be an important function in their lives. This custom was surprising to me, having grown up in a country where alcohol played no role in ordinary people's lives. Muslims did not drink, and only on very special occasions was a little wine served in Christian settings. Strong Turkish coffee served in tiny cups was what people drank in Arab coffee places, which were strictly for men.

Mother's letters to me were full of descriptions of festive services in church or about the spiritual books she was reading or which guests and tourists from Europe visited, adding interest to daily life. But most of all, she admonished me to be careful in that distant sinful world of America and reminded me of the importance of my religion and frequent attendance at church services. Then she started to ask if Wayne was serious about our relationship, especially in view of his worldly life experience and being several years older than me. "You have not mentioned what his religion is, and whether he has honorable intentions," Mother wrote.

Engagement and Graduation

One evening Wayne's best friend Otto Zaff invited us to dinner at his apartment. Otto liked to prepare elaborate meals and loved filling his guests' beer mugs over and over again. He was a bachelor, who after serving in Normandy, France, during World War II, traveled around the world on a mere one hundred dollars! He enjoyed talking about his adventures and especially about the invitations he got in India to dine with maharajas, no less. We never knew whether he expected us to believe it all, but the better one got to know him, the more credible his stories became. He was a wheeler-dealer type, but always with a joke. However, one thing was very real about him: it was his fondness for Wayne and that he remained his friend throughout their lives.

Noticing the affection with which Wayne treated me that evening, Otto suddenly asked, "How long are you two going to continue courtship? September is almost here and Anya will soon return to college for her final semester exams and graduation ceremony. I know you two are in love, why don't you get married?" After the dinner party, on the way to the subway, Wayne suddenly said, "I always wanted to have children, but the law says I first must have a wife. Will you be my wife?" Then he stopped and gave me a big hug. Of course, I could find no words for an answer but silently clung to him and when we entered the subway hand in hand and stood facing each other in the jam-packed car he asked again, "Yes?" I answered, "Yes."

The next day I called Father Antony to tell him my news and ask him to arrange for Wayne and me to meet with Metropolitan Anastasy to request his blessing for our decision to get married. I knew that for Mother this would be of paramount importance from the spiritual point of view and would put her mind at ease. We were invited to the Metropolitan for a cup of tea over which we discussed our future plans. He told me he knew I was old enough to make my own choices in life, but that he hoped Wayne would understand that first he must be willing to accept the Orthodox Christian faith. Because Wayne was never baptized, he would need time to prepare, and only after his accepting baptism could we decide when to be wedded. The Metropolitan then blessed us to start moving toward this holy endeavor.

Father Antony later informed me that for those who were never baptized there a three- to six-month period was required to study the faith before espousing it. He pointed out that the time I needed to complete my final semester and graduate from college would give Wayne enough time to become an Orthodox Christian. Then he encouraged me by saying, "Think of your parting as a time of Lent and sacrifice. Meanwhile Wayne will prepare himself, upon your return to New York, to be baptized and your Orthodox Church wedding to be celebrated." Wayne was willing to start studying Orthodoxy right away, while I was to take the train back to college in Kansas.

When I went to work the following Monday, it was my last week at the Tolstoy Foundation. I told Prince Teymouraz and my supervisor Elizabeth Tomashevsky about Wayne's proposal of marriage. They both expressed their approval, saying that he made a good impression when they met him the first time. They told me that an office farewell party for me was planned at which my news could be announced, and that I could invite a few of Wayne's good friends. What a wonderful party it turned out to be! Wayne's closest friends who could make it at such short notice came. The staff at the party included the president, Alexandra Lvovna Tolstoy, while Prince Teymouraz and Elizabeth Tomashevsky acted as hosts. My co-workers congratulated me on my engagement and on the possibility of thus being able upon graduation to remain in peaceful, prosperous America. Wayne's friends smiled approvingly at the Russians' spoken English, and the Russians were delighted by a black friend of Wayne's who could speak some Russian. I, of course, was deeply touched by this warm and unforgettable gathering.

When Wayne and I parted at the train station, we promised to write, which we did and sometimes overdid, as I had at this time an especially heavy load of studies. In addition, I was anxious about my future considering that I was on a temporary student visa. Wayne also informed me that there would be a problem keeping his top secret clearance status for work in the State Department; he could reapply for work there only after I had become a U.S. citizen.

Such problems were like freezing wind blowing in our faces in late spring. Yet Wayne's letters, along with the anticipation of graduation, energized me and brought hope, such as when he suggested that our marriage would open the possibility of bringing my mother to live in this country. His devotion and longing to be together was reassuring, as expressed in the following letter:

My dear Anya,

Your letter was waiting for me this evening when I came home. I'm glad things are going along fine with your studies and other duties at the college. Has your mother written and is the situation in Jerusalem stable and she is well? I miss you and keep reminding myself that when your studies are over you'll be able to come back here. I only wish there was some way of making things happen faster. It seems that you have been away already a long time. I have not been doing much without you, and I'd rather be here saving money waiting for you and going to spiritual instruction meetings with Father Antony at the church headquarters. I will write in a few days.

All my love,
Wayne

Marriage in Manhattan

I graduated from St Scholastica College at the end of 1956, with a BA in English literature with a minor in biology. In the meantime, Wayne found an interesting new job and described how it happened. He walked into an employment agency for an interview wearing the English tweed suit that I liked. It was a rainy day, so he carried a closed umbrella that gave the appearance of someone with a cane. The agent took one look at him and said, "You are the type of man I was looking for. Do you speak French or perhaps German?" Wayne handed him his résumé. The position required knowledge of European museums, art galleries, and names of some of the artwork on display in them. He needed to be able to talk about famous Viennese and Parisian landmarks and parks as well as about monuments and statues on the grounds of European palaces and estates. Wayne's experience living in the capitals of Europe, he was told, would perfectly qualify him to sell indirect lighting to wealthy property owners.

Indirect lighting was an expensive innovation in the late 1950s. The sales pitch worked like this: Wayne's office was in the company's elegant headquarters in a downtown Manhattan skyscraper. Upon entering the foyer, in the center was a small water fountain surrounding a beautiful statuette that was lit up with indirect lighting. From his office, he contacted rich and famous

New Yorkers, as well as the same class of people living in Chicago, Detroit, Washington, D.C., and Florida with whom he made appointments for artistic lighting consultations. Some of those people had acquired priceless paintings and other precious objects from war-devastated Europe that they wanted attractively displayed in their homes or in art galleries and museums. Other jobs for which he signed contracts were monuments, mausoleums, and city libraries. It was amazing what famous people he met at those job sites. The only drawback was the frequent trips that he had to make to properties outside New York City.

Soon I found a job too, but it was not as impressive as Wayne's. It was a secretarial position in the Garment District on 32nd Street, the last stop on the subway. There were many restaurants on 32nd Street, and some only for men. I discovered this by walking into one of those eateries, because the food looked so scrumptious. Inside there were no seats; everybody ate standing around high tables. Then an older man approached me saying that it was not a good place for a lady. He said it was for men belonging to unions. At that time I knew nothing about work unions or places of special preference for various people, other than what I learned in Kansas about segregation of blacks. My co-workers had fun later explaining things to me and laughing at my naïveté.

By the time I had returned to New York from school, Wayne had completed his religious studies and was ready to be baptized in the Russian Orthodox Church. Mother wrote letters full of excitement about what to her seemed the most important event in life: Wayne's baptism. A special white gown had to be sown for Wayne, which was to be worn in church after baptism, when with a lit candle in his hand he would stand the next day during the service in church. On the Sunday following Wayne's baptism, we had a beautiful Orthodox wedding at the Synodal Cathedral of the Sign. The officiating priest was mother's old friend Father George Grabbe. How I wished she could be present at this ceremony, a once-in-a-lifetime event as the Orthodox Church strongly discourages divorce and remarriage.

We found a one-bedroom sublet apartment on Tiemann Place near the Hudson River, not far from Columbia University. We bought an aquarium with tropical fish and spent evenings just watching the fish and enjoying each other's company; this was our honeymoon. Finally I started to feel that everything was becoming right in my life. I had a college degree and a husband whom I loved. We were both employed and could start to help mother financially. Her quota waiting time,[2] I hoped, would quickly pass, and she would be allowed to join us in America. Whenever I wrote to mother,

Wayne would send her his regards and asked me to tell her that he was looking forward to meeting her. Wayne's parents wrote to ask us when we would be coming to visit them in Tacoma, Washington, where they had moved from Puyallup.

Beginning a Family

Soon after our marriage, I was expecting our first child. I put myself in the care of a lady doctor who made sure all was going well. Wayne was ecstatic; he wanted so much to have a son. "But the other alternative is okay too," he would say. He was ultra-nice to me the whole time of my pregnancy. He waited on me hand and foot. I felt like it was my birthday every day, just as I sometimes felt in my childhood when I was commended for good behavior. Writing to my former high school teacher, Father Arnold, I tried to describe how special I felt. But he tempered my elation by writing back that this was temporary; after becoming a mother, I might face all kinds of difficulties. Even the love between parents may change because children sometimes create divisions between them. I wondered why he would be so sure of all this having never been married himself. Was it something he was told by married couples, who had confession with him before communion?

I went through several hours of hard labor before our first baby boy was born. While I was still in the hospital bed, I wrote the following letter to my mother:

Dearest Mother,

I will start with the most important: that is Wayne's and my infinite happiness. We wanted so much to have a baby boy and God fulfilled our wish. I am still not quite myself after this most happy event of my life. So great is the joy that one quickly forgets the pain. We agreed on naming the baby after my father. Baby weighs eight pounds and it is not clear whom he resembles, his eyes are blue and he is fair. I am the only one nursing my baby, the other mothers in my ward feed their babies with a bottle.

Wayne was with me till the last minute. He was required to be dressed in a white gown like a doctor's, in the hospital. Now he visits daily after work and he glows with happiness when he is shown his little son from behind a glass wall to safeguard the baby from germs. Wayne eagerly awaits our homecoming so he could hold and feel the warmth of his precious son. After baby's arrival I started to feel myself a different person and Wayne says he also feels he is a different person. Our love for each other doubled as we waited for our baby's birth. It kept growing, bringing us closer and closer to each other and now we feel the three of us are like one being—a trinity. For now this is all. Stay well and happy my dearest Mother.

Your loving daughter

The first weeks at home were difficult without outside help. However, Wayne was on vacation for two weeks and was the best mother's helper. Baby and I had to get used to the nursing schedule, and so did daddy, who was eager to be able to do something for the baby. Neither of us had sisters or brothers, so we had even more to learn about nurturing a baby by practicing on our firstborn. We also found help by reading Dr. Spock's famous book on the subject. By the time our baby was three months old, life became more normal, and we started to notice how with every day he became more and more lovable.

He gazed at us with his deep blue eyes, and later learned to know the difference between us by the sound of our voices. At that time Wayne's bachelor friends were eager to come see the baby. I may have given the impression of being very unfriendly but that was because I was overly protective of the child. I remember how one of Wayne's lonely friends, who attended our Tolstoy Foundation party, kept dropping in and trying to be helpful the best he knew how, but I could only silently tolerate him.

Although Baby was generally good, to our great distress there were times when he cried and cried without an obvious reason. We tried everything imaginable to make Baby comfortable, but to no avail. To survive New York's steamy hot summer, we kept all our windows open, and when our darling continued to cry after the 2 a.m. nursing, some woman from a nearby building would scream, "Shut that kid up!" We would hurriedly close the window because we understood how noise tended to resound across the empty spaces between the tall buildings. I am sure many New Yorkers who couldn't afford air conditioning lived through such times of physical as well as emotional discomfort. However, when Baby was happy, he lay in the crib cooing and emitting little sweet sounds and kicking with his little arms and legs. He especially enjoyed it when I put him in the pram and we went for a walk. It would amaze me how he looked at the trees and other things around him and made new joyful sounds; this was a time of infinite joy for us parents in spite of inevitable sleepless nights.

Mother soon began reminding me of the importance for Orthodox families to have the baby baptized as soon as possible. She urged us to start arranging it, and suggested that Prince Teymouraz be the godfather. When

I discussed it with Wayne, he said we should wait until the baby was older. He was concerned about sanitation in the church baptismal font. Of course, I did not mention this to my mother as I knew she was too great a believer in God's grace to understand such a secular outlook. I decided to leave the matter to time rather than argue either point with the two persons dearest to me. I wanted Bishop Antony of Los Angeles to conduct the baptism service. I knew his position in the Synod of Bishops sometimes required his presence in New York. How I wished he would come and explain to Wayne the spiritual significance of this Orthodox tradition.

Summer rains brought cooling relief; often a breeze would blow from the nearby Hudson River, and fortunately one of our windows was facing that way. Wayne's office had air conditioning that made it tolerable to work. However, the city air was so full of pollution from industry and cars that the white shirts he wore to work had to be laundered daily. Baby and I took daily walks in the mornings. After dinner all three of us went to the park, where Wayne played tennis and I nursed the baby while sitting on the grass. On rainy days, we stayed in our two-room apartment with the tropical fish in their lit aquarium, potted plants, a caged canary, and especially with our darling son; we were in our own little paradise.

Doing laundry in the apartment's basement laundromat, I met an Irish American couple whose baby was close to the age of our baby, and soon we became good friends and swapped babysitting. They were Catholic and on Sundays wanted to go to early Mass, so we took care of their little boy. When we went to the Orthodox Church, we could leave our precious little boy with them, and whenever Wayne was gone on a business trip they were my mainstay.

In her letters, Mother reminded me again and again to have her grandson baptized. She also was not feeling well, her blood pressure was too high, and the American consulate was not responding to her application for a visa to America. I wanted so much to lift my mother's spirits and to be able to give her a date for Baby's baptism but nothing was happening on our end. Even when Father George Grabbe telephoned to say that he was at our service whenever we decided to arrange a baptism, Wayne's response was that he did not like to be pressured into things and that he would call if and when he was ready.

Then one day Father George called and said that he could stop by that day and talk to us about baptizing our child. He arrived with a parishioner who drove him over and spoke better English so he could make it all clearer to Wayne. Father talked about the importance of early baptism so the child could sooner benefit from God's grace passing to him through baptism. Then the driver inquired if Wayne wished to wait until the child's age of maturity as some Protestants do. This question irritated Wayne, and he said, "This is a personal matter I do not wish to discuss." Then he got up, thanked them for their concern, and escorted them to the door. After they left, I avoided the subject in an effort to keep peace at home, but for a long time I suffered deeply from embarrassment and humiliation at the way this visit of the well-wishing priest, a friend of my mother's, ended.

In my letters to Mother I wrote about the daily changes in the baby's development, how every day he became livelier so there was more work to do, but, of course, there was also more joy to experience. Now when he smiled he lifted one of his eyebrows; it looked so amusing and at the same time clever. After being gone for only two weeks on a business trip, Wayne noticed a lot of changes in the baby in such a short time. I wrote to Mother about how our little one liked to be on the davenport with his favorite toy, my colorful apron, loving its bright colors and pulling it over his little head and emitting funny noises. He was such a darling that she would fall in love with him and perhaps soon we might be able to come and bring him to her in Jerusalem. I wondered if I had been just as lovable at one time and if Mother played with me and hugged me the same way as I did my baby. At that time, Wayne had said, "Only when you become a parent yourself, do you begin to really treasure your own parents."

Time was flying. Our baby was growing. Wayne was doing well at work, although his days in the office seemed to get longer. Every two weeks I received a sentimental letter from Mother; she wanted so much to see us. I also tried to write every other week, so when Baby would take a nap I sat down to describe for Mother our life:

Dearest Mother,

How is life on the Mount of Olives? Yesterday we bought a wooden playpen for our little boy. Here everyone gets them for their babies to start learning to crawl and lift themselves up and hold to the rails. It is safer this way as he already turns over by himself and the other day when I put him on the davenport, to my great alarm he rolled down on the floor. Both Wayne and I would like to see you come here very soon, although Wayne is a little afraid of family trouble. But he also says he would like us to take care of you and give you a chance to be secure and comfortable.

With all our love,
Your family

Baptism and Struggles

One morning Prince Teymouraz called to ask how we were doing. After telling him how happy we all were, I shared with him my concern about my mother's health and asked how to speed up efforts for her to join us in New York. I knew that through his work with Russian refugees he had experience in such matters. I also told him about my mother's frequent questions about our baby's baptism and how we would all be honored to have him be the godfather. He said he would like it very much and asked whether a godmother had been chosen. When I responded that I had had no time to think about it, he suggested Mrs Elizabeth Tomashevsky, my former supervisor, as a possibility, and added that she often talked well about me at the Tolstoy Foundation. Because he was calling from work, he said he would talk to her and that he would arrange it with the church and the whole thing could be accomplished as soon as this afternoon. "No sooner said than done" was an ancient Russian fairy tale refrain. Around 2:00 p.m. that afternoon, Prince Teymouraz and Mrs Tomashevsky picked me up with the baby to go to church.

The baptism took place according to tradition, except that Baby screamed at the top of his lungs after he was deftly dunked in the warm font water three times in the name of the Holy Trinity. I was glad Wayne was not present as he would not have been able to bear Baby's crying. I suffered too but I was raised believing in God's grace, which is a spiritual help to parents at such moments. Father Antony Grabbe put a little golden cross around the baby's neck that, according to early Christian tradition, would be worn on the chest inside the shirt for the rest of one's life. Afterwards the godfather and godmother were busy drying and dressing the little darling in a lovely white outfit they had brought. Later, Baby was happy to be back in my arms and nursed with gusto as the cab drove us back home. That evening when I told Wayne about the afternoon's events, things did not go so well for the family. He was deeply hurt that I did it all on my own. He even said, "This is what your mother did to our happiness: she ruined it. Now you can return to your mother in Jerusalem, but the baby will stay here."

I was devastated by his words and totally confused. I began to ask forgiveness and admitted to acting impulsively. I said that I truly believed it was God's will that my child be baptized and therefore accepted the kind offer from friends to help me. I told him I loved him very much, but that I also loved God and my mother. I said that I assumed he was so busy at work he had little time left for other things, and so I took advantage of an opportunity.

I remembered back in Jerusalem when my mother returned from work-ing in the children's ward at the Augusta Victoria Hospital in the vicinity of Jerusalem that she joyfully told me how she had secretly baptized three dying Muslim babies. She said she did it by making a sign of the cross over them with some holy water she always carried with her to work. She said she wanted to give them a chance to meet Christ, as their pure little souls were surely deserving of life in the kingdom of heaven. This was the reason why Orthodox Christians baptized babies as early as possible after their birth lest they die before getting a chance to be baptized. I continued to plead with Wayne to forgive me for this misunderstanding, but he would not respond; instead he sat down at the table and wrote my mother an airmail letter, which I saw and read only many years later after I found it among books and old letters I inherited from her:

Mrs. Berezina:

It appears to me that upon your insistence Anya had my son baptized without my consent. I was not in favor of this and it was done without my knowledge. Anya assured me if I would become baptized and would marry in the Church it would make you very happy and I thought there would be no other such requests made as baptizing the child. This I did for you. This was not understood by you. Anya says she could not make you understand. Now that I am very angry with your insistence and the instructive telegram you sent, I hope this letter will give you my feelings— of course it is now too late. I would like to have Anya return to Jerusalem, where a child can be taken care of properly! Please insist, as you have in the past, that she return to you. I do not now, nor do I ever intend to have any religion for my son.

Wayne

The atmosphere was so tense at home that after putting the baby to bed, I burst out crying and told Wayne I wanted to go upstairs for a while to visit our Irish neighbors. I felt I needed outside help to sort out my thoughts and feel-ings. They listened to me, allowing me to cry my heart out to them. Having been raised in a strict Catholic country and family, they understood my confu-sion and sadness. They told me to go back to Wayne and first of all give him a big hug. Then they said to tell him that this is the first and last time I would do something without first talking it over with him, again and again if neces-sary. "Tell him how much you love him and his wonderful son and that you cannot live without them." They knew that one of Wayne's parents was from a Catholic family and the other from a Protestant family and that perhaps this was the reason Wayne was never baptized; it was to avoid conflict. This was the first real discord of our married life, but that same evening it ended.

A Growing Family

Our first child was born in 1957 and in that same year Soviet Russia became the first country to launch an earth satellite. The president of the United States now often addressed the nation, and there was talk about the Air Force being on alert in strategic points of Europe and the Middle East. For some reason, the newspapers wrote about a possible war with Syria. This, of course, made me worry about the safety of my mother and my friends in Jerusalem. We heard news of attempted assassinations against King Hussein of Jordan, who was still a very young man, and I questioned why anyone wanted him dead. I was always interested in hearing the news, but had to remind myself to stay calm as I was expecting a second child, who we thought might be a little sister for our baby boy. Wayne said that it was better to have children while we were younger, and so we should be happy. My mother meanwhile wrote that it was much too soon and not too good for my health or the baby's. I did some research and started attending young women's meetings where midwives taught natural childbirth without anesthesia. It could be done at home with the help of a midwife and was found to be psychologically better for both the baby and the mother. I had to preregister with the New York City Health Department and be assigned a midwife. With every day, I felt it harder to lift my little boy, who was still a baby himself and required a lot of basic care. I adored him and enjoyed every minute with him and could not imagine how I would divide my love for him with another baby.

Two weeks before my due date when I went to the clinic for a routine check-up, my midwife listened to the baby. Then she suddenly walked out and returned with a colleague who also listened, smiled, and announced that they could hear a second heartbeat. "You are going to have twins," she announced and said that according to New York City Health Department regulations, a medical doctor's presence at the home was required during the natural childbirth of twins. Our friends were just as excited as we were about this very special gift of God for us, and both of us glowed with pride. But there was much to plan and do right away. Wayne took time off from work to look into moving to a larger apartment in our neighborhood. There was a vacancy on Morningside Drive, just a few blocks away. This was the street on which the Columbia University president lived, and the campus grounds were conveniently close by for us to take walks. Wayne's bachelor friends again offered to help us move after painting the new premises for us. At his workplace, the employees got together and acquired two identical cribs for the babies, and the owner of the business gave us a set of monogrammed silver spoons for the new arrivals.

I was getting heavy, and all I could do was take care of my firstborn son, who at thirteen months was just beginning to walk. He was still wobbly but determined and kept having spills. The day of the move to the other apartment the weather was windy and rainy. My little boy and I stood out of the way and only watched the movers. Then one of the well-meaning movers dropped the big mirror at the doorsill of the old apartment, shattering it to pieces. Someone else, while carrying the aquarium with the tropical fish, slipped and spilled the water with the fish on the ground at the entry of the new apartment building. In Palestine, Arabs used to say that when something breaks during a wedding party, especially if it is a mirror, it is a sign of good luck. So we told the movers not to worry about it, and we thanked them for their help and the good luck it might bring us.

The first night in our new apartment we slept in a freezing cold room filled with a heavy smell of paint. The next morning our little boy woke up with a slight temperature from all the commotion, but it proved inconsequential. Our new fifth floor home was bright and roomy, and from the children's room, he enjoyed watching the pigeons that walked along the roof ledges. He was getting intelligent and knew his boundaries and that the telephone was not a toy. In our building we met friendly neighbors who were graduate students at Columbia University. They even offered to babysit our child during the birthing of the twins if it were to happen during the day and he needed care.

It was getting to be evening when labor pains started, and Wayne called the midwife. She arrived accompanied by a helper and a doctor; meanwhile an ambulance stood at the entry of our building. Wayne was sitting beside me holding my hand, and the doctor sat quietly across the room. The midwife and her assistant coached me in deep breathing, encouraging me to bear the pain without an anesthetic. This continued long into the night, while our little boy was asleep down the hall in the children's room with the door closed. When the pain appeared to exhaust me, Wayne got nervous and turned to the doctor for help. To our surprise the doctor suddenly addressed me in Russian, telling me that Russian women are strong and that they never give up. At this point the midwife explained again how to push as hard as I could, which I did, and soon I saw a tiny baby boy in her arms. Then there was a pause for a few minutes and I pushed again with all my strength, and another lovely baby boy appeared.

Meanwhile our mere thirteen-month-old first child, on hearing noises but not seeing anyone come for him, somehow climbed out of his crib and onto the floor, opened the door, and holding onto the wall, slowly took his first independent steps down the hall to our bedroom. Seeing two tiny babies on both sides of me, he hid his face with his arm and laying it on the edge of the bed, began to cry so sadly that his daddy hurried toward him and put him closer beside me. With time, this older brother, still a baby himself, became fascinated with his adorable new playmates. He watched me nursing them and changing their diapers and tried hard to be helpful. He was very lively and cheerful most of the time but occasionally felt left out, and then there were tears in his big blue eyes.

Early on the morning of their birth while the newborns were being cared for by the midwife and her helper, the doctor said he believed that the second baby should be taken in an incubator to the hospital for a brief time. He said that because there had been a delay in the baby taking his first breath, this would be beneficial to strengthen him. This alarmed me, but the doctor soothed me once again in Russian, saying that meanwhile I should rest and later the father could go to the hospital to bring the baby back home. Soon there was a knock at the door, and two tall African American men in white hospital gowns walked in. With great anxiety I watched them put my baby in a small incubator, and then all together the medical staff left in the ambulance. Only after Wayne brought our second twin back from the hospital did I feel our family complete and I was able to relax.

Those were days when I wished Mother was nearby as she would have been the only one besides their father who I could truly entrust with my babies when needed. I was unable to keep pace with our correspondence as I did before, yet in every letter from her I sensed a tone of urgency for her to be with us now, not later. When Prince Teymouraz called to find out how we were coping with a double addition to the family, I told him how busy my husband and I were with all three of our babies. He said he would soon be going to Jerusalem for a visit to his mother, Abbess Tamara, on the Mount of Olives, and hoped to talk to my mother about her plans to join us. He never had children of his own so was eager to see his godson and the twins, expressing concern about our rapidly growing family and stressing that I needed paid help with the babies.

In her last letter, Mother sounded downhearted, not only because the American consul in Jerusalem was stalling in issuing her a visa, but also because she was not feeling well. Wayne wrote a personal letter to the consul, who answered that he was waiting for my mother's blood pressure to go down. In those days, a clean bill of health was mandatory for entrance to the United States. At sixty-three years of age when we parted for the last time in Beirut, Mother did not seem old to me. In fact, it never crossed my mind that she might someday become mortally ill. Instead I worried more about political issues that could endanger her life. I wanted so much for her to have an opportunity to enjoy not only the peace in this country but also the physical comforts of life that we had. Now I felt I had so much more in common with her, and I wanted to share with her my experience of being a wife and a mother, to tell her that now I understood life and knew what she went through with me.

Meanwhile, at Wayne's work much of the big business was coming from the Midwest, and Wayne's presence in Chicago was often needed. So his chief suggested we think of moving there in the near future. On one of his trips, Wayne found a nice apartment for us in a small university town not too far from Chicago—South Bend, Indiana. Such a move I thought would be reasonable because Wayne would be able to be home every night with me and the babies. We decided to move in October before winter set in, which we were told could be harsh in that region. Before leaving, we went one more time to the residence of Metropolitan Anastasy and asked for his blessing, and I told him about our efforts to bring my mother over. He said we should leave this up to God's will, but to continue to pray for His help. This was the last time I saw the Metropolitan, and I also bid farewell to the Grabbes, father and son. On the way home that day, we saw a motorcade with President Eisenhower pass us so close that I noticed his sympathetic smile, something that I wrote about to Mother to keep up her hopes about travelling to America.

Moving with three babies was not easy, although at the airport people helped us, and stewardesses gave us two additional seats for our babies. Our possessions left New York in a moving van ahead of us, and we hoped its arrival would be timely and moving furniture into our apartment would be manageable. Somehow everything worked out, and we were able to settle down comfortably in our new home. Next we needed to acquire a car as this was the only mode of transportation we knew of that was available in this town. We bought a slightly used but beautiful pale green 1957 Chevrolet and began to live like our neighbors. I found it difficult to believe that I was becoming a real American, at least as far as worldly lifestyle was concerned.

Some days later while the children were taking a nap, I was able to sit down and write to Mother. I told her that we had arrived at our new home, where we hoped she would soon be able to join us. I described how on the airplane the twins were quiet but that their brother either played hard or fussed, and that the rain was pouring hard as we got out of the cab feeling exhausted. That in spite of all the small difficulties we had on the way here, it was worth it. Now in the fall, the trees were golden; the homes in the neighborhood were neat and had pretty gardens. The apartment building we settled in was only three years old, and all the appliances were still new. Then I added and underlined that we had a special room for her with a picture of old Moscow on the wall.

Our first trip in our 1957 Chevrolet was to the Roman Catholic University of Notre Dame. As we walked across the campus, our older boy enjoyed shuffling through the dry leaves on the ground and stopping to look at the ducks in the pond, but the twins were not yet aware of such things. At home, Wayne typed business letters or made phone calls, then took off to nearby cities to meet his clients. I was glad it was not like when we lived in New York and he had to travel so far on business and be away for several days at a time. If only Mother would hurry and come to us, my family would be complete, I thought.

Then I received a letter from Mother, the tone of which surprised me because it sounded almost tragic. She was suffering from neuralgia, she thought, and had terrible headaches. She was impatient to come see us, but wondered if she could make it at all. I never saw her ill or despondent before; I even thought to myself, what was the point of being so deeply religious if religion did not give health and inner peace to a person? Why couldn't Mother stay hopeful that soon everything would work out, and why be so upset that the mail was slow both from me and from the American consulate? Perhaps, I thought, she just forgets how busy I am. I wrote to Mother that a couple of days earlier we had received a telegram and that before opening it I was sure it was from her informing us that she received her visa and was on her way, but to my disappointment it was just a business telegram for Wayne. In another letter I enclosed photographs of the children and twenty dollars:

Dear Mother,

I am anxious to hear that you are on your way, my dearest. You can notify us through Alex Eddy & Co. in Beirut, who is holding your ticket and can make adjustments to it. You can either fly or go by ship, which of course is slower. We shall meet you in New York.

Love from your family

A Death in the Holy Land

Just a few days later, I wrote my mother yet another letter describing the children and our lives and told her that we found a Serbian Orthodox church in our town that she would likely enjoy praying in with all of us. I added that we could send medicine for her headaches by express mail, but Mother never read this letter. It was returned to us by the post office with the notice *RETURN TO SENDER: DECEASED*. Within two days, we received two consecutive telegrams: the first said, "Your mother is gravely ill. Pray for her." The second said, "We buried your mother at 4 o'clock this afternoon."

Upon receipt of the first telegram, I wanted to call the convent and tell them that I would immediately fly to Jerusalem. In those days one needed to reserve a time for overseas long-distance calls. I was given the time to call at 4:00 a.m. It was still dark as I left the apartment and went into the corridor where, attached to the wall, there was a public telephone. I called the Mount of Olives and asked for Mother Taisia, assistant to the abbess. She came to the phone, and I hastened to tell her that I would fly out immediately with my older son. I could barely hear her voice across the miles as in a sing-song tone she answered, "Our own dear Anya, do not wear yourself with excessive grief, we already buried your dear mother. No need to come now, your place is with your infants. I'll write you a detailed letter." Later that afternoon the second telegram arrived to tell me what I already heard from Mother Taisia on the telephone.

Words cannot describe my shock at hearing what she said. All I could think to say was "What can I do for Mother now!" At this moment the telephone operator said, "Your time is up," and I heard the telephone click. I walked into the apartment completely dazed and fell into my husband's arms crying. This was the first grief of great magnitude in my life. I felt I could never get over it, although my husband did his best to soothe me and tried to share my sorrow. I longed to talk with someone who knew my mother, and I wished he had known her; then he would really understand how I felt and would really be able to share my grief. Finally a long letter from Mother Taisia came with all the details I needed to know for a proper closure to take place. Between caring for my babies and crying, I managed to write her a letter in which I poured out my overwhelming sorrow. This is how she answered:

Our dearest Anya!

Yesterday I received your bitterly sad letter. Yes, my dearest it was I who talked with you on the telephone, but we were allowed a short time and this is the reason I was unable to tell you all that I am writing to you now. Probably you already received Mother Antonia's letter. However I did not write sooner because I was hurrying to inform our bishop and abbesses of our various religious communities, such as Mother Theodora in Fourque, France, Mother Ariadna in Novodiveyevo Convent in New York, and your mother's other spiritual friends. I wrote so they could immediately start to pray for the peace of her soul and for you in this time of your great sorrow. I shall describe in detail all that I witnessed and know about your mother, in her final hours and minutes, as well as about the last months of her life.

On Saturday, November fifteenth, with God's benevolent guidance, I went to spend the night at the Life Giving Sepulchre of our Lord. I did not know that your mother also intended to be there at the same time. I stood during vespers on Golgotha (the Lord's crucifixion place) and did not see your mother there. Then I descended to the Kuvuklia (the Lord's burial place) intending to pray there until the matins service. In the total stillness of Resurrection Cathedral, I read prayers and silently prayed and did not see your mother.

Not long before the beginning of the midnight service, I came out of the Kuvuklia and sat down to rest in front of it on the benches there, hoping to have a rest and doze. I sat with my eyes closed and therefore did not see who was entering and exiting the Kuvuklia. Soon, however, I started to hear life around me. The Greek *ponomars* (votive lights attendants) and the Roman Catholics began to light candles, but I still sat there and for some reason started to think about your mother. I was thinking that because of poor health she was already unable to come to pray at the Holy Sepulchre as often as before.

Soon bells started to ring summoning everyone to prayer. I quickly rose and went again to the Kuvuklia so as to kiss the Lord's Sepulchre one more time. Upon entering I suddenly saw your mother standing inside. I was very glad to see her there so unexpectedly, and I exclaimed, "Sister Masha, how wonderful that you came. Where were you all this time?" Your mother looked happy, calm, and with a glow on her face she answered, "I was all the time at the Golgotha praying there so well, I read all the *akathists* which I brought with me. You remember how Vladika (Bishop) told us above all to pray at the Golgotha. Then, together, we venerated the Lord's Sepulchre and exiting went in the direction of the restrooms. Suddenly I heard a noise like snoring. I turned and saw your mother down on her knees. I burst into tears and called for help.

Greek monks ran towards us from Resurrection Cathedral where matins already began. Roman Catholic monks also hurried toward us, and together they carried your mother to the exit, and laid her on the bench, where Muslim guards usually sit. Here they started to give her first aid, but in spite of all their efforts she remained unconscious. I telephoned doctors, but it being midnight there was no response. Finally having summoned the police, it was decided to carry her to the nearby Old City of Jerusalem Hospital on the Way of the Cross. The monks wished to carry her there themselves as cars could not drive through the narrow streets of the old city. The doctor on duty took her blood pressure and diagnosed her to have had a stroke and said her condition was hopeless. The appropriate injections did not help her regain consciousness. Her breathing became quieter and quieter until at 3:15 a.m. she quietly passed away.

At daybreak, I returned to the Mount of Olives and reported the sad news to Archimandrite Dmitry and Mother Abbess Tamara. Being aware of Mother Antonia's weak heart, I did not dare inform her, although she was your mother's best friend. Everybody in the convent was shocked at this news. Our sisters cried and with deep sincerity grieved at this unexpected end of life of their beloved nurse, Sister Masha. But at the same time they wondered joyfully at Our Lord's benevolence in that He granted her such a marvelous end.

The monks who served the liturgy at the Holy Sepulchre, Father Kiriak and Bishop Stefan, all said that such an end of life is a great gift of God. In Augusta Victoria Hospital, where your Mother worked, doctors and nurses and sanitation workers and even the guards who knew her were deeply saddened but also expressed that same thought about God's great gift to her to have had such a death. Even Muslims like the postal workers in the city and others in the villages repeatedly marveled at God's benevolence to your mother.

Do not grieve, dear Anya; the Lord gave your mother a truly Christian end of life because the last hours of her consciousness she spent in prayer, and in no other place but in one of the holiest places on earth, the Holy Sepulchre of Christ. One of our sisters, Mother Evpraksia, who was also the same evening at Golgotha, related that she saw your mother all that time praying with tears in front of Christ on the Cross. When finally I told Mother Antonia this news, we decided together to let you know about your mother not at once, but through two telegrams: one about her serious illness and next day to send a second telegram about her death.

Your mother lying in the coffin was so beautiful that Mother Abbess Tamara even exclaimed, "I never saw Sister Masha looking so beautiful." It is true she lay there with such a good expression on her face, all white and with the faintest smile. Sisters approached the coffin and looked with tears at her kind and loving face. They decided to call a professional photographer in order to capture this look, but alas the photograph did not capture the authentic expression and the smile. We did it for you in case you would have liked to have the photograph; however, if it would be too painful for you to see it, we would keep it for us.

Dear Anya, we sisters cry not for your mother because we believe that she went to the Lord with repentance, ready for passing into the next life. We cry because we lost an understanding nurse, a person with a loving heart for fellow human beings, who always had empathy for the sick and elderly, both nuns and the villagers around us. From the bottom of their hearts, the sisters and villagers feel and understand what you are now going through. They ask questions such as "What is Anya writing, how is she coping with her loss?" You became an orphan but console yourself by praying for your mother and thanking God for His mercy so evident in that she left this world on her own two feet.

It is true that lately she did suffer from headaches because of high blood pressure. She went to doctors, took some kind of pills, but she did not go to bed; she walked everywhere and frequently was seen in church having communion. However the thought of her possible sudden death never occurred to anyone. How could we write to you to come here, when we all were certain that any day now she was to join you in America?

You ask me, "What do you think my mother would have wanted me to do for her in this life?" During her life you did everything: you wrote her frequent tender letters expressing your affection and concern about her. I do not think that your mother was disappointed that you married not a Russian, but a foreigner. Her wish was to have your family live without cutting itself off from God, the Church, or from the Mysteries of the Faith through which we unite with God. Of course she did worry a lot in the beginning of your marriage, about the question of Wayne's baptism and your church wedding and your baby's baptism and later the twin babies' baptism. She prepared for them baptismal gowns and crosses which she had blessed on the Lord's Holy Sepulchre. She also prepared a Russian embroidered shirt for Seriozha and an embroidered book mark for Wayne. She planned to bring all this herself when she would come to you very soon. Well, now we shall send you all this by airmail and the rest by ordinary mail.

Now Anya, your question about your mother's health requires a detailed answer, and before responding to it, I must mention something about her concern lately. She spoke about it to me, to Mother Antonia, her dear friend, and to some other sisters. Sometime before her death she came to me and among other things asked, "Mother Taisia, do you think the Lord accepts my repentance even if I do not do it as I should? I still believe in His mercy and that He will not deprive me of the Kingdom of God." She often referred to herself as a great sinner, and in casual conversation she often referred to death.

You understand that you were everything in her life, but it did not interfere with her preoccupation with her soul and passage to eternity. She knew she was getting older and realized something was wrong with her heart. Nevertheless she was getting ready to relocate to America, and it never entered our minds that she might soon die. Even on the last day of her life she went to Jerusalem a couple of times. She went to the post office in the morning and then in the evening she went to the Holy Sepulchre for the midnight service, where she collapsed.

The nearer the day of her departure to America came, the sadder was her disposition at the thought of parting with the holy places of the Holy Land. While loving you with all the intensity of a mother's love, it appears she loved the Lord more than you, and for this great love the Lord deemed her worthy of Him. He said, "He who loves his father or mother more than me is not worthy of me." In her death, He revealed to us all quite clearly how dear to Him is such love and commitment to the holy places of the Holy Land.

Believe me, Anya, that if she would have actually come to you, no doubt she would have soon begun to long for the Holy Land. It would not have been easy for you to see her in such a state. Because of her failing health, she also used to express her doubt that she would be capable of physically assisting you in your busy family life. Perhaps she even feared becoming a burden for you. She paid little attention to her own health, but devotedly cared for the sick and was loved for her simplicity of character and empathy for the problems of others.

There was one other factor that disturbed your mother, her inability to speak English and that she would not be able to communicate with Wayne. The other consideration of life in America was her reluctance to trade her Red Cross nurse's uniform for American civilian clothes. She loved her World War I nurse's uniform and her Red Cross medallion given to her in prerevolutionary Russia on behalf of the Russian Empress Alexandra. Your mother was buried in her uniform. In short, her great desire to be with you was overshadowed by both worldly and spiritual considerations. The Lord sent her such a sudden death undoubtedly because it was the best for her. Incidentally your mother told many about her wish to die in the Holy Land.

We decided with Abbess Tamara that we should request that on the fortieth day after your mother's death a special service be served at holy Golgotha. After the service, we will arrange to have a memorial meal for the brotherhood of the Holy Sepulchre for their kindness to your mother. She was well known to the brotherhood because of her frequent visits to the ailing patriarch and older monks in the hospital. This is why Greek monks attended her funeral and wished to carry her coffin to the grave site and sang for her in Greek "Eternal Memory." Afterwards, Archimandrite Dmitri and Abbess Tamara invited them to dinner at the abbess's residence, where she thanked them for their devotion to your mother.

All the sisters send you their love and share with you your sorrow. In moments of sadness, dear Anya, write to me and Mother Antonia, when you want to share with your spiritual friends your joys and sorrows. We all consider you our own, one who belongs to our mutual experience of life on the Mount of Olives—as an *eleonskaya*,[3] a sojourner in the past—and we shall unite in our mutual prayers. I hug you with deep love, so does Mother Antonia, who more than anyone understood and loved your mother and was her faithful friend.

Your sister in Christ,
Mother Taisia

It took a long time for me to recover from my emotional state of mind. I struggled daily with moments of anguish that now and then struck sharply within me. Was it my mind or soul that was hurting? I asked myself. I could not tell the difference because I had never hurt this way before. But I remembered how my mother would say, "My soul hurts for Russia and those close to my heart whom I left there." But there is truth in the saying that time heals. Thanks to my husband and three lovely babies who needed me all the time, I slowly began to feel normal. My former attachment to my mother turned toward my husband and children so that they became everything I needed and dearly loved. In some ways, my emotional attachment to them perhaps became too great. I loved all my children but I felt a special bond to the past I shared with my husband and my firstborn child. With my twins, I felt that same way only after we had lived together with them as adults in Birzeit on the West Bank in Israel, because that was when they understood where I came from.

After a short stay in South Bend, we moved to Chicago to be closer to Wayne's work. Here I met my in-laws for the first time when they came from Washington state to visit. They had not met me and had not seen their only son since his return from Indo-China five years before. It was a good visit; they enjoyed the children and kept bringing up their memories of Wayne at the same age. They said they were pleased with his choice of a European wife who spoke English. They feared he would marry an Asian girl with whom they would not be able to communicate.

We settled in the Chicago suburb of Oak Park, a good place to walk with small children. By now Wayne became more understanding of my cultural background and what seemed to him to be its idiosyncrasies. As gently as I could, one day I brought up the subject of visiting a local Russian church, with the pretext that it would be a good place to meet new friends. The next day when he returned from work, he informed me that at lunchtime he visited a nearby Islamic mosque. He said he asked what it takes to be a Muslim, and that the answer he got was that Islam is for blacks and whites are not welcome. He then added smiling, "I guess we'll have to baptize the twins in a Russian Orthodox church," and hugging me added that we could go there that coming Sunday.

Wayne liked joking to such an extent that it often left me confused, especially as I still did not always understand all the nuances of American English. But his sense of humor was a great gift that was admired by friends and acquaintances who said it was part of his charm. In church we met the future godparents of our twin boys: two sisters born in Paris to Russian parents would be godmothers, and a high school Russian teacher and another young man, son of the church warden, would be godfathers. This time around, Wayne not only accepted the idea of baptism but even arranged a fancy dinner for the godparents and guests. They hoped that as the twins grew up they would be able to spend good times with them, helping their parents with raising them.

Another happy event for me took place while we lived in Chicago. It was a visit from Bishop Antony, the former head of the Russian Mission in Jerusalem and now Bishop of Los Angeles, a dear old friend from my past. It felt like a bit of my mother came with him. He told my husband how when I was little he spent summers with us and his younger brother at the Sea of Galilee, and he commended me on my fluent Russian, saying it was a surprise for him as he remembered me speaking mostly Arabic. He asked, "Do you remember how your mother struggled to make you speak and read in Russian?" Many years later I met him again at a convention at Seattle University, where he gave a lecture on Orthodox Christianity. Afterwards we sat together to talk but somehow I started to cry and could not stop. Perhaps it was because his manner of speaking reminded me of my childhood in the Holy Land and made me realize how much I had changed since those innocent years.

Not too long after our relocation to Chicago, the head office in New York informed us that the owner of Wendell Artistic Lighting for whom Wayne worked had unexpectedly died of a heart attack. Several months later it was announced that the business was sold and that employees would be paid three months of their salary as severance pay. Now Wayne's office in Chicago was not needed, and we were compelled to begin planning a new future for ourselves. Although I had not yet seen the Pacific Northwest of the United States, where my husband was born and raised and where his parents lived, we decided to relocate to the state of Washington. Here we settled on a small farm, from where we commuted to work and pursued higher degrees while raising our three sons.

Visiting the Holy Land

When my older son turned sixteen years old and arrived at the often difficult teenage years, I thought it would be good for both of us to travel to Jerusalem, my former homeland, where on the Mount of Olives I could finally visit my mother's grave. Wayne approved of this and promised in our absence to take good care of the rest of the family and our home.

The belfry of the Russian Orthodox Convent on the Mount of Olives where we stayed was topographically the highest point in Palestine, now the West Bank in Israel. The window of our room opened in the direction of the Jericho road winding through the desert to the Dead Sea, which we could see in the distance. "Mother, now I am quite sure we are in a very foreign land," my son exclaimed on his first trip abroad; but for me, after a twenty years' absence, it was a homecoming.

To my great delight, home looked almost the same and the few changes did not make me feel like a stranger. Perhaps this was possible because I did not grow up in an ordinary home, whose owners could sell it and move away so only memories would remain the same. However, now there was one most important difference: the physical absence of my dear mother. We occupied the same room in the guest house by the convent gate in which years ago mother and I lived. We were able to visit her grave nearby and sit on exactly the same kind of wooden bench where I sat with my mother when I was the age of my son.

The Russian convents, the Mission residence in old Jerusalem, as well as my former school in Bethany were still almost the same. Of course, there were improvements in the school but classrooms were not much different. The teachers now were mostly Arab with only the headmistress being Russian and the director of the school still English. As we visited those places, the spirit of Old Russia remained very much alive, in spite of its virtual absence in the Soviet Union. My generation of Christian Arab nuns raised in this convent were at home here. Russian Orthodox traditions of church reading and singing in Slavonic, ancient icon painting, and various other rare skills were still practiced as I remembered them.

My son was fascinated with the caves where some of the archeological treasures in the convent's museum had been found. There was a deep cave in the garden down a hill that he wanted to explore. He entered it with a tiny flashlight brought with us from the United States, as he wanted to be sure he had a light at night in case there was no electricity the way it used to be in my childhood. When he finally emerged from the cave, I thanked God with a sigh of relief, as I had never myself explored this cave in the past and was never fascinated with caves. Perhaps this is the difference between being a boy and a girl.

In the Old City of Jerusalem, in the place known as the Russian Raskopy on the way to the Holy Sepulchre and surrounded by the noisy Arab *suq* (bazaar), now resided the Mission chief and monastic brotherhood. This was Father Antony Grabbe, who baptized Wayne and my older son in New York and later took the place of Father Antony (Sinkevich). He invited us to have dinner with him and the brotherhood; he told us about all the administrative changes and about some of their more secular activities such as managing the business side of monastic life amid the Jewish and Muslim populations. Thinking about it all later in the evening in our room, I wondered how with God's help they were surviving. I wrote home the following letter:

Jerusalem, March 13, 1973

Dear family,

We are having a great time, busy all day, but in the evening we get homesick for the three of you. Life begins early here: at 5 a.m. the sun shines, church bells ring, the muezzin calls Muslims to prayer, buses honk to signal their first departure time to Jerusalem and we too wake and get up. By 7 p.m. in the evening all is quiet, it is dark everywhere and everyone is preparing to go to sleep. Of course it is not so in the new part of Jerusalem in the Jewish sector. Life is no different there than in the U.S. or at least this is how it looks from a distance. Someone told us, "While

Jerusalem prays, Tel Aviv plays." Skyscrapers and buildings are going up like mad in the Jewish sector of the country, but I am glad to say that the Arab sector has not changed so much that I could not find my way around. We have crisscrossed old Jerusalem on foot and after praying at Christ's Holy Sepulchre, we went this afternoon to the Wailing Wall, where we watched the religious services including the traditional Hebrew form of prayerful lamentation.

The Arab bazaar is as fascinating as ever. Your brother impressed me today when he bargained trying to buy a mother-of-pearl inlaid chess board. He offered forty-two lire instead of sixty and won the bargain! He walks around like an Arab in their kind of checkered head cloth on his head, which is good protection from the hot sun. He understands all about the local money; lire, agora and so on. Now there are no dinars or piastres as it used to be during the rule of the Kingdom of Trans-Jordan the last years I lived here.

Yesterday we were in Jericho, the Dead Sea, a fascinating Greek monastery built in a dried river gorge or canyon with monks' cells as if glued to the cliffs. Tomorrow we plan to go to the Mosque of Omar and to Bethlehem, while on Monday to the Archaeological Museum and Hebrew University. The Russian places did not change much except for the improvements, some new faces and much older faces of old friends. I have been kissed and hugged so much by the Russian nuns, French nuns and Arab villagers my face is red! Abbess Tamara on the Mount of Olives, Abbess Barbara in Gethsemane and Father Antony in Jerusalem treat us like family. We are invited to so much Russian tea and Turkish coffee which Arabs drink that we get tired of it all and scheme how to slip away and be alone exploring the old places whenever we can manage it.

The weather here is like spring, clear blue sky and warm in the sun but cools off in the evening. We are getting used to the lack of central heating indoors and do not shiver the way we did the first days. This is a very desirable country, especially the Russian properties and the climate. Both the Arabs and the Jews as people leave something to be desired, Americans are much easier to live with. The many hours we have been spending in church don't seem to tire us, and both of us equally fulfill church customs of venerating the icons and genuflecting. Communal life is appealing both at meals together and because they treat us like the family they lost and found. But we wish the rest of the family members were with us here, we miss you all.

With much love,
Mother

From Jerusalem to Denmark

We were flying back to the United States through Denmark so that we could stop for a few days in Copenhagen. A close friend of my mother's, Sister Ulrica (de Mylius), lived here in an old castle together with her cousins, relatives of Danish royalty. The mother of Russia's last tsar, Nicholas II, was also born a Danish royal. During the revolution in Russia, together with her young daughter she was able to return to her homeland, where she eventually died. For years after my mother's death, Sister Ulrica corresponded with me and always invited me to visit; so when she heard of our trip to Jerusalem, she insisted we visit her also.

During my early life in Jerusalem, medical nurses were known as sisters of charity and therefore were addressed as sister and their first name. When my mother worked in the clinic for Arab villagers and in Russian convents, she was called Sister Masha; similarly Sister Ulrica worked in a Lutheran hospital for lepers near Jerusalem, which was supported with private funds from Denmark as well as by the Lutheran Church. They were both working in missionary establishments and on occasion met at functions in common, thus becoming good friends. Sister Ulrica attended Orthodox churches as well as her own and felt comfortable with Russians revering the memory of her distant Russian relatives, the martyred imperial Romanov family.

While living with her mother in Denmark, the younger sister of Tsar Nicholas II, Grand Duchess Olga Romanov, befriended Sister Ulrica. The Danish royal family and the Russian royals were close relatives. Then in 1948, Grand Duchess Olga married Mr Kulikovsky, a Canadian-Russian, and before leaving to live in Canada, the two friends were photographed together and Sister Ulrica sent me this photograph. After Mother's death she continued to correspond with me for the rest of her life, trying to replace my mother for me and remembering me as a little girl. When we let her know that on the way back from Jerusalem we would stop by to visit her, she made a point of reminding my son not to forget to pack a nice evening jacket. She wrote, "Here for dinner we dress up, men usually dine in a suit and a butler serves the dinner."

When we arrived at Vemmetofte Kloster, we were each given an elegant room. We were invited to eat breakfast daily in Sister Ulrica's private rooms, whereas lunch and dinner we would eat in the regal dining room. My son acted as if he was a bit uncomfortable in this place of pomp and ceremony, but quickly got used to it, especially because he said the food here was so much tastier than at home or even in Jerusalem. After meals, we were shown around the beautifully kept grounds and the quaint house in which the butler lived with his family. The sons of Danish nobility came here to be trained in horseback riding, in working with tractors and other farm implements, and how to become managers of their family estates. One day Sister Ulrica took us for a walk toward the Baltic Sea. Pointing in the direction of Russia, she told my son to look in the distance where she said we could catch a glimpse of our motherland Russia. "Now when you go home you can tell everyone that you saw Russia," she told him. Sister Ulrica was already in her eighties at that time and didn't live very much longer, other than in both my son's and my fond memories of her.

The Writings of Alexander Solzhenitsyn

At that time, there was a lot of talk about the great books written by Alexander I. Solzhenitsyn, a talented Russian writer who revealed the truth about the horrific life of the Soviet concentration camps known as gulags. After reading his *A Day in the Life of Ivan Denisovich* and the short story "Matryona's House," I decided to start taking courses toward a master's degree in Russian language and literature. I knew Russian well but had no higher academic degree in this. Solzhenitsyn's philosophy of life and the positive personalities he described attracted me. This writer opened my eyes to the reality that in distant villages of the Soviet Union survived truly good Orthodox Christian Russians. They were not changed by the atheist communist ideology practiced around them and embodied the ancient ideals of Holy Russia about which I heard so much in my youth in Jerusalem. They were hardworking, honest people without whom, Solzhenitsyn wrote, no human community could survive whether they were communist or capitalist.

So far I lived convinced that everything and everybody in the Soviet Union were evil because of the cruelty and inhumanity of what happened during the revolution. Of this I heard a lot throughout my growing-up years. The books I read were primarily nineteenth-century classics about life before the revolution, and a few short novels written by Russian refugees living in Europe, some of which were full of horrors they witnessed in the wake of the Soviet regime. I was convinced that any good in communist Russia was nonexistent, and only the resurrection of Old Russia, so tenaciously believed in by those who raised me, would restore it to its past righteousness. Solzhenitsyn's contemporary heroes and their positive ideals were a revelation to me, and I became deeply immersed in his works.

I was fascinated by how he described one such character, Ivan Denisovich, who was always serene, collected, and calm, in spite of his continuous concentration on the task of staying alive. Survival in a labor camp demanded a practical ability to say and do the right thing at the right time. However, side by side with his practical sense lived his primitive beliefs in peasant lore and in the existence of God. The story was told from a point of view very close to that of the prisoner, who hour after hour had to fight his way through the working day of a camp inmate. Although his body was weak, his spirit was strong, and he showed his leadership in coming forward at work as a specialist, a skilled mason and carpenter. He was proud of his trade and showed devotion to his work.

The idea of work as an honorable and honest endeavor seemed to encourage him. According to an ancient Russian belief, work and prayer represented moral force. This implication became particularly strong in the story "Matryona's House," a slow-moving story of the day-to-day life of an elderly peasant woman in a remote village of Soviet Russia. In the morning she greeted her tenant teacher in a dignified, unhurried manner, then made a clumsy attempt at preparing breakfast, and went about her household chores. All this was told in a deliberate, mater-of-fact style so one almost saw the old woman with her round, wrinkled face, her tired smiling eyes, her hands always at work.

In describing the wretched poverty and squalor of a peasant's hut, the author wrote that it was the direct result of the inefficiency of the collective farm management. Illogical actions of the authorities made Matryona regret the passing of bygone days, when things were less complicated and one did not have to cope with so much bureaucracy. However Solzhenitsyn wrote that she never expressed bitterness; instead, she looked for consolation in work. When she finished her portion of work, she would help others finish theirs, and although unconscious of it, she lived as a true Christian. She did not exhibit her righteousness other than by her good deeds to those around her and unwittingly by keeping a *lampada* votive light lit on holy days and Sundays. These and other stories about good people existing somewhere in the vast spaces of Soviet Russia made my desire to visit my parents' homeland stronger than ever. At this point in our life, however, God willed otherwise, and another more practical though equally desirable trip became a probability.

CHAPTER 5

✠✠✠

Work on the West Bank

Returning to Palestine

After our older son graduated from high school and his brothers were in the process of finishing their studies, we saw in an academic journal interesting positions advertised for professors and librarians to work in building a new university on the West Bank. It was after President Jimmy Carter was elected president of the United States and expressed an interest in giving the Palestinians a chance to form their own state similar to the State of Israel. When Wayne was between jobs, I encouraged him to inquire about the job openings. There were several jobs he had applied for at different colleges and universities in the United States, but the first response he received was from Birzeit University in the vicinity of Ramallah, a Palestinian town on the West Bank. We heard that President Carter was putting forth an extra effort to bring peace to the Holy Land and we hoped that he would be successful. And what better way was there to do so than through education for young Palestinians? I was filled with hope that finally a possibility would open up for me to be able to help spare Jerusalem from the constant threat of war and devastation of its holy places that remained dear to me and to Orthodox Christians in general. I was overjoyed when Wayne received a response to his inquiry about a job on the West Bank.

We were invited for an interview by a professor of higher education at Kent State University who held a position at Birzeit University as dean of liberal arts. He said that preference was given to couples with families who would be willing to spend several years at the new job. My knowledge of Arabic was an asset as well as my MA degree in librarianship. I was offered the position of reference librarian and library science instructor. Wayne's higher education doctorate, for which he only had to finish the dissertation, qualified him to be library director. It was explained to us that to some extent this was a hardship post because of the political situation of being under Israeli

117

occupation. Salaries were much lower than in the United States but we would be given a free furnished house, free lunches in the university cafeteria, and our children would be able to enroll in the university free of charge.

There was bad news at that time about unrest in Israel, especially the constant struggle between the Israelis and the Palestinian Arab population. I was looking through our local newspaper *Centre Daily Times* when I came across the following short article titled "Solution for Conflict." This is what an educator from State College, Pennsylvania, wrote:

> Like all good American citizens I have been horrified by the recent increase in hostilities in the Middle East. I propose then the following solution to the Arab–Israeli conflict.
>
> A Swedish U.N. police force should be assigned to the Middle East with the task of overseeing compulsory bussing of Arab and Israeli children to the same schools. A common school system and a common educational background for Arab and Israeli children are bound to decrease the terrible tensions which now exist between the Arabs and the Israelis.
>
> It would also decrease the present educational gap by raising the intellectual level of the culturally deprived Arab children to the middle class Israeli standard.
>
> To forestall possible misunderstanding, the language of instruction should be a neutral Scandinavian tongue such as Swedish, Danish or Norwegian.
>
> The efficiency of the proposed solution to the Middle East crisis would of course be evident only in the long run, but in the meantime a sufficiently large police force should be able to keep the Arab and Israeli children in the same schools (and their parents at bay).

This idea for a solution to the Arab–Israeli conflict reminded me of the time near the end of the British Mandate in Palestine. In 1942, General Wladyslaw Anders made it possible for a division of Polish troops, former prisoners of war under Stalin, along with their wives and babies to spend time in Palestine on their way from Siberian captivity to Europe. During our three-month summer vacation, the big classroom building of Bethany School was emptied of desks and rented as a home for those mothers and their babies. Suddenly job availability boomed among the Arab villagers of Azarye; lots of diapers to wash and help to be given to the young Polish mothers, and plenty of building maintenance jobs for the men. There was elation on the walkways of the impoverished village as finally there were plenty of paying jobs to go around. Best of all was the amusing phenomenon that took place that summer: practically half of the village began to speak Polish and enjoyed it.

Problems arise not only because of the foreign language or religion of an occupier but because of differing concepts of human rights and belief in racial equality. Arabs and Jews are equally Semites: so why was it allowable for one and not for the other to have a state, and where should people's loyalties lie in case of dual citizenship? In another letter to the editor in the *Centre Daily Times* I read the following under the heading "America First":

> To the editor: I am thoroughly disgusted with the chauvinistic pro-Israeli attitude taken by many American Jews. Do they give any thought as to what's best for America?
>
> There is a long-standing controversy as to whether the Jews constitute a religious affiliation or a national grouping. If the former, one would assume that the political loyalties and priorities of American Jews lie with the American state, as would those of a member of any other denomination. If the latter, then I suggest that they change their citizenship and their residence to the state that holds their true loyalty: Israel.
>
> American interests can only be served by a just, stable peace in the Middle East that accommodates both sides. I do not want to see my country suffer from involvement in a war from which it has nothing to gain at the instigation of American citizens who place another state's welfare above America's.
>
> Each American Jew is going to have to decide for himself what his Judaism means to him. If he feels that as a member of the Jewish nation he must ultimately support Israel, I trust that he would do America the justice of not clutching on to her only to drag her into his nation's quarrels.
>
> Fourth-year undergraduate student in political science

We talked to our boys and their grandfather about the possibility of moving overseas. Grandfather stated that he would go wherever we go as he was a widower. Our twin sons said they were eager to see a new country but our older son said he had already been to Israel and preferred to stay on the West Coast on his own. With heavy hearts, we embraced our independent older son; this would be our first long separation, and for me especially unnerving. Wayne gave him our car and put five hundred dollars in his hands, saying, "We love you son, be careful, and write"; meanwhile my heart was breaking at the thought that we would be so far from each other.

We planned to arrive at Birzeit University a few weeks before the beginning of the fall quarter. When I resigned from my job, it was with a certain amount of anxiety; what if things did not work out where we were going, and both of us became unemployed? Yet even though Wayne was over fifty years old and I was over forty, we were both still courageous and optimistic about the future. We hoped that Wayne's eighty-year-old father, who wanted to go with us, would be happy in Palestine. We had been encouraged to come to the Holy Land by Father Antony (head of the Russian Mission in Jerusalem), who told us that if things did not work out for us at Birzeit University, he could always find work in Israel for us. He offered me a position teaching Russian at Bethany School and said Wayne could help in the difficult job of administering Mission properties such as banana and orange orchards in Jericho and vineyards in Hebron, both places maintained by local Arab villagers.

Our former next door neighbors in Oak Park, a history professor and his wife, offered our twin sons a stop in Oxford, England, on their way to Israel. Here they could stay for a month in their daughter's home and help her paint it, as being diabetic and losing her sight, she could not manage this on her own. The boys gladly agreed and consequently got to stay a month in one of England's nicest towns.

Arriving at Birzeit University

Upon arrival at Birzeit University, we were warmly welcomed by the vice president, and we were escorted to our new house on Attara Road, within walking distance of the university. In our yard, we had our own well, several fruit trees, and some artichokes growing here and there. As the house had only two bedrooms, we gave one to Grandfather and the other to the boys. Wayne and I slept in the living room. Our bathroom had a shower and the kitchen had an electric refrigerator and a gas stove for cooking. On top of the flat roof stood a big water tank for use in the kitchen and bathroom. A low stone wall separated the house and yard from a field in which Arab peasants worked with their donkeys, separating wheat grains from the chaff. They used an ancient method of doing this before taking the grain to a mill where it was ground into flour. From our back porch, we watched this procedure with great interest.

We had been expecting to hear from our twins about their flight to Israel so as to arrive in August for the beginning of classes in September. The last time we had talked by telephone they were still in Oxford and were planning to leave shortly. But time was passing and we were not getting information as to when to meet them at the airport in Tel Aviv so we could then drive together to the West Bank. We began to wonder and worry about what might have happened to them.

Wayne went to the American consulate in Jerusalem to ask for advice. It was determined that they had not arrived in Tel Aviv nor purchased tickets on airlines flying there. We never thought that they might have decided to take the cheaper flight that would land in Amman, Jordan, and that from there they would cross the bridge to the Israeli side. The consul advised us to check with airlines flying to Amman, which we did and were told that the boys did arrive in Amman and were last seen going through the Jordanian immigration checkpoint.

Apparently the Jordanian authorities made them check into a local hotel to allow time to determine whether they really were American students on their way to a West Bank university or American Jewish troublemakers trying to infiltrate into areas populated by Palestinians. No one in the hotel knew how to help them, and meanwhile days were passing by. For almost a week the twins waited for permits to proceed to their destination on the other side of the Jordan River. They were unable to go anywhere while they waited for someone to do something for them. The Birzeit University vice president suggested Wayne travel to the Allenby Bridge that crosses from the Kingdom of Jordan to Israeli territories and wait there on the bridge. Finally a telegram from the university vice president to some important immigration officer activated my sons' case, and they were able to cross the bridge to the West Bank.

Upon finally arriving and seeing our house, the boys exclaimed, "What a charming stone house!" and hurried in to tell me and Grandfather all about their long wait to see us. The weather in Birzeit was glorious, with clear air and sunshine daily from 5:00 a.m. to 7:00 p.m. Our location was near the low mountains with a beautiful view of hills and villages; on clear days we could see Tel Aviv and the Mediterranean Sea in the distance.

This university was small by comparison with universities in the United States. The university library was comparable in size to a public branch library where we came from, but contained books in both Arabic and English although a portion of the card catalog was still only in Arabic. Most of the professors and students were bilingual, speaking English as well as Arabic. Wayne and the boys immediately started taking Arabic language lessons as all the signs on the streets and on the university campus doors were in Arabic. The students, who were mostly dark skinned from the sun, otherwise looked very much like American students; they were well dressed, often in good quality jeans, girls' heads were uncovered like American women's, and they were motivated to learn English.

As library director, my husband was responsible for the building of the library on the new campus grounds that were under construction. The staff liked his management style and his occasional show of humor. I started to teach a course in library skills and research methods, and it being a required course, the classes were huge. It was also up to me to teach the students to write term papers. Soon I discovered that teaching was my forte and decided that someday back in the States I should teach full time to really enjoy my work. The students called me Miss Anya, and with time I felt a bond forming between us. A couple of students once approached me after class and asked, "Miss Anya why do you always carry a small notebook with you? What are you always writing in it?" I answered that I write down everything I need to remember such as all the names of my students, especially because there were so many of them. I told them that besides memorizing each student's name, I needed to remember something special about each one of them.

We arrived in time to attend the graduation ceremony, which was impressive and with nationalistic overtones. NBC reporters and cameramen were everywhere, and we were told that Americans would be viewing the ceremony on television. We were new in town and were invited to many faculty social events as well as to the residence of the university's vice president. The president himself was in Lebanon, where we were told he had been exiled by the Israeli authorities. There were parties with Turkish coffee and local sweets served, and in the evenings there were copious Mediterranean dinners.

In general, social life here was quite active in spite of political repression and military occupation. We attended a wedding that lasted all night at which women provided drum and chanting music, and men did all the dancing in groups. One could sense it was a male-oriented society. On the streets, men walked hand in hand or with arms around each other's waists, and so did women with women. Each sex kept to itself, people were predominantly heterosexual, and families were large. There were lots of taxis called "Service" as most people had no private cars. The buses were very old and rickety. Only United Nations personnel and Israeli government employees were driving Mercedes-Benz cars.

The new university campus was to have a beautiful territorial view from most classrooms. The library building was second on the agenda to be completed and overseeing this was Wayne's responsibility. Before our arrival, the exterior of the future library was already designed with the library committee's approval. Now Wayne had to meet with the architect to draw up plans for the interior. Periodically Wayne was to go to Tel Aviv to deal with the

Israeli bureaucracy in connection with construction materials imported for building the library and items for various special projects.

Besides teaching research methods to all students, I was to supervise and guide librarians and library assistants in cataloging newly purchased books according to the Library of Congress system and recataloging the old book collection, thus creating two card catalogs, one in Arabic and one in English, which was necessary for adequate use of the library. With my help, the staff was to review and reorganize the serials and reference collection. There was plenty to do, and I may have appeared to the staff somewhat like a slave driver.

Sometimes my Palestinian co-workers would say, "Miss Anya, why do you hurry so much to get things done? Anyway the Jews will come and destroy all our work." Many difficulties were expected at work; they could be caused by a different standard of living, unpredictably very hot or cold weather, and the hardship of living under Israeli occupation. This last factor could cause much unnecessary red tape. The "regime," as far as we could see, was at that time characterized by the Israeli military presence made up of mostly very young, eager soldiers with guns. They patrolled the area that used to be Palestine and arrested anybody they considered troublesome. Meanwhile, helicopters overhead, which were alien to us, were so common-place here that the natives seemed not to notice their constant drone.

Our twin sons were quite happy with their new life. They faithfully attended classes and tried hard to learn the local language. One of them was proud of his first language exam and said he thought he and his brother should be good in Arabic by the end of the two-year contract we signed for work at Birzeit University. They were hearing the local language all around them outside home. They spent free time with their new friends and often were invited to dinner or some cultural festival, where they tried hard to communicate with the little bits of Arabic they were learning every day.

Occasionally they complained that the university administration was lax when it came to scheduling Arabic language courses for foreign students. Why they did not equip the language laboratory for self-help or offer intensive English or Arabic courses remained unanswered questions. The boys said that they would do their best with what they had and keep trying to work for a little more than was assigned in class. The older twin was always interested in sports and was one of the best students in gymnastics. During what was called Palestine Week, he was impressed by how well the student council put together programs of local art and crafts. The cafeteria was full of products made by West Bank artisans. There were books written by local writers on various subjects, some with political and historical topics as well as a few on religions. There were poetry readings, games, and contests as well as political speeches expressing love for their country, Palestine.

In winter there was no central heating in the stone buildings, so layers of woolen clothing had to be worn. But other than comparing the situation to living in old English castles, where they said they would not have chosen to live in winter, our boys for the most part said life was generally all right. Often when the Israelis wanted to punish a village because schoolboys in the streets sometimes threw stones at the Israeli military vehicles passing through, they cut off the electricity or in summer the water to that village. These were very uncomfortable times, especially during exam weeks.

On Saturdays, we enjoyed shopping at the big market in Ramallah, the biggest town in our vicinity. It was a very colorful and noisy place, where a lot of the produce came from Israeli *kibbutzim.* I never understood how these transactions occurred when produce crossed the roadblocks and barbwired borders. In the *suq,* there was much to buy and bargain over, as was the local custom. If we were the first that day to buy something, they charged us more for good luck so that their trading day would be successful. We were glad to bring them luck with a few extra shekels.

On Sundays, we drove in our tiny Japanese Subaru to the Russian Convent Church on the Mount of Olives in Jerusalem. As in my childhood, we stood during the long services because in Russian Orthodox churches there are no pews to sit on. We were invited to dine in the convent refectory, where during meals the lives of saints were still read, replacing conversation.

At other times, being American, we were able to more easily cross over to the Jewish side of Jerusalem and went shopping for Western-style goods in a Jewish American department store. There was a restaurant on the top floor where European meals were served. This was a treat and a pleasant change from the Arabic food we ate every day. In the parking lot here, if we were noticed exiting our car that had a West Bank license plate, passersby would look at us with apprehension. Then noticing our American appearance they would ask why we had such a license and if we were Americans why we did not drive a big American car. We would tell them we lived and worked in an Arab village on the West Bank. With an alarmed expression on their faces they would ask if we were armed for our safety, and we would explain that we were teachers and the people there were pleased to have us teach their young people so they respected us. There was no police force in Birzeit, and we rarely heard of theft or disruption among the locals. Their traditional respect for their elders helped restrain their youth, but, of course, it was not always so when political situations arose.

Professors working at Birzeit University were from various European countries as well as the United States. An older French professor, who taught French as a required second language course, was self-sufficient enough not to mind the lack of European entertainment in Birzeit. The younger Americans and British citizens tended to become bored and restless, and although we had parties among ourselves, this was not always enough. A British couple, who had two small children, became close friends of a young American couple who had a new baby. They wished they could go for walks with the baby's pram, but there was no park and most roads were not paved and there were no city store windows to enjoy. Those two young mothers naturally couldn't help hoping the two-year contract would quickly pass.

Some weekends for a change we would go to Jerusalem to visit the Russian properties and shop in the old and new sectors of the city. Once when Wayne and I went alone to the Mount of Olives, we visited Abbess Tamara (née Romanov), who was already quite old and ill in bed. She remembered me, and giving me her hand with a warm smile on her face said, "Anya I am so happy that you came to see me." It was the last time we saw each other, and not too long afterwards she died.

Wayne was trying to spend some of his free time from work doing research for his PhD thesis. He also enjoyed sitting toward evening on our front porch with a glass of beer when it was available, which was rare. He would watch the passing townsfolk on their way to Attara, a village beyond our house and last on our road. They would be chattering in Arabic and usually nodded and greeted him with a *Marhaba*. In the afternoons, I could take a bus to neighboring Ramallah, from where another bus took me to my former Russian school in Bethany. Here I was teaching Arab girls several times a week Russian language reading and writing. In addition to going some Sundays to church, volunteering my time this way kept me in touch with the Russian Orthodox community.

Letters from friends and former co-workers in the United States added to our pleasurable moments, and Wayne sent back home descriptive letters that answered questions asked about life in the West Bank:

Dear Art,

It was good to hear from you recently. Unfortunately your acquaintance did not contact me after he reached Jerusalem, but the fault was not his. He did call me from Tel Aviv and said he would call the following Wednesday. By that time, either due to the storm, the students' failure to maintain peace with a bit of decorum, the telephone lines were cut and the interruption lasted through the following Friday. A few students who were apprehended by the military authorities (allegedly those who sang the songs and wrote the slogans) are still in the local slam in Ramallah. The parents are required to pay 2,000 IL [Israeli lira] towards the release of their son and a like sum if he is ever picked up again for questioning.

Concerning the Friends School in Ramallah it is in full swing and enjoys a student body of not only the faculty children from Birzeit, but many of the children of families of Consulates in Jerusalem. I do not know personally if there are Friends' meetings, but with the popularity they enjoy, I would be surprised if there were none. Ramallah is somewhat higher than Jerusalem and Birzeit is still higher, consequently the summer months although warm are much more pleasant than the rest of West Bank. In Jericho you suffocate, but that's about 1,300 feet below sea level.

I imagine you may have heard about the soldiers that patrol the neighborhood with helmets and batons. On the West Bank acquiescence and fear are maintained by threat of physical violence. In Israel proper this fear is illustrated by the following episode which happened to Anya and me at the end of October. We were returning from Nazareth to Birzeit. The main road runs through Nablus, Janine and finally Jerusalem. Just outside Nazareth you leave the State of Israel and enter the West Bank. At a check point on that road south of Nazareth we were stopped by the military authorities.

It was just dark enough so they could not see our blue license plates, but our small white car was clearly new and we certainly didn't look Arab, ergo, we must be Jews. One soldier spoke excellent English and asked for identification. We displayed our American passports. He asked how long we had been in the country and I mentioned merely a few months. He became quite friendly and after a few questions concerning our health and the level of pleasure we were deriving from Israel, he asked if I had a weapon. For me to be found with even a pocket knife if I were arrested in a disturbance would result in me being in prison or at least deported.

He suggested I buy a gun in Tel Aviv. I knew it had to come and besides I was getting bored with exchanging tin-pot homilies with this albeit likable chap, so I asked, "Why do I need a gun?" "To protect you," he replied. "But why?" I asked, "Why do I need a gun?" I asked a bit more incredulously than before. "Because you are going through Arab territory," he explained. Then with a smile I asked, "Protection from whom, the Jews or the Arabs?" He stood up from the car window and replied, "Why, from the Arabs of course." At this point the come-on became apparent to him.

He walked to the front of the car, looked at the blue license plate and with no more a pleasant smile he waved us on. These small isolated episodes slowly add up to become greater than the sum of all the parts. But life can be enjoyable and Anya is happy to be able to see and visit many of her old friends, both Russian and Arab.

Still this culture is not one that either of our sons is used to, and I often wonder how soon the novelty will wear thin, if it already hasn't. If I can be of any help in your coming over for either a summer or a year or two, let me know.

Best regards from all of us,
Wayne

Another letter written to some friends and co-workers, American Jews who were quite interested in coming over to visit Israel and us on the West Bank, read as follows:

Dear friends,

It was good to get your letter and to learn that you found something else and a bit closer to New York. The situation here has not changed, and the general feeling is that the only change which will take place is that when the talks have formally broken off, the military will become even stricter in the future than they have been in the past. As you can well imagine the Palestinians want to be independent, and were against Sadat's visit. It was well known that the demands of Sadat would not be met by Begin. Apparently none of the territory now held by Israel will be returned. In fact the settlements are becoming more numerous all the time and they will continue to increase. These small groups become a thorn in the shoe of the Palestinians, but there is nothing they can do. There is only one possibility of solving the problem, and that is sad to consider. Once you've seen this rocky part of the country, you wonder why God promised it to the Jews. But there are some beautiful places of irrigated land where a great deal of produce comes from and they are controlled by the Israelis.

Anya and I just received our work permits a week ago and now we are waiting for an extension of our visas. This is the first time such permits were not given and no one seems to know what this means. We have been on the West Bank illegally now for about four months. The mill-wheels of the authorities grind extremely slow. We have been to Jerusalem many times, both to the old and new city, but the old city seems to be a tourist haven and the new part seems to be somewhat soulless. With an annual inflation rate of 42% last year, it takes something other than money to keep one amused. The cinemas have closed in all of Israel, I heard because of some additional tax for something. As I type this evening in my office, I can hear the heavy artillery of the Israeli army at their base beyond the next hill. The usual practice I guess.

For Anya, as you know, this was almost like coming home. We have been to the Russian places many times. She speaks the language and has many friends, but I think she has lost the old feeling she once may have had. For me I would much rather do what business I have to do with people in Israel than with the Arabs. They seem to have a simple hearted pleasure in finding out what the traffic will bear so to speak, and the initial experience of being taken is still unpleasant although it doesn't happen anymore. Lines to buy a ticket for the bus, even getting on the bus, going through the cafeteria line here for lunch, cashing our check at the bank, all of these turn into a shoving bout with no respect for anyone.

Of course this behavior is not restricted to the Arabs; all of the Middle East has this "modus vivendi." It does not seem to be as pronounced in Jerusalem or Tel Aviv, but when it does take place, it is mostly immigrants from America who become heavy-handed. The Israeli bureaucracy is no more efficient than the Arab way of shuffling papers, and when one form of confusion is superimposed on another the result is frustration. I some-how find it difficult to believe the Israelis want to continue to administer more than one million persons who do not want their administration and consider them foreign occupiers.

The job here is pleasant and there is always something new to keep one busy. The new library building is moving slowly; the plans and the cost esti-mates should be here shortly, and then maybe a trip to the states will be neces-sary. I am trying to buy a large collection of books, I have in mind a complete library of some small college, but I see no "ads" for anything like that for sale.

Good luck in your new job. I hope your wife can find something around the area. Stay in touch.

As ever,

Wayne

Thanks to our little Subaru, on long weekends during holidays or between quarters, we took short sightseeing trips with the boys. One interest-ing trip was to the desert of the Sinai Peninsula, location of Mount Sinai—in Arabic *Jabal Musa*, meaning Moses' mountain, where according to tradi-tion he received the Ten Commandments from God. Here also is an ancient

Greek Orthodox monastery, St Catherine's Monastery, with one of the oldest libraries in the world. A very small mosque stands in an open plaza across from the church and belfry. In times of intertribal conflicts between Bedouin caravans passing through this wilderness, the feuding parties assemble here and request that the monastery abbot act as impartial judge in settling their disputes, often about the availability of water in the dry desert. According to Muslim tradition, this custom was sanctioned by the Prophet Muhammad.

From there we drove to the Red Sea where Wayne and the boys went snorkeling and admired the beautiful shells, corals, and exotic fish under water. We also saw gorgeous tropical fish of all colors and shapes in an undersea observatory at Eilat, a new Israeli town across from the Gulf of al Aqaba. This is where Israel, the Kingdom of Jordan, and the Sinai desert of Egypt meet. As we began our drive home through this arid wilderness, we saw desert gazelles and flocks of young camels. We fraternized with their masters, the Bedouin, who invited us to visit with them in their tents. My Arabic without a foreign accent delighted them, a proof of the importance of teaching foreign languages in first grade, as happened in my childhood. My oral muscles were still flexible enough to conform to the local speech pattern.

The scenery in the Negev desert was fantastic; barren rocky strata of all colors, canyons, and sandy desert in eighty-degree heat were a sight to behold and provoked wonder about their history. When we reached the Dead Sea, we decided to take a dip but could only float on its very salty water. We visited Masada high up on a mountain accessible by cable. Jewish King Herod (reigned 37 B.C.–A.D. 4), a very long time ago, built a fortress here, the remains of which we came to see and ponder. On the way back home, we stopped in Jericho, one of the lowest and warmest places in the country. It is situated below sea level, and here in the valley we saw a big Palestinian refugee camp. Above it stood an old Greek Orthodox monastery that was built on the rocky incline of the "Forty Days Mountain." It was so called because, according to the Gospel, this was where Jesus Christ fasted and prayed for forty days before he began his ministry.

Jericho, a typical small Palestinian town, was pleasant as a vacation place. Water ran down narrow canals alongside its main streets. Palm trees lined the streets as well as buildings that stood surrounded by all kinds of greenery and fruit trees. Here birds sang incessantly and water gurgled as it ran down the canals. The Russian Mission owned two lush gardens that the Mission chief entrusted Wayne to oversee in his spare time. A faithful Arab guard was also the gardener who took care of the fruit trees and the stone house with a small chapel and rooms to rest in. Our family took advantage of this and occasionally spent weekends there during the cold and wet winters in Birzeit and Jerusalem. Here monks and nuns from Russian monasteries in the Holy Land took turns spending the winter.

After this pleasant trip, we were glad to be home in Birzeit and back in the academic routine. But Grandfather, who was already eighty, was getting homesick for his real home and lifestyle in America. I knew he did not want to disappoint his son and part with us, but on the other hand he did say that at his age he might not last long enough to see us all return together to the United States. Our sons said that America was his country and he fit in there; the people here were just not his type. We were all younger and could adjust and hopefully would like it here. But it would not be as easy for him, so we agreed that I would take a short leave of absence from work and fly back with him to his home. Later Grandfather wrote to us about his pleasant moments in life and how happy he was to be in his native land. He lived to be eighty-three years old and after our return to the Northwest stayed with us in Everett, Washington, till the end of his life.

At Birzeit University the twins were making progress in Arabic, but, of course, other students like Armenians and Greeks who were born in Palestine had an advantage over them. Besides their own languages, these students already knew both English and Arabic as it was taught in local public and missionary schools. However my sons were determined to succeed as they believed that if they learned a second language as difficult as Arabic appeared to be, they would be able to secure good jobs in the United States and represent American companies in Egypt and other Arab countries.

They were encouraged in this thinking by the university president's mother, Mrs Naser, who lived on university grounds in a wing of the oldest building, which originally belonged to her family. She and her sister-in-law often invited us for coffee and sweets, realizing that our family probably felt homesick sometimes. They were well-educated elderly Christian Arab ladies, who at one time ran a girl's school in this formerly all-Christian town. They told us that the art teacher in their school was a Russian gentleman, Georgi Aleéff, a popular teacher. They were delighted to hear that he taught art also at Bethany School where I studied. This formed a bond between us, and they enjoyed talking to us about the good old days in Palestine before it was overrun by refugees from territories now occupied by Israel. They said that at that time both Christian and Muslim families lived together peacefully respecting their traditional patriarchal way of life.

Old friends from Seattle who were touring Europe, while in Greece took advantage of its proximity to Israel and came to visit us for a few days.

At home in Seattle they had four grown children, who at one time were our sons' good friends. With them we went to most of the West Bank's biblical sights and then drove to Tel Aviv by the Mediterranean Sea. Its location was beautiful; its skyscrapers were impressive but seemed incongruous with the rest of this ancient land. Not too far from there, in the vicinity of the Sea of Galilee, we ate St Peter's fish in a restaurant that served it as the specialty of the house—a whole baked fish for each one of us. Tourists usually enjoyed this dining excursion as it took them back to the days when Christ walked around this countryside with His fishermen disciples. This area was known as Galilee and encompassed ancient ruins and remains of cities such as old Capernaum, the Mount of Beatitudes, and nearby the Church of the Multiplication of the Loaves and Fishes.

During winter in Birzeit, the weather during the day could be sunny and fairly warm but at night was very cold in spite of several layers of woolen clothes we wore to bed. Then the electricity often was off for three days at a time, and we were unable to turn on our small electric heater. This was how the Israelis often tried to send a message to the Palestinians. On and off, the military government picked up a few students for questioning, and the *Jerusalem Post* had an article that there were protests because yet another settlement of Jews was being built on land the Palestinian villagers considered their own. As the Jewish settlements went up, the Arab villages came down. It was believed that in a few years there Jewish settlements would cover the entire West Bank. In the distance, we often heard explosions and shooting and wondered if a war had broken out or whether it was simply soldiers practicing.

We went to the Russian Church in Gethsemane for Easter midnight service. The weather was still wet and cold. Some houses at that time of year even had mold growing indoors, and this included our home. I was eager to attend the midnight service, which in Russian churches is of special beauty. The choir singing sounded heavenly, everything looked bright and festive as with lit candles in our hands we stood praying and listening to the Gospel words describing Christ's resurrection. The church was full of believers; many of them came all the way from Tel Aviv, as among the Jewish Russian families one parent was often Orthodox Christian. The atmosphere was that of sincere elation when the serving priest addressed the crowd with the words "Christ is risen!" and everybody responded in unison "Indeed! He is risen!"

Several days before Easter, I caught a cold but I did not pay much attention to it. I also noticed that when I was in the house I sneezed a lot. In a few days I was awakened at night by a feeling of suffocation, and I struggled for breath. Wayne immediately called a taxi, which drove us more than ten miles to the French hospital in Jerusalem. Luckily that night there were no Israeli roadblocks, and we reached the hospital in the shortest time possible. I was told that being somewhat frail and underweight my body was unable to fight the allergens in the air coupled with the cold I already had. The doctor added that stress related to the volatility of the political situation around us might have contributed to this asthma attack. After a ten-day hospital stay, my lungs cleared up, and it was recommended I go back to the United States on sick leave to gain some weight and undergo allergy testing. I followed these instructions and returned home to the West Coast, where in our home on Silver Lake my older son met me. I spent the spring quarter gaining weight as I recovered. The asthma never returned, and I learned a lesson in taking care of my body, something I had given little thought to before.

While I was in the United States, Wayne and the twins continued to live on the West Bank, and we kept the post office busy delivering mail thus keeping us all linked as a family. Wayne did the work of both of us at the university library. Before getting ill, I was putting together materials for a library workshop and was teaching as well as continuing to be a reference librarian. He had to take over all my duties himself until other arrangements could be made. This was what Wayne wrote about it:

Dear Anya,

The workshop finally came to an end, which it was bound to do, and I am glad it's over. Issuing certificates was done with input from all three Deans and the Vice President. Everyone had a different idea. Finally the printing was done and there were thirty-three participants who received them with only one who did not deserve it. We should have had more practice sessions!

The boys and I drove to Tantour Monastery today to see the library there. Jerusalem is filled with tourists. A bomb was found near Jaffa Gate and another exploded somewhere in Jerusalem, but no one was hurt. For a while there have not been any disturbances, just the usual road blocks.

I made arrangements to go to Cyprus for a week. It costs $333 for all three of us and the car round trip. We will borrow a tent and try to camp out. Hotels cost only $15 a night, so we may sleep inside if we have to.

Aside from the weddings, engagements, and wheat harvest that go on next to our house, the place has not changed. In the evenings our road becomes a "Boulevard" for those taking in the night air. The usual "Har yoo" (how are you) rings out loud and clear as the assorted groups pass in review. The Russian lady married to the Arab doctor stopped to talk for a few minutes, they are cleaning a house down the road, they will have only one room she says, and they and their five kids will move in when she comes back from Moscow in about three months.

Did I mention the Englishman with whom I went to Hebron one afternoon? We were impressed with the city and its narrow streets that are covered with grape vines and attractive arches that connect parallel streets. The local Arabs considered us Jews, of course, and I felt uncomfortable. I'd like to go there again with an Arab. The glass blowers were not operating because of Ramadan, but they asked about you and they send their regards. At the Russian Orthodox Monastery, the few monks there were very hospitable. This reminded me of our family trip there with you. They showed us the church for the Englishman's benefit, then we were invited to the refectory. Here they treated us to their homemade wine and sent us off with a basket full of grapes from their large vineyard.

I received a letter from Kessler, our Jewish friend in New York City who gave you the book by S. L. Frank, "God with Us." I do not know if he would want to come here for a visit. He's working at a library in the Ben Gurion University near Birsheva. Now that I have more time, I realize in many different ways that you really are not here, but I know time will pass quickly. The twins send you their love and I also send all my love.

Wayne

I could not have described our academic life at Birzeit better than Wayne could. He was so much more involved with the university administration than I was. He had to account to all three deans in addition to the vice president and his wife, who was the registrar and head of the enrollment division. This is what Wayne wrote:

Dear Anya,

Things here are about the same as when you left, except that the Vice President is getting "funny." For the past three weeks I have been trying to get in contact with him to talk for just a few moments about how he wants the budget taken care of. He never bothered to return my call. I tried several times. Finally, when I had to take the car to Cyprus for a week, he wondered why I hadn't let him know earlier that I was going. Of course he is the boss, but I don't have the slightest intention of having communication a totally one-way operation.

Also it seems as if the library skills course is going to be offered again this year from the library. The Vice President needs to know if and when you're coming back. I told him you were better, but it was suggested that you remain in the United States rather than return and become ill again. You should write him a letter and explain the situation.

I just checked with the Vice President and found that the Library course is going to be given with approximately 400 new students. An exchange type of arrangement could be made. If you could find a qualified fellow librarian at the Everett Community College or elsewhere who would be willing to fill out an application the same as any other applicant for a job here, it would be similar to an exchange type of arrangement. Anyway, I will have to be prepared to take over teaching your course until I find someone here, so between the two of us we may manage to muddle through. This situation as well as my necessary trip to Cyprus has caused a small flap, but it could not have been foreseen and prevented even if it caused a big flap. Now I'm beginning to understand the reason for the faculty action. It seems as if this "sandbox" is run according to the Vice President and the three Deans, causing gaps in communication.

The trip to Cyprus was enjoyable, as far as it went, but we were all happy to be back in our own trundle beds. I was given one week to keep the car because that was the length of time it would take for my "dirty" passport to expire. You remember we have to have two passports, one to travel to Israel and the other to travel to the Arab countries. When I was parked by the tax office in Jerusalem a few days ago, someone soundly ran into the back bumper and dented it. The West Bank license plate with Arabic language on it must have caused the accident. It probably was difficult for an Israeli to resist the opportunity to hinder; now I have to fix it.

Have our son go to college for a change. He can always work for a living. His brothers here are quietly getting somewhat "antsy," but bearing up well.

With love,
Wayne

Observations on Local Life

The following sections are excerpted from a diary kept by my husband while we lived and worked at Birzeit University. It mirrors the daily life and disquieting times of West Bank inhabitants when we lived there.

PRACTICALITIES AND POLITICS ON THE WEST BANK

Today a small article in the *Jerusalem Post* reported on a trip of several American lawyers who were checking on civil rights on the West Bank. The lawyers stated that as far as Arabs were concerned, they could not find any civil rights. One Jerusalem newspaper refered to them as leftists and radicals. Some member of a government office said that the group got their information from the usual totally unreliable sources. A London newspaper published an extensive article on mistreatment of the Arab population in the West Bank. As might be expected, the local administration merely called the entire thing unfounded assumptions from the usual unreliable sources.

The religious makeup of this small town [of Birzeit] is split between the Muslims and the Christians, Orthodox, Protestant, and Catholic each being about a third. The Orthodox and Protestants are smaller groups, but it is obvious that this general statement will not go without some argument by those who presently live here, or those who have lived here.

$$* * * * *$$

Many Palestinians were educated in foreign countries, and having been exposed to a culture that was different from their own, they notice what amenities foreigners, in this case Jewish immigrants living in Israel, have. For example, in Israel there is no shortage of water as there is in the West Bank. For those living in Birzeit, water is available two or maybe three days a week only. This necessitates reserving water in tanks on the roofs of houses. Electricity is shut off several times during the week, often for unknown reasons. Other times for only a few hours, while some repairs are being made or new lines are being installed along another road.

Equipment is somewhat old, and the large spools of cable and electrical wiring are slowly rolled along the road by several men, then placed under the metal light poles. Often the need for water pipes to houses at the edge of the town, such as ours, is satisfied merely by connecting a galvanized pipe to the last house closest to the water supply. Because of the rocky terrain, the pipe is laid on the surface and covered with a few stones and dirt. The water does not come directly into the house but is brought up to the reservoir tanks on the roofs.

The tanks are equipped with a simple float, similar to one found in a toilet bowl, which stops the incoming water when the tank is filled. With the scarcity of such a valuable commodity as water, it is sad to see water running onto the ground when one of the floats in the tank has become faulty and no one is available to repair it. There is, however, a meter on the pipe, and a faucet that allows water to be shut off if the residents are aware of the loss of water. Unfortunately, the water is supplied sometime during the night when everyone is asleep and not aware of the loss.

For those Palestinians who are aware of the standard of living beyond the restrictions and bureaucracy of the West Bank, and [the restrictions] are many, they make an effort to be what they are not. I do not mean to imply that this group is large nor that it is losing its national identity. Merely that this is something in the line of personal business, because any improvement in their standard of living requires Israeli permits or other administrative papers. The realization that a few Israeli lira (IL) under the counter will accomplish more in a few hours than legal procedure will in a few months has become a way of life. "Under the counter" deals are known to have taken place, but I have absolutely no reliable evidence that any have taken place. In many transactions, the person whom you know may be in a position to aid you and there is nothing new or irregular in any such operation, otherwise even shuffling of papers would have come to a complete halt.

* * * * *

My position in the Palestinian culture is certainly not an enviable one, for my ability with the language, at this period in history, is extremely limited. By that I mean my language and knowledge of Arabic will hopefully improve. It is no secret that living in a foreign setting for any length of time without learning at least some working knowledge of the language is analogous to being physically transplanted without benefit of mental transportation. More could be learned leafing through travel catalogs!

When meeting friends we have known in the United States whose families are here, either in Birzeit, Ramallah, or Jerusalem, their pleasure at seeing us again is obvious and sincere. They are willing to be of whatever help they can in getting our household effects through customs, taking us on a tour through the Old City, and generally wanting to help. These offers of aid are appreciated, but the underlying theme seems to be not so much the actual physical aspects of such operations as revealing the possibilities of how to bypass the officials. Further help is offered on how to go to the official who is apparently in charge of some realm of the bureaucratic operation.

The first step in accomplishing some business relating to transfer of property, obtaining a car, or getting either a visa or an airline ticket is to start with the highest official to whom one has access, and then working down if all fails at the top. After having lived under occupation that relegates the Palestinians to a rank lower than any *Alia* (Jewish immigrants), or even those who returned by choice, there remains little else in the way of getting something done other than having connections in high places.

* * * * *

In most sovereign states that refer to themselves as democratic, there is an unquestioned respect for the integrity of universities and institutions of higher education. Yet on the 9th of November, this respect was violated again by the military occupation, or "liberation" forces. They entered Birzeit University campus by jeep, without presenting any authorization or directives issued from the military headquarters. The reason they gave was to see if any slogans with a "meaning" had been written on the walls. There were no specific names of students asked for, and only one student was shoved around. Of course, all six of the military men carried their ubiquitous machine guns.

The same acts of disrespect took place at Bethlehem University and the Teacher Training College in Ramallah. The last time this type of military "show-of-force" took place at Birzeit, it resulted in several students spending several days in hospitals and many more spending several months in prisons. The cause for this military action was based on the fact that anti-Israel slogans had been written on the walls of Birzeit University.

On November 2, the anniversary of the Balfour Declaration, the military forces entered Bethlehem University campus and removed several posters relating to this declaration. On November 3, a larger group of military—still carrying their machine guns—went directly into the classrooms of Teacher Training College in Ramallah, disrupted classes, and took names and addresses of students. This time the military governor was with the military forces of liberation!

On November 8, the military attempted to enter a private house in Ramallah. Being unable to get the people inside to come to the door, they broke the glass, then left. The UN has been informed of these actions but apparently these acts do not qualify as transgressions of either privacy or civil rights. Quite obviously neither do they fit the category of military actions. When such events are mentioned in any press release, the military authorities pass them off as groundless rumors, emanating from the same "source-less" source.

Birzeit University is attempting to provide the students of the West Bank with the knowledge and leadership that is required for the administration of their own affairs. Such incursions by the military have taken place many times in the past and will doubtless take place in the future. There is, unfortunately, no way that these incursions can be stopped, unless the local so-called democratic sovereign state allows the students of the West Bank to choose and plan their own course for providing their own welfare. One of these courses of action is establishing a university to fulfill these needs. It is indeed questionable how a university education can be considered anything but beneficial to any part of any democracy, even a military one.

* * * * *

Jerusalem Jews, although they are not barred from taking the Arab buses, prefer their own services. Along the road, within the city limits of Jerusalem, are many homes that display a refinement and sophistication that seems almost out of keeping. There is presently one private residence being constructed for an Arab millionaire, all being made of the ubiquitous stone and in a baroque style that is a beautiful blending of both the traditional Arabic and European modern. The only attribute that would indicate this affluence in America is a swimming pool. Such a snob feature is not required to indicate affluence here. An owner has other displays of his affluence.

The road enters Jerusalem by passing several consulates. The American Colony Hotel, the British Council, and the YMCA are also there, whereas the American consulate is on Nablus Road. Along this road there are also different Christian schools, the Italian Silesian Music School, Les Pères Blanc Archeological Institute, and at the end of the bus line there is Schmidt's School for Girls. St George's English School for Boys is near there. At this particular bus terminal, there is a W.C. that is nicely built and maintained. Whether or not you are like King George, whose first question at any gathering was "Where is the toilet?" such facilities must not be overlooked.

* * * * *

The local administration is in the process of annexing the West Bank. Still with their definition of military administration, the question seems merely of semantics. It is unfortunate that the descendents of Abraham cannot only beard the lion in his den, but can tweak his nose as well. But maybe the United States is not the lion anymore. Whether or not it is the lion obviously seems to be of little importance here today.

The *Jerusalem Post*, one of the only means of obtaining current information that I am able to obtain and read in English, continually indicates plans to rally the forces of American Jewry into more commitment to the cause of annexing the West Bank. It also reveals the intransigence of the Arabs in dealing with the situation. The editorial comments from the papers as presented by the morning news in English suggest that it would be best for all parties concerned if nothing was said about this annexation at the present time, or probably in the future as well. This would give the concerned parties time to appraise and properly assess the situation. For the second time in about two months, code numbers have been announced over the radio that coincide with certain groups or individual soldiers who are required to report someplace for military training. The comment was that the number of soldiers reporting was quite good.

Continually the military administration is working on new settlements for Jews who are planning to move into them. These settlements are not restricted to the borders of Israel but are scattered all over the West Bank. The thought of paying the Israelis for these buildings, of course by the American taxpayer, in the event they should be forced to return to 1967 borders is staggering.

On August 18, the salient news over the radio mentioned the concern other countries have about providing equal facilities to the residents of the West Bank. No one has sanctioned such a move locally, although it could be considered a humanitarian move. The three new settlements that are to be started have been explained as projects of the former government, and therefore no one can actually be responsible for the ongoing plans.

The present administration is merely following what the former started and therefore is no longer responsible for what was started. Perfectly clear? The small element of question at the beginning of the U.S. Secretary of State's advance visit regarding the West Bank has disipated into vapor. There was a slight chance that the West Bank was getting some recognition, but that no longer exists. Even the local news no longer express any doubt as to the outcome of whatever talks may take place about the West Bank. The "straws" of "Carter's broom" apparently wore out rapidly! Further, the administration is quite active in the air, with both planes and helicopters. More trucks are moving the soldiers around and there was some tank activity a bit north of Birzeit a day or two ago. Someplace there is heavy artillery practice. Directions are difficult to determine but the noise is clear.

* * * * *

On Sunday, army pilots were practicing bombing maneuvers north of Jenin. Low-flying jet planes made a great deal of noise. There seemed to be a pattern established; on Fridays, they used to fly low and fast to create noise for the Muslim holy day, and then did the same thing on Sunday for the Christians. Was this planned? Or was it a coincidence? The news that morning told of the superiority of the administration forces over their Arab neighbors. What they failed to say was that these were combined forces against the West Bank. For the past few days the news primarily covered the cholera epidemic in Syria, parts of Jordan and Lebanon, and even Kuwait! There have been two known cases in what is now referred to as the West Bank when there was cholera here, but Judea and Samaria when there was none.¹ Local administration news just mentioned two cases this morning; such news would have had an adverse effect on tourism had they been announced earlier in the year, but then there was no cholera, of course.

The last few days there has been a great deal of air activity and I would guess a great deal of ground activity to match on the other side of the hills to the west of Birzeit from where heavy gun action could be heard. It was announced that there would be equal medical facilities for all inhabitants of Gaza and the West Bank, which apparently meant equal medical care and other social benefits that the people of Israel enjoy. However, a day or two later, as an austerity plan, it was announced that due to financial exigencies, further programs for social welfare would be cut back or stopped. No new hospitals or schools would be built. The Gaza Strip and the West Bank are right where they started, except now they know what they aren't going to get. The water has been shut off for about a week now because water diversion to new settlements was going on. We still have water in the cistern and managed to pump the two tanks on top of our house full. The refugee camp next to the university will soon have the same disease [cholera] as they have in Syria unless clean water is provided. According to the news from the Jerusalem radio, by their own admission, the local authorities are continuing to allow settlements on the West Bank and giving apparently little or no attention to the opinion of the rest of the world. If the Gush Emunim² are as concerned with settling in the West Bank as they appear to be—on territory they call Judea and Samaria—why does the land have to belong to a nation or state with any name at all?

It would seem to me that the Gush Emunim would be fulfilling the will of their "ancient real estate dealer" by merely living there, being able to have their prayer meetings or whatever, and not caring who controls the land, as long as they were allowed to live there in peace. By placing the law of their faith first and the law of the land second, they would be considered religeous people first and Zionists second. For me it is difficult to understand why one must necessarily be tied to the other. I guess those are reasons enough as to why I would never be a good Jew, or even a bad one either. If I were a 100 percent five-star Israeli, I would be a bit more than somewhat perturbed by the goings on throughout the world and especially at the United Nations regarding the "plight" of Israel. It seems as if the Jews are desirous of having the full and complete backing of and treaties with the United States government, which would allow them to do as they saw fit regarding not only the Palestinians but the West Bank as a whole. Anything short of this arrangement with the United States seems not only unacceptable, but sufficient grounds and reasons for continuing the intransigence that Israel has displayed.

* * * * *

The Israeli lira was decontrolled this weekend, and the banks will open this morning for business as usual, if it could be called that. The dollar went to 115 lira to sell and 150 lira to buy. On Friday, the price of car gas went from 54 agorat (cents) a liter to 66 agorat starting at six the next morning. Fortunately for a few Israelis and others who were in on the ground floor, they did indeed make a small bundle, or most probably a large one. The immediate result for those who have to work for a living is bad both for Arabs and Jews, as well as, for example, immigrants from Russia. A woman who has been living with her son and Jewish husband in Tel Aviv for the past five years had been given three years to convert to Judaism if she wanted to be allowed to have a job in her profession as a musician. Remaining a nonconvert, she is now working as a maid, whereas she is educated to be a concert pianist. Her Jewish husband understands her disappointment and does not accept the situation, but now they have to remain in Israel as second-class citizens. They wish they could go back to Russia and tell the rest of the Jewish people there how unfair life could be in Israel.

But think what a dull world this would be if there were "liberty and justice for all." I always did think America, even with all its faults and iniquities, was a pretty decent place to be, but time spent in Europe and the rest of the world had at times made me more or less forget this. Would democracy sometime in the future bring a semblance of justice for all, and would it reach beyond cultural and religious inequalities in both Israel and Palestine? In villages, and not only in all-Muslim ones, when a girl is seen walking with a boy her age and probably considering healthy biological thoughts, she is regarded as slipping in her behavior. The hangup with sex is startling here and for such a young woman can be harmful for her life. This to me is not an understandable aspect of local culture. On the other hand, there seems to be nothing wrong for the Muslim minaret to be equiped with loud speakers and colorful neon lights so it looks like a modern merry-go-round at some carnival.

ATARA VILLAGE ENCOUNTERS

About five miles beyond Birzeit, going north on the only road there is, exists the village of Atara. The total population I would guess to be about fifty souls. For the first time since we have come here, I visited Atara. The bus that goes between Ramallah and Birzeit goes to Atara every other trip. Our house is the last one on the top of the hill next to a large open field on the road to Atara. On my way to Ramallah this morning, the bus was coming from the opposite direction toward Atara, and I decided to take the trip just to see what was there.

The road stops in Atara, and I guess it's all for the best, because Atara doesn't seem to be going anyplace anyway. The road enters something similar to a square. There are two or three shops, or stores of some kind. There are a few paths that lead back between the buildings, and a short road that leads downhill and to the left. This road is about fifty feet long, and then turns into another path. The town square is also about fifty feet long and wide and has a low wall on two sides.

The people of Atara are Muslims, I was told. It is beautifully situated on the top of the hill with a view in all directions into the surrounding valleys. There are several well-built houses with gardens that could also be beautiful if water was available. If I could only communicate with the people, I'm sure I would find them interesting. Living in Atara alone might be one means of learning a working vocabulary in Arabic. I have the feeling that living with someone out of wedlock, which is something of an acceptable custom in the Western world, would not be tolerated in this village. One might remain anonymous in a large Arab city, not in Atara.

The bus then drove a few feet down the road to the left and about three persons got off. Then the bus backed into the square and drove forward a few feet back into the road by which we had just come. By this time, I was the center of attraction. Some foreigner had obviously come to town and wasn't getting off the bus. It was about eight in the morning. Another scheduled bus had been there at six the same morning, and the people getting on now were few. Sunday is not a day of rest for Muslims.

The bus filled to about half, and by 8:50 a.m. we were ready for the trip to Ramallah. A young boy of about eighteen decided to sit next to me rather than by himself or with one of his friends. I was already uncomfortably warm and still had a slight cold that made me feel tired, and I knew he was going to talk in English to me. His first question was "Har you?" I acknowledged his question with a smile and "Fine" and looked back out the window. We had started slowly down the road now, and despite the bumpy bus, I feigned extreme interest in a pile of stones in the field. I heard him ask what my name was, but my interest in this unique stone pile grew in direct proportion with my annoyance. There was a pause as the pile of stones passed slowly to my right and out of sight.

Then I felt an elbow in my ribs: "Watzur nem?" I thought that if I indicated his English is inadequate by asking what he had said, he would be discouraged. I scarcely felt like listening to an effort in English, but my ploy failed. He repeated his second question. I told him my name, which he manfully attempted to repeat. My name to him was obviously as alien as his name was to me. My total inadequacy with Arabic was again a source of annoyance to me. If I were only able to ask him the same questions in Arabic, I am sure, the rousing conversation would have stopped.

The bus had picked up a few more passengers, and two or three were aready standing in the aisle. My young friend was talking to his friends in the seat behind us and enjoying the part of translator immensely. The next question indicated he had remembered another word, and I wondered what class technique had been used. "You married?" I answered yes, and his final *pièce de résistance* was "Why?" Normal conditions would have indicated I was sitting next to a *vieux roue*. His English teacher apparently had not had time to teach another response to any question that required a "maybe" answer, but I knew saying that maybe wouldn't be fair on my part, no matter how little I wanted to continue this dialogue, so I smiled and said, "Why not?" He found that answer totally acceptable and so translated it to his friends behind us. I was pleased to see the prestige of the young man rise to above a scale of merely one-to-ten among his friends, and the light of worship in their eyes, but his cup that already was running over received another abundant slosh of pride.

An elderly gentleman got on the bus, who was a friend of this boy, and the boy immediately stood up and offered his seat. With the desire to show off to his friends and to maintain our camaraderie that had been by now well cemented, he tried to prolong our conversation. Finally, I guess to indicate to his older friend these undeniable attributes, he leaned over to me and pointing to his friend, now sitting beside me, said quite loudly and more plainly than anything before, "He speaks very good English." My estimation of the boy immediately dropped, for obviously the man could not speak any English at all. The man did understand enough to wave his hand back and forth as a sign of negation, which caused the boy and his friends great glee. I am afraid I will see that boy again.

The local people of Atara were similar to those found in any small village. The older men were sitting on a low stone wall along one side of the square, and several small children were playing with their homemade wheels, which constituted the only toy available for most of them. Most children wore the usual tattered shirts and pants or some form of short pants and sandals.

A few were barefoot, and one poor little rascal had the viscous substance from his nose securely cemented on his upper lip, resulting from a husky three-day cold. The residue continued to remain just out of reach of his tongue. I was more bothered by this than anyone.

We were halfway back to Birzeit from Atara by now, and the bus driver stopped under the shade of a fig tree to collect the fare. Since I had stopped him going to Atara, the opposite direction from Ramallah, I assumed I would have to pay additional for that impromtu excursion, but he charged me the usual 20 cents fare. Besides, this type of tourist trip is doubtless not one of any itineraries offered for the usual sightseeng. The driver, Muhammad by name, has a fair command of English and has been helpful in the past. I would like to think we are friends and have an understanding that transcends the usual utterances required for oral communication. The Ramallah bus to Jerusalem stops on the opposite side of the circle in downtown Ramallah.

From the discharge point of the Birzeit bus to Ramallah, the fare to Jerusalem is 20 cents. It requires the usual checkpoint stop by the military just at the city limits, beside the small alcoholic spirits plant that makes arak. At one bus terminal in Jerusalem, about two blocks from Damascus Gate, the buses from the West Bank arrive. The Israeli buses also have a terminal here. I took the Israeli bus to the new part of the city, and another young boy sat down beside me, red-haired and with a yarmulke firmly bobby-pinned into place. With practiced Hebrew, he asked for directions. I told him I did not know Jewish, which was an unfortunate choice of words. He said he was British and suggested that most Americans did not know the difference between Hebrew and Yiddish anyway. I said that unfortunately he probably was correct, but those Americans who were aware of the situation in Israel certainly did.

He was planning to stay for a year and was interested when I mentioned I was living on the West Bank. He said he had no idea how to get there but would like to visit. "For you," I said, "with the official stamps in your passport, you will have less trouble travelling throughout the West Bank than the natives, or," I paused, "the people who were born there." I looked at him. "I don't like to call them invaders, but I don't know how you refer to them." He now looked at me with some question. His age and exuberence are the seed that will maintain the Jewish cohesiveness and clanishness in whatever part of the world the diaspora is found.

UNIVERSITY LIFE

The application for admission to Birzeit University is a well-defined operation by both the administration and the students. Because of the exceptionally high standing of the university, both academically and prestige-wise, the applications always outnumber the space available. Presently there are only five students enrolled who are not able to actually follow the courses in Arabic but they do have a speaking ability in the language. An important aspect of admissions is the English language examination that all students must take. It is a foregone conclusion that every student entering Birzeit University speaks English with merely a question of their fluency and ability. An entrance examination determines the level into which the entering freshman will be placed. Courses are taught in English except for those that deal primarily with Arabic language and literature. Without exception, every member of the faculty speaks English. The catalog of the university, like any catalog of a university, describes the courses taught.

School officially started here at Birzeit University the first of October, but registration is still taking place and a few students still are floating around like feathers in the wind, wondering where they need to go. There has been a substantial increase of students this fall term, and most appear to be students that have been in America. If there should be some change in the status of the West Bank's administration put in effect either by the Jordanians or by the Palestinians themselves, those who were not here in 1967 do not want to be someplace else even if the same conditions would prevail. It is possible that merely being here and being a Jordanian would be sufficient to entitle the local people to either vote in a referendum or plebiscite, which will determine the future type of government for this area.

It is unique to find classical Arabic being spoken by those students that come from the most remote villages, not the larger towns and cities in the West Bank. In a few isolated examples, certainly not the rule, a few Arab students who are in a position of authority, such as working with a faculty member, tend to be unable to handle the responsibility of their job and as a consequence act and talk to others somewhat rudely. But you do not have to be an Arab to do that, and my attitude is still positive; I like the job, I like the people. Even the continual "Har U" or the less frequent "Shalom" doesn't bother me as much as it once did.

Many of the girls are very attractive, and the boys are well dressed and presentable. I guess I won't find the type that might be easily seen, say, at Ohio State who play on the football team, but I doubt if I'd find that type in France either. Throughout the Arab world, from what I recall of the past, there is the opposite of respect for a waiting line that leads to anything. Either to buy books, to eat lunch in the cafeteria, or to board the bus results in minor chaos if more than five people congregate. Registration was, of course, tight balls of ten students blocking a doorway, which resulted in the impossibility of anyone either leaving or entering the office. No one seems to be able to figure out a working solution. Maybe next year!

The first day of the new quarter could be considered nothing even slightly aproaching the beginning of classes for both students and faculty. The students call it a "strike" against the operations of the cafeteria. It seems as if the students want the all profits to go toward a scholarship fund for students who are unable to pay. It amounted to a general meeting in the assembly room where it was decided to boycott the cafeteria for three days and post students in front of the counter inside.

Of course, it was all right for students to use the facilities of the cafeteria for study, smoking, toilet, and just relaxing, but no one was allowed to buy any soda pop, juice, coffee, candy, etc. Quite obviously the handful of leaders had really not the slightest inclination to think such a program through. Tuition amounts to approximately $150 a quarter for up to eighteen credit hours a quarter. Food in the dining hall is good and inexpensive, and the ratio of PhDs to total faculty is higher than in any other university I can recall. Graduates from Birzeit University have a good reputation and are accepted throughout the world. More than a thousand students were refused admission because there was no space, and somehow a few who enjoy doing anything more than studying already decided to let the university administration know that they won't be pushed around.

About three students were quite rude when I acted as though I had no idea what was taking place and walked up to those seated around the counter. The window outside the kitchen was open, and students and help were able to buy coffee, etc., from there. I objected to going ouside, and while I talked to one of the student leaders, the fellow in back of the counter handed me my cup of coffee. I paid through the grill that had been closed by the students, gave them a questioning look, shrugged my shoulders, and walked out. The regulations of the university strictly point out that such unexcused absence from class is not acceptable. The university administration knows who these handful of students are, but I doubt if any action at all will be taken. Sort of like America dealing with the Israelis.

Looking at it from another point of view: if the university vice president should take action against any of the students, his house is unprotected. Anyone who wishes to know can find out where he lives. An expelled or suspended student could break several windows, and there is absolutely nothing that anyone could do to either catch the students or to prevent such an occurance. The local security guards are hired by the military force and patrol the streets on scooters, and are unarmed. The only other type of force is the Israeli soldiers, who cruise around the towns and villages, usually with four in the back of a little pickup-style jeep with the driver and passenger in the front seat. On the passenger side in the front seat there is a machine gun, mounted obviously on the frame and extending over the hood. It looks to be a fifty caliber and has the cartridge belt in place, and the belt running from a container; it seems operational. They are ready to put the butterfly to the rack.

The faculty of Birzeit University seem, for the most part, to have come here either for a summer lark or because their parents live a few miles in either direction from Birzeit. Others have come for a sabbatical from their comfortable position in an American or European university, maybe because they were interested in the Palestine question. They are a likable group and all seem quite competent in their field of expertise. I am not qualified to judge, but I would like to think I am correct, as they all seem nice. There was one chap, whose name is not important, who managed to get himself admitted into the AA [Alcoholics Anonymous] chapter of Ramallah—an English-speaking branch? But most were very professional.

MORE TRAVEL IN ISRAEL

Late one August, the main sports instructor at the university arranged a bus trip to Tiberias for a picnic of sorts. One of the twins was one of his best sportsmen and sat next to him at the front of the bus. It was very hot, although all the windows were open. Anya, the other twin, and I were sitting at the back of the bus, where the uneven surface of the road was felt rather strongly. Just as we were ten miles from a small Arab town called Jenin, Anya started to have stomach pains, and then became nauseated. She changed seats for more comfort and sat in front of the bus with the first twin.

Then she began to feel even worse and started to sense she was fainting. The first twin later said he noticed his mother's eyes roll back. He quickly pulled out from his rucksack the first aid kit that his favorite history professor in the United States gave him for the trip to Israel. The sports master touched Anya's nose with the smelling salts vial and she slowly started to return and came around all right. Later she related how just when her discomfort became unbearable, she started to hear a distant voice as if coming toward her saying, "Wake up, Anya," and thanks to the smelling salts she could feel relief. We decided to get off the bus in Jenin while the rest of the group in the bus continued on. Soon we came upon the archeology students' camp, where a Birzeit University archeology professor from the United States worked on a project. At night, students were staying in tents nearby but now were out working under the direction of the professor, a famous archeologist. We were able to rest for a couple of hours in one of their tents, and after Anya started to feel better, we took a taxi to the doctor's clinic in Birzeit, where she was told that she was dehydrated from the extreme heat.

* * * * *

Several days ago we went to Hebron. All four of us got inside the small two-cylinder Subaru and traveled due south of Jerusalem. About two hundred years earlier, the same trip would have been made with a two-eared donkey, but that's progress for you. The road follows the valley for the most part, amid twists and turns that aren't too difficult to negotiate. The little car makes one a bit more conscious of the possibilities that could occur if a Mercedes truck and the car should find themselves both at the same spot on a curve. If it's a tie, of course, we lose.

Along the road, there were several persons who were selling grapes, both the dark and light yellow, and something that resembles the Tokay type. A few kilometers south of Jerusalem is Bethlehem, and on the way there is apparently the burial spot of Rachel, or Rebecca, or probably Hagar. The place was filled with those of the Jewish faith, it being Saturday, and instead of stopping we continued driving, although Anya said that visiting that place was definitely necessary as basically it was sacred for all three major local faiths: Jewish, Christian, and Muslim.

South of Bethlehem the road was clearly marked. I stopped at one of the stands to buy some grapes and was addressed in Hebrew. Of course, since I do not look Arab at all, the next reasonable guess is Jewish. I couldn't understand the price he was giving me in Hebrew and told him I wasn't Jewish. He shrugged his shoulders and said it did not matter to him what I was, the price was staying the same. Although the grapes were large and sweet, they were about half again as expensive as they were in Ramallah.

Just before entering the outskirts of Hebron, we were stopped by the ubiquitous Israeli checkpoint. One of the reasons for our trip was to visit a glass-blowing factory and shops that are in Hebron. The first glass-blowing business was near the checkpoint. We stopped to see what it was like. The greeting again was of course "Shalom"! The factory consists of a vat or tank about four feet square on the inside and made of fireproof bricks. It is covered with a curved dome about two feet above the molten glass and heated by a forced gas jet.

Access to the inside of the tank is by means of small doors that are opened by a lever from the floor attached to a cord up, over, and down to a small door that is about eight or ten inches square. The blowers have a shelf that extends out about two feet from the tank of glass. This shelf is apparently part of the fireproof brick, and the small opening is built into the curved dome that covers the vat or tank where the glass is. A long, hollow glass rod is inserted into the molten glass and the blower makes what he wishes. The finished product has a rather rough appearance and certainly has that handmade look. Pitchers, glasses, and various goblets or wine glasses are for sale. It turned out that the owners of these small factories are all related and all are Muslims.

On the way back from Hebron, we stopped to visit the Russian monastery and church where Anya spent part of her time as a girl. The old father, having a little trouble getting around, of course rememberd her. Together we toured the grounds for about half an hour. We saw the large church with beautiful icons on the walls. Such elaborate settings in the midst of such barren countryside is startling and difficult to adjust to quickly. There are about thirty acres, I guess, and there are three monks, who take care of the entire grounds and buildings. One of the monks is unable to do anything and is barely able to move around. The other two are too old to do much outside; however, they still make their own wine. There is an Arab caretaker and his wife who guard the gate and allow people in and out. They have eleven children, and the youngest is still in diapers; maybe they don't realize where babies come from. The Russian monk-priest said that the grounds and building will continue to fall into disrepair. It is not a question of money but rather of finding young people who are willing to devote their life and love to the service of God. I guess there aren't many of that type left around. The curtains are becoming tattered from the constant light wind blowing. The heavy iron doors are moving with difficulty now, and the locks are stiff and hard to turn. In many of the lower windows there are iron bars because someone tried to break in.

If the Russians should ever abandon this piece of property, the Jewish authorities would immediately take it over from the Arabs living in the surrounding village. To save this place, someone of the Russian Orthodox Christian faith must support it and be there all the time. The Greek Orthodox church is supported by its country. The Lutherans have support from many countries, as do the Catholics, but the Russian Orthodox Church Abroad is struggling to keep their properties. Those on the Trans-Jordanian side of Palestine survived, while some of those that remained under the rule of the newly created State of Israel were passed on to the Soviet Union in the days when the two countries were holding hands.

* * * * *

During the feast days of the Muslim faith, Anya and I have been taking small trips in our faithful Subaru. One time all four of us decided to go to Tel Aviv and drove from Birzeit by way of Latrun, a beautiful Catholic establishment where one could buy good wine. Tel Aviv is a nicely planned Israeli city with wide streets that are kept clean, many sidewalk cafés, and people trying to outdo each other just like in any other normal city. We wanted to have lunch along the Mediterranian Sea and finally found the street that would take us there. The coast along that part of the city from Tel Aviv to Jaffa was formerly a well-to-do city of mostly Christian Arabs. It is what one would expect to find at any waterfront. The only difference is that there were no ships to add a little bit of picturesque scene to the drab view. A jetty was being built that consisted of dumping enormous stones several meters out into the Mediterranian.

There appeared to be only one section of the beach where people were in bathing suits but here no one was in the water. There were several large signs in English, Arabic, and Hebrew. The English sign said it was dangerous to swim. I did not know whether it was because of pollution, some vague belief about an undertow, or merely there was no lifeguard around. No restaurants were there aside from a small place that sold soft drinks and falafel, but there were other "items" of marketable value that added a bit of interest to the countryside. They came in three assorted sizes, each representing a different area of the world. Two of them were standing smoking in front of a "London café," and about two doors away in front of a "Bucharest café" other international "items" of varied value were available. With the employment situation being what it was in Israel, everything had to be available to catch the early afternoon trade.

Finding no appealing place to eat, we drove farther down the coast. I do not mean to even slightly imply that the coastal drive to where the city of Jaffa once stood was anything even remotely resembling something found along the coast of Oregon or Washington. Remains of once splendid homes were still quite visible, and there were the shatterd remains of a mosque. What remains of the ancient city consists of narrow and somewhat winding streets with very dirty stores. I saw very few signs in Arabic. There was a plethora of Israeli soldiers everywhere. That section has been the center of much drug trafficking among the Arabs since they were forced into this ghetto-type of existence. The Israelis do little to stop such traffic; they merely contain it in that section. Closer to the water, there were several expensive restaurants that doubled as night clubs featuring belly dancers and high-priced watered-down booze. Tourists always were fair game.

Because nothing here seemed to please us, we decided to go directly to Jerusalem and avoid possible traffic delays as the Egyptian president's visit ended and he was leaving via the airport in Tel Aviv. We were directed to a bypass leading to Beersheba, which I knew to be many miles to the south. Anya decided we should eat there in the company of noble and proud Bedouin sheiks, and in their tents to boot. Apparently I was to finish the meal of roasted lamb by smoking the argile and being fanned by either two or three Nubians with banana leaf fans while reclining on several pillows of goose down! I was wondering if dancing girls were provided at a small additional charge, but at such a time crass materialim had no place. If such a place should exist even in my wildest flights of desire, it would not be a fitting place to go with one's wife and children. As it turned out, this was a wild flight of imagination on Anya's part. We drove through a rambling city that did not seem to have a center and ended up at a bus depot. Anya did manage to say a few words in Arabic to a disheveled Beduin who must have thought she was a Jewess because he immediately turned and hurried away. We had a small meal in the Beersheba bus depot and then headed north toward Hebron.

The next day was a bit better planned. We left for the Sea of Galilee about 10:30 in the morning and headed toward Kinneret and Tiberias. The highway runs from Ramallah through Arab towns such as Nablus and Jenin, and then forks at Dafur and meets again at Nazareth. From Nazareth, there is a road to the city of Tiberias. We decided to have a look at Nazareth, which turned out to be an interesting place to visit. Quite imposing on the top of the hills north of the city there are several churches, but probably the most impressive was the one built by a group of French Catholics. The present church was rebuilt five times over the home where Christ lived. This present manifestation of man's love for God consists of four levels; a center circular opening connects to a cone-shaped dome some 700 feet above the original level where in His childhood Christ lived.

There were various grottoes and chambers, each donated by different religious groups. The main floor was furnished with large wall plaques from America, Japan, Germany, and about five other countries, each submitting representations of the Virgin Mary. I managed to get in with a group of visiting Germans, and the tour guide provided us with all the financial aspects relating to the present edifice, which are quite impressive. Here a real symbiosis exists between the Jews and the Arabs, as both sell their wares of souvenirs and trinkets to those who wish to buy them. Further up the hills and still to the north were other churches, but the road was crowded and difficult to get to, so we continued to Tiberias. It took about thirty minutes to descend to the level of the sea from the top of the hills. We had a lunch of grilled freshwater perch, salad, hummus, beer, and bread. The waterfront cafés were situated about fifty meters north of the cruise boats that went in different directions. Three of them at least were at the dock at the same time. After the expensive and not necessarily well-prepared or served lunch, we drove north to Capernaum.

Before leaving, Anya asked about the house and big garden that formerly belonged to the Russian Mission where in childhood she with her mother spent summer vacations. Father Antony, now in Los Angeles, was at that time chief of the Mission. We were told that now the property belongs to the Soviet Union and is rented to the director of the YMCA. The waiter at the restaurant gave us this information. The former Russian Mission property consists of about three to four hundred meters along the water. It is difficult to judge when there are so many banana trees and orange trees between the road and the lake, but there are at least fifteen acres there. The potential for development is excellent, if only the Soviets can somehow figure out a way to keep it from the Jews, who are trying to keep it for themselves since they gave it to the Soviets in 1949 when things were much cozier.

In Capernaum we managed to get in with a group of French tourists. Here we heard the Israeli version of the persecution of the Jews, which we were told was due to the preaching of Jesus that led to the eventual destruction of the synagogue. There were Stars of David to be seen on the ancient pillars, and there was no doubt that a very long time ago the Jews were there. It seems, however, that Jesus was the one in trouble as his own people condemned him to be put to death; apparently what Jesus Christ taught about love and forgiveness did not appeal to them.

* * * * *

Here ends Wayne's diary, and I return to my story.

Both tourists and pilgrims to the Holy Land usually arrive in Tel Aviv from where they proceed further. Their first impressions often sound in favor of Israel: "Look how organized and well-kept the Israeli territory is, whereas places and things in general are run down and neglected on the West Bank." This impression occasionally leads them to make political conclusions such as "If the whole land is given to the Jews, they would put it in order." Such an outlook is expressed due to lack of understanding and knowledge as to what happened in Palestine in 1948: Indigenous people were driven out or were pushed aside if they remained. Their centuries-old achievements in coastal cities and other places as well as sumptuous homes fell into the hands of Zionist occupiers. Villages surrounded by fertile fields and orchards inherited by the Palestinians from their forefathers were taken away from them, appropriated by outsiders who still hold on to them and pass them on to their children and grandchildren. This was wealth misappropriated when the British Mandate ended, and what belonged to Palestinians became free for all who spoke Hebrew and had a gun.

In areas populated by those newcomers, why is the grass around their homes green while Palestinian homes are surrounded by bare rocks and barren land? It is because the local inhabitants saw their best lands taken away; water was misappropriated by the settlers who built themselves swimming pools and indiscriminately used water for their lawns while Palestinians had to buy their water a canister per week in order to wash themselves and drink. Refugees were driven to live in camps as in Jericho or the camp near Ramallah, or even worse the Gaza Strip of land walled off from the Israeli sector. Prosperity achieved by dint of someone else's misfortune cannot bring lasting happiness, much less allow for peace. To continue building settlements for newcomers on land mostly misappropriated from the native population without remuneration of some sort fosters hatred for the occupier, which is passed on generation after generation, giving little hope for peace in the foreseeable future.

CHAPTER 6

✠✠✠

Russian Encounters

Returning to America

In the summer of 1979, I was still on sick leave at our home in the Pacific Northwest. I received a surprise letter from one of my two twins saying that they had decided to return to the United States whilst I was still there. Their father was to remain on the West Bank until he completed his contract with Birzeit University.

I was delighted to have all my boys back safe and sound with me in our home. But our family was only complete a few months later when we all met Wayne at the airport. I asked him, "Where do we go next?" He answered, "We've arrived." I looked at our grown-up sons standing beside us and realized that we were not young anymore; Wayne and I were entering the twilight years of our lives. Meanwhile our sons were on the way to achieving their personal goals, one of which was graduating with a university degree and beginning to look for a job. We agreed that the two years spent in Birzeit not far from Jerusalem had made us all not only older but above all wiser.

Our oldest son, who had not gone with us to Israel, was gainfully employed near where we lived, and he soon met a pretty young woman who became the mother of his son. Our enjoyment of this lovely little boy, who was named after his father, was endless and we showered him with love. He was so tiny when he was born that he could be bathed in the kitchen sink. Whenever he was with us overnight, Wayne read him stories. He could not resist inserting in the text a joke here and there, so I would hear my grandson's laughter with the words, "Grandpa, it does not say so in the book; you made it up didn't you?" and I would hear again the childish bursts of laughter. With time, grandfather Wayne taught his grandson how to swim in the lake, and their laughter could be heard echoing across the water. Our grandson grew up to be a tall good-looking young man; he married a bright young woman, and they had two lovely little girls. I never thought that I would live to see my great-granddaughters and to enjoy them as much as I enjoyed their father when he was their age.

Wayne was looking for work in higher education but to no avail. Times then were unlike when we first acquired our graduate degrees and were promptly hired by universities. Having had a civil service job previously, he applied for state and federal jobs. He was a veteran of World War II, which was helpful in his job search. Before too long he was offered an administrative position at the local juvenile prison. I remember how on his first day of employment he proudly brought back a new uniform in which to start work.

It so happened that on his first day he witnessed the harsh treatment of a young man who was reentering prison for the third time and still acted defiant. One of the staff had to be rough with him and told Wayne that if one "spared the rod" in such cases, he would never have control over an inmate. That night when Wayne came home, I noticed from the expression on his face that something was not right. Then I observed how carefully he folded his new uniform and then said, "I will return this uniform tomorrow, because I do not want to go back to work in prison, I am out of my element there. I thought things over and will start looking for a job in a less violent environment." Following this experience, he found employment at the local post office, where he worked until his retirement. The time here was added to the time he worked in the State Department before our marriage, thus making him eligible for a federal pension. Soon one of the twins married and had a son. In his spare time, he continued to study first toward one master of arts degree and then a second one, and with two he was moved up at his work to a general manager's position. Meanwhile his son grew up, married, and had a baby girl, thus awarding me the pleasure of becoming a great-grandmother once again.

Russian Relatives

In 1989, just before the Soviet Union fell apart, it became easier for Russians living in exile all across the world to return to Russia on extended visits. That year Wayne and I went to Russia by invitation of a distant relative I never knew I had. She came to New York City to visit her son, who had married an American student studying at the same university. At a party, she showed around a photograph of my father as a young man hoping to meet Russians from Belgrade who might know something about him and whether he married and had offspring. Here an elderly lady recognized him, exclaiming, "Oh, yes, I knew this handsome young man, he was in my class and we were all in love with him!" She suggested searching for my father's progeny, if any, through the Russian churches on the East and West coasts of America. Soon thereafter Father Antony (Sinkevich), Bishop of Los Angeles and former chief of the Russian Mission in Palestine, directed her to me in the Northwest.

She sent me and my husband an invitation for a six-month visit to Leningrad. Here I met more relatives on my father's side. I discovered I was aunt to our hostess as well as to three middle-aged nephews, whose grandmothers were daughters of my grandfather, the general. These newly discovered relatives were all professional people. She was a musician and an accomplished singer, popular in Russia and Europe. A nephew was a geologist with a wife and daughter. Another nephew was a journalist with a wife and two daughters. The third nephew was a physical education teacher and coach with a Ukrainian wife whom he met at Leningrad University and with whom he had a daughter and a son.

Of course, it was very interesting to meet them, and we regretted that it did not happen earlier. I also met my father's youngest sister, who grew up with him and was now ninety-two years old, bedridden and living with her daughter, my cousin. Although she was very frail as she sat on her bed, her mind was perfectly clear, and she asked my husband in which language he preferred to be addressed, in French or German? She was fluent in both languages besides Russian. As a farewell gift, she gave me her graduation pin from the Smolny Institute in St Petersburg and a small crystal Easter egg, which my father had given her the last Easter they spent together on their family estate.

We arrived in the Soviet Union a few days before Easter with a group of pastors from Seattle for whom I interpreted. They were members of the Seattle–Leningrad Sister Churches Committee, who were invited by Archbishop Alexei of Leningrad, the future Patriarch of Russia, to spend Easter as his guests. I met the archbishop earlier in Seattle when he was visiting this organization. At that time, our St Nicholas Cathedral had not joined the Moscow Patriarchate, and officially the Russian Orthodox Church Abroad was not in communion with the Church in the Soviet Union. Nevertheless the archbishop and those travelling with him stopped at St Nicholas Cathedral for a short while on their way to the airport before flying back home to Leningrad. As head of the sisterhood at our church, I was allowed by our bishop to walk out with the visitors and offer to show them our church hall, where on the walls we had hanging old portraits of Nicholas II and his family. On the way I expressed to the archbishop my regret that we were unable to offer an official reception to him because we were not in communion.

With a warm smile on his face he responded, "Soon, very soon we will be united, and together we will be one Russian Orthodox Church." It took fifteen years for this prediction to be fulfilled. After the collapse of the Soviet Union, Archbishop Alexei was elevated to the rank of Patriarch of Russia, and our Orthodox Churches officially united.

In Leningrad, Archbishop Alexei invited our group to attend the midnight Easter celebration at St Alexander Nevsky Cathedral on Nevsky Prospect. There were numerous members of the clergy serving with the archbishop. That Easter was the first time in history that a cardinal from Rome attended. We were given a place to stand on the left side of the area next to the altar while the cardinal was on the right side. From where we stood, we could observe the beauty and pageantry of the Russian Orthodox Easter service, which was attended by a multitude of Orthodox Russians filling the church to capacity.

The cathedral and the open square around it held several hundred prayerful Russians who stood throughout the service, which was several hours long. Occasionally someone in the crowd fainted, and medics came in and helped them out to the first aid van that waited on the street across from the cathedral. The choir, made up of at least a hundred well-trained singers, sounded magnificent. At midnight there was a procession around the cathedral with everyone carrying a lit candle in their hands. Upon reentering the cathedral, the archbishop facing the crowd exclaimed, "Christ has risen!" and everyone loudly responded, "Indeed! He has risen!" An indescribable moment of elation filled the church as expressed on the faces and in the voices of those present. After the liturgy, people hugged and kissed each other three times on the cheeks repeating the words of the good news that "Christ has risen from the dead, conquering death by death."

After the service, around four in the morning, the clergy, seminarians, the Roman Catholic cardinal, and the guests from Seattle were invited to the Easter breakfast in the seminary refectory. This was a sumptuous meal of *kulich,* a cylindrical loaf of sweet bread, and *paskha,* a sweet cheese made in the shape of a white pyramid to be eaten with the *kulich.* There were multicolored eggs, cheese, all kinds of fish, and various kinds of salads. In addition to all this, there were various wines and liqueurs on the beautifully set tables.

The hours of standing at the midnight service and fatigue we felt after the sleepless night seemed well worth it, not only from the spiritual point of view but also from the purely physical. We thoroughly enjoyed the meal, and my husband especially enjoyed the assortment of drinks. Even his legs stopped hurting, he said, from standing for so long because he was not accustomed to standing the way Russians were. When at the exit we stopped to thank our host, Archbishop Alexei presented each one of us with a red egg with an inscription in gold "XB," which are the first letters of the Russian words meaning "Christ is risen!"

During our stay in Leningrad, we became good friends with the family of a nephew who lived near St Isaac's Cathedral, close to Nevsky Prospect. It was conveniently located close to the subway and was in walking distance from Palace Square. The father was born in this apartment when his great-grandparents lived in it. After the revolution, the Soviet authorities allowed his family of four to live only in two rooms of the apartment; the other was occupied by a total stranger. Only after the death of the latter was the maternal grandmother allowed to move in with them. She was a model Russian *babushka,* kind and hardworking beyond compare. She not only cooked for everybody in the household but also did the laundry by hand and kept the place in order, having only a rug-covered bench in the kitchen to sleep on. Yet in the late afternoon before everyone returned from work or school, she dressed nicely and went to sit on a bench with her friends near St Isaac's Cathedral. She did not talk much, but quietly smiled whenever our eyes met. Once she told me how during World War II in Ukraine she was taken by the Germans as a prisoner of war. She said she was sent to work on a farm in Germany, but she was not mistreated by anyone and the owners of the farm were sorry for her and treated her kindly, and after the war she was able to return home to Ukraine.

My cousin, daughter of my ninety-two-year-old aunt, was grandmother of this family. Born and educated in old St Petersburg, she spoke French and was an accomplished pianist. After the revolution, young women like herself, who belonged to the intelligentsia of old Russia, were forced to do hard menial labor. During the deep winter snow, they put on their fancy fur coats and every day went to work digging tunnels for the future Leningrad underground subway. It was the only means of support available in order to earn a daily ration of bread. Then during World War II, her infant son was evacuated for safety with other small children to distant parts of Russia. After the war, his mother searched for him a long time before she was able to find him; when she did find him, he was already five years old.

We were renting a studio apartment in the outskirts of the city on the subway and bus lines to Nevsky Prospect. Our apartment was on the second floor of a typically Soviet era building and consisted of a small living room with an extendable couch, and in the hallway a full bathroom and small kitchen. The entry door was made up of two separate solid doors for safety. The hall outside was dark as the electric bulb was always burned out and there was no replacement available. On entering the building, one could smell a rather heavy unpleasant odor in the hallways.

Living here we experienced the communist way of life just a few months before the beginning of its downfall. After we moved in, the relative who had invited us and arranged our sublet brought her boss to meet us. He was the director of a government-owned radio station where she worked as a musician. She had asked us when we came to Leningrad to bring with us a synthesizer from America because they were not available in the Soviet Union. It was needed for broadcasting music at the radio station. When they arrived at our apartment, he carried a briefcase. After greeting us, he looked around the room and said, "We'd better sit with our backs to the window." Then he opened the briefcase, and we saw that it was full of paper money. Counting out the stacks of rubles, he asked Wayne to recount them for accuracy. I looked and did not know what to make of it. This took time because he was stacking several thousand rubles, which he said were a gift for us to spend during our stay in Leningrad. He said it was just an expression of his gratitude and to show his appreciation for the gift we brought. Our eyes were open wide as we looked with disbelief at all this money. Wayne smiled and jokingly said, "I never thought I had to come to the Soviet Union to become a millionaire."

Thus we started life as guests in the once magnificent St Petersburg that was now rather impoverished Leningrad. We needed to live like our new neighbors and shop where they shopped for food, toiletries, and other needs of daily life, but we soon found out that there was not much one could buy in stores with rubles. Bus and subway transportation was very cheap; the rent was only the equivalent of two hundred dollars a month, but restaurants would not accept rubles and would let you in only if you could pay in dollars. Of course, for a newcomer to this gorgeous city, there was so much to see and explore even on foot and for free, and entertainment was no problem. Meals, however, were rather problematic; it reminded me of Palestine after World War II. Fresh fruits and vegetables were scarce, and the same was true of meat and other items we were so used to finding all in one place at any supermarket back home in the United States. Bakeries, I must admit, were found in most neighborhoods, and bread was good and plentiful. Beer, however, was difficult to find, and even for wine and vodka one had to stand in a long line, if you were lucky to get to it before it was all sold out. People's friendly attitude to newcomers like us was encouraging, and it made us feel like we were all one big poor family and therefore happy to be helpful to each other.

In the mornings, some kind person living in the same apartment complex would stop at our door and loudly inform us on which street of our neighborhood sugar or frozen chicken was being sold that day and not to wait too long or it would all be gone. People could tell we were newcomers by our clothes. When my husband walked up to a group of local men standing in line in front of the state liquor store, they would give him their place in the queue. Those men, with pale exhausted faces after a hard day's work building something or eternally repairing roads damaged by Russia's extremely cold winters, would offer him their place in line. Not having a language in common, they smiled at Wayne as if acknowledging they had something in common.

In the afternoons, Wayne liked to sit on our small balcony, facing the path through which children came home from school. He would sit and write letters while I would be in the kitchen trying to prepare a halfway decent dinner. Noticing him writing something, they would stop and call to him "Dyadya," the word for uncle, a common way for children to address male adults, "What are you always writing?" Then they would burst out laughing without waiting for an answer. To their delight, Wayne would sometimes try to tell them something in his broken Russian, and then the laughing crowd of kids grew bigger beneath the balcony, behaving as if it was the funniest entertainment of the day.

We noticed that if I spoke Russian to a guard at the door of a museum, restaurant, or other such public place, he would be unfriendly. Sometimes he would even refuse us entry to the place. If when walking on the street we needed to ask for directions and I did so in Russian, a passerby would rudely answer, "Can't you see the street signs?" He would walk away giving the impression that he thought I was a local pretending to be a foreigner in my foreign clothes. Salespersons in stores were especially unfriendly and acted as if we were bothering them. They had no notion of pleasing the customer as we were used to in America. One day my husband got tired of it and told me that from now on I must forget my Russian; he would be the one to address people in what little he knew of Russian. So after that searching for an address or asking for permission to enter a restaurant, perhaps inadvertently exposing a dollar, became a fun time in Russia as people became somewhat open and jovial, giving the impression of preferring to deal with foreigners than with their own people.

West from Russia

About the third month into our stay in Russia, we felt things were moving forward much too slowly. Wayne said he was getting tired of it all and we should be getting back home. The next day we went to the travel agency to update our tickets back to the United States. We were told that all return flights through Denmark had been filled by summer vacation travelers. We were advised to return through Europe by train, from where it would be easier to get to Denmark and board our return flight. We understood that there was nothing else we could do and so bought train tickets to Paris. Then we were informed that before boarding the train we had to obtain Polish transit visas because those would be required on the train to let us pass through Poland. So we went to the Polish embassy, told the secretary we needed transit visas, and would like to have them as soon as possible. The rather unfriendly young woman said that it would take time, and we had better come back tomorrow to fill out the required forms as there was no one now to help us.

The next day we got up bright and early and went to the Polish embassy, but again we were told to come back another day. Wayne took out his billfold and offered to pay ahead so she could start the process, to which she stated, "Americans also make Polish people wait a long time for visas." This reminded us of what we had heard earlier, that a bribe must always be paid to get anything done in the Soviet Union. So now Wayne took out dollars and handing them to her said, "This is for you," and then, giving her the required stack of rubles, added, "This is for the visas." That same afternoon the visas were ready for us to pick up!

We bid farewell to our new relatives and gave them all the rubles we had left—and there were many of them because we could not find enough goods to buy with them. We boarded the train and entered our private cabin with clean, narrow beds between which there was a nightstand and passage to the door. Someone brought us hot tea to drink before bedtime, and we peacefully went to sleep. Suddenly at midnight there was a loud knock at our door, and opening a crack in it someone yelled in Russian, "Everybody, grab your suitcases and hurry to the end of the train. The railroad lines will change as the Soviet line stops here." I explained to Wayne that we were told to get up and carry our things to the very last car, but unperturbed Wayne simply answered that he was not getting up in the middle of the night to carry our heavy suitcases all the long way to the end of the train. He added that what we were told made absolutely no sense and that we both should simply go back to sleep, which we did.

After some time the train stopped with a jolt, and it was loudly announced that we had arrived in East Berlin and that this train went no farther, and therefore we must exit at this station. It became apparent that we missed going through Poland on the direct line to Paris when we did not obey the order to walk to the end of the train. So now we had to go out with our heavy suitcases whether it made any sense or not. We found ourselves standing before the Berlin Wall, and hundreds of people were rushing past us in its direction; they were in a great hurry, and on their faces one could see an expression of intense concentration. Nobody seemed to notice us, and although Wayne spoke German and tried to ask for information, no one had time for us. Finally, a middle-aged man stopped and listened to Wayne, who told him that we had no German money and did not know what to do or where to go. This "Good Samaritan" told us to follow him quickly so we could cross together with him to the other side of the wall in order to enter West Berlin. He said that on the other side of Berlin everything would be possible for us to continue our return to the United States. He gave us some German money saying we would return it to him when we got back home. He suggested we leave our suitcases in the locker at the train station on the other side, where they would inform us at what time to get on the train to Paris. We thanked him warmly, hugging each other and exchanged addresses.

As we had a couple of hours before boarding our train, we looked at our surroundings and noticed the tremendous difference between East and West Berlin. In West Berlin there were bright lights everywhere, restaurants, stores, smiling people, elegant tall buildings, and at the end of the wide street a beautiful, old Gothic-style church stood with its doors wide open. We started to walk toward it and could hear the inviting organ music. It stirred up in me a feeling of joy that we were back in the free world. We sat down on the wooden seats; I closed my eyes and fell into a deep sleep, feeling almost like a child on its mother's bosom. Wayne woke me up saying it was time to hurry back to the train leaving at midnight to eventually bring us to Paris. From there we took the train to Denmark and flew back to Seattle as initially planned. The memory of the gray drabness of the poorly lit streets of East Berlin and other signs of poverty and long-standing neglect witnessed throughout our stay in the Soviet Union made me pray for the speedy end of such an intolerable regime.

Bereavement and New Life

My children each chose a different lifestyle, something typical of young people born and educated in America, but thank God without the decadent pastimes that entrapped some young people. Russian ethnic activities did not fit into their busy schedules, although they enjoyed our trips together to Russia. Closer to our retirement years, my husband started to accompany me to the Russian Orthodox church and its social activities. He enjoyed our farm, which in the past we leased out but now used as a *dacha* or country home.

During the spring and summer, Wayne grew a big kitchen garden with beets, cabbage, potatoes, and onions for the borsht served in the church dining hall during the yearly Russian Ethnic Festival. A big crowd was usually expected, and he helped cook favorite Russian dishes. He prepared the dough for the *pelmeni* and *piroshky,* which were served with the borsht, and while working in the kitchen he entertained other volunteers with his usual sense of humor. When he became ill, he received a get-well card from the sisterhood signed "From your harem at St Nicholas Church!"

For Russian immigrants, church was a home away from home. This was where their native language was spoken and where parents took their children from a very early age. Children were used to having communion in church and behaving well as they stood next to their parents amid all the other standing adults surrounding them. When the children grew to be seven years old, they would start to say confession before going to communion. This helped them feel closer to "Batushka," our pastor, who helped them understand Christ's teachings and know the difference between good and evil.

During my eleventh year of service to the church in the sisterhood, my always healthy and strong husband was diagnosed as having prostate cancer. If the doctor had not told him this, he would have never known it. He felt fine, nothing hurt, and even if something did hurt, he would joke and say, "It comes with the territory," referring to his age. He was in his seventies and since his retirement liked to spend his days on the farm. He enjoyed the vegetable garden, where the corn grew taller than him. He loved the sheep he fed and sheared, and liked to clear the woods for them in the back of the property. After work, friends liked to stop by for a glass of his home brew. No matter what the weather was like, he loved the outdoors and his farm animals and birds. He often told me that these were the happiest years of his life and how much he enjoyed coming home to the lake house, relaxed after a day's work on the farm. "I am a very happy man," he would say. But the doctor kept reminding him his PSA was elevated and treatment was necessary. To this he once exclaimed, "PSA is nothing but a number!"

Getting ready for Christmas season that year, he sent the following group letter to our friends, not suspecting that it might be his last Christmas:

Our Dear Old Friends and especially you . . .
   In a few days it will be "that time" again to place myself before my flawless typewriter, prepare a cooling libation merely in the unlikely advent

of a buffalo stampede (one can't be too careful, you know), and make an honest endeavor to sincerely wish everyone of you all the best in the best of all possible worlds for the Christmas Season and the coming New Year.

(You will note I have sat myself down before the allotted "few days" have arrived.)

However, to update you: Anya, always the stalwart organizer, keeper-of-the-keys, the ONE that keeps clan Derrick on an even keel—sometimes I think I list a little to starboard—is in disgustingly good health. Aside from still feeling the stress and responsibilities of teaching two and a half hours twice a week, she now translates three days of the week. Then there's the Sisterhood of the Russian Orthodox Church of which she is the head, should provide sufficient stress for any eventuality. During her free time, Anya tries to attend a conference on something to do with an academic subject. I've been to a couple with her, and I'm always impressed with the prolix of an overabundance of intellectual cotton candy. Has it ever been otherwise?

Concerning the Lord High Executioner, the Great Pooh-Bah, I'm enjoying the aches and pains that come with old age and the accompanying territory. The past year was a mix of joys and displeasures concerning the events of the old farm. The cats ate the baby chicks and now the owls are feasting on the few remaining grown hens. Starting with twenty-four, there are six left. A pesky coyote or two has also influenced the present hen population.

The sons are doing quite well. The oldest works as a programmer and has married and now has a daughter one year old. One of the twins is second in command for a local Waste Water Management district and has acquired a second master's degree. The other twin is working for a Medical Insurance Company. It's good to have our sons within driving distance, but with the super-development of our neighborhood, we wonder how long our little farm will manage to stay out of the greedy hands of developers. Probably until we become greedier than the developers. Suppose?

We visited several friends in Florida recently. A change of environment and climate, however, is good any time of the year. Next year we'll have to check on the same conditions in Europe. It is our sincere desire that your wishes for the coming year become a reality. Best wishes to you from the Derrick family.

Hearing that San Diego, California, had several excellent clinics specializing in cancer, we decided to board the train going south to find one. On the train we had our own two-bed cabin and a tiny bathroom with a shower, all very comfortable. We were served three meals a day in a nice dining room, where we had a happy hour at 5:00 p.m. with an entertainer. During the day we could ride on the upper vista level from which we could enjoy looking at a magnificent view of the terrain.

In the interim, I was reading Thomas Mann's exhaustive but truly interesting book *The Magic Mountain,* the work of a German genius. Even in the paperback English translation, it was a fascinating tale of human faith. I was encouraged by the description of how full of hope of recovery were patients with tuberculosis, at that time a disease believed to be incurable. Young and old patients, regardless of their status or nationality, never lost hope while residing in European mountain sanatoriums. This took place during the years before World War I, when people seriously believed that just breathing the fresh mountain air would heal them from this terminal decease. Their courage somehow empowered my own hope for finding the right clinic for my husband's terminal condition. But alas, upon arrival and visiting the clinics, as well as talking with several physicians, it became clear to us that their help would be only palliative.

Upon returning home, both of us felt refreshed by the trip, although it did not change Wayne's condition for the better. Chemotherapy was completed and an operation was endured, but it seemed as if all those medical treatments just made things worse. I began to notice how quickly Wayne got tired, and his zest for life was waning. After the last operation, he had increasing difficulty walking or eating. As his illness progressed, many of the trappings of who he was fell by the wayside. He used to love to cook and be a generous host. Now he was unable to enjoy doing most of what he did in the past, and near the end of his life, he did not want to have visitors other than his sons and one or two close friends.

I treasured the time I spent with him during the last months down to the last weeks. He became a much quieter, softer, gentler version of himself. His humor became more subtle; sometimes he made a joke with only one or two words, or just a hand movement. The nights were difficult for me, and with time I started to feel exhausted without a full night's sleep, as he was restless and needed my help at night. September was approaching, a time for me to decide after a year's leave of absence if and when I would return to work. Then one day sitting at the kitchen table with Wayne nearby in a wheelchair, I was leafing through my Russian class textbook and looking at the new teaching schedule. Wayne asked me what I was doing and I said, "I am getting things ready for going to teach a Russian class." Looking at me sadly he said, "I thought you are going where I am going." Another time he said, "Anya, you are not the same anymore, things have changed"; then he added, "I want you to be with me, I am afraid of going alone where I am going." He seemed to be hinting at something I couldn't foresee or understand.

After this talk, I asked our parish priest to come and help Wayne to say confession and receive communion. They had a good talk together in the living room while I stayed in the kitchen. Wayne asked the priest what to do so his sons would understand him better and forgive him. He said he wanted his sons to realize his deep regret for whatever he may have done to hurt their feelings, especially one son he was suffering for, his oldest. The priest replied that Wayne should pray for them, that parents' prayers are powerful. "Pray for their souls to open up to your soul," he said. The next day Wayne told me referring to his dead father, "My poor father, everybody took advantage of him." I asked how, and he answered, "He always did everything they asked him, he lived for others more than for himself. I did so little for him, how will I be able to look him in the face? Oh, if only he were here now, things would be all right. I loved my father very much." Sometimes I was not sure if it was him or the morphine speaking. He seemed to be facing the end of his life, but I could not accept it because I remembered how strong he always was.

Now he often cried and simply had no strength to fight for his life. He said, "I am tired of it all. I want to do what I want to do!" Then he asked, "How painful will death be?" I said, "Through your illness these last months, you have suffered enough and absolved any wrongdoing you may have done throughout your life. You should have a clean slate and a peaceful transition." He seemed to like my comment and said, "Anya, I feel so much better now that you told me this, but you don't pray enough with me." This last sentence baffled me as it revealed a different Wayne than I was used to; he wanted us to pray together? He was now even a greater believer than I was? I put a string of olive wood beads in his hands, which long ago my mother sent me, writing that it was blessed on Christ's Holy Sepulchre in Jerusalem. I told Wayne to repeat to himself the Jesus Prayer as his fingers touched one bead at a time, something I learned to do in my youth. Afterwards, he held the prayer beads anytime he was alone and anxiously looked for them if he couldn't find them right away.

Throughout his illness, I used to give him a hug while he sat in his wheelchair, and we cried together. He often said, "Anya, you have the patience of an angel to put up with me like this." All this time our oldest son was in New York working hard at his new job and concentrating on his family's new life there. Wayne asked, "Does my son not care at all that I am so ill?" Now he was skin and bones and hardly ate anything, but slept often. Later one day he woke up from a nap crying and said he had a terrible dream: that he was on the shore of some huge lake that he was supposed to cross. It was absolutely necessary for him to cross to the other side, and he had a canoe but no oars. The people around him said that I had the oars but that I was not there. He tried to call me but had no voice, and so I could not hear him. "It was terrible, it was terrible," he repeated.

I was getting emotionally drained and thought that perhaps going to teach two evenings a week would give me some relief. That week Wayne asked again about his oldest son and added, "I want everybody to be here on Sunday. I want all three of my sons and our closest friends to be here." When all who could come had gathered in the dining room, I wheeled Wayne in his wheelchair into the dining room. He looked steadily at every one, then paused a minute and without saying a word turned around in his wheelchair and returned to the bedroom. It was the first time in his life that he did not say a word to those present, something that left them stunned; they all were so used to his usual jovial personality.

The next day, an Irish friend flew up from Los Angeles and stayed over-night with him in his room. While we slept, Wayne made a supreme effort to get up and somehow started to walk, although for the last six months he had been unable to walk without a walker. One of the twins, who stayed with us for the weekend, hearing a commotion jumped up to help his father and awakened me and our guest. We saw an amazing feat of courage on Wayne's part, to gather all his remaining strength, to get out of bed unaided, then try to walk one more time in his life. It was unbelievable. At daybreak his Irish friend needed to leave, and in a barely audible voice Wayne said, "I am so very happy you came to be with me, Patrick," and embracing each other, they parted with tears.

That day Wayne refused food and all medicine. At 4 p.m. a friend and former student came to help me and stayed with Wayne so I could take a few hours off to go teach my class at the college. When I returned I asked my friend to stay overnight with me as I could see a change I feared I could not handle alone. I was told that Wayne did not eat but continued sleeping. My dear young friend had this special God-given gift of compassion that made her always ready to help, so after calling her family at home, she stayed for the night. We were up all night with Wayne who was restless and breathing heavily in a strange way I never heard before. I called the nurse about it, and she advised me to put a small morphine tablet under his tongue to help him feel better.

As he struggled to breathe, twice he exclaimed, "Oh, boy!" The night dragged on until sunrise, when in a loud voice he said, "Now, don't panic!" It was not clear whether he said it to us or to himself. We were beside him, propping up the cushions from which his head kept sliding. Then just as I walked out of the bedroom, my friend called me back. "Hurry back, something is happening." When I walked back in, I heard Wayne exhale his last breath. My dear helper ran to the icon corner, lit a candle, and we started to pray together. Soon one of my twin sons walked in; he had just arrived from the Catskills, in upstate New York, where he had been helping his father's closest old friend. He had missed his father's last moments by only a few minutes. He checked his father's pulse but could feel nothing, and as we stood in disbelief, the morning nurse arrived and told us that it was all over.

I looked at Wayne, and what the nurse said became reality. It seemed to me as if I was waking up from a bad dream, which culminated in last night's mutual suffering. The now lifeless being in the bed was not my husband anymore. The pale void on the face was nothing like him with whom I had fallen in love many years ago. He was the reason for switching my life's path in a totally different direction from where I started. He was always either good or bad, always had an opinion or a joke. We had a forgiving sort of love between us, which was rekindled almost to its full youthful zest after our sons grew up and each went to live his own life.

Now there was no trace of a soul in the still body I was looking at; it must have returned to its source, where I knew mine would someday follow, and we and our sons would hopefully meet there. How strange that we do not wonder where we come from at our birth, and we tend to feel that we always existed and find it hard to imagine not always existing. If the mystery of what happens after death remains a mystery, death is frightening. What gives us courage is the faith-given hope, passed on to us by the Church, that if we try to live right and ask forgiveness for what we have done wrong, we might deserve an eternal life in the heavenly kingdom of God.

I stood there and thought about an incident only a few days earlier when Wayne needed help; as I grabbed him, he fell, full length to the floor. In a low voice he told me to hurry up and get someone to help get him up. "Run out in the street and ask a passerby to come in and help you lift me," he said. I rushed outside, but there was no one on our quiet one-way street. I telephoned 911, and as the fire station was very close, soon three husky firemen walked in. They lifted Wayne onto his bed, and as he lay down and closed his eyes in exhaustion, the medic turned up one of his eyelids up to check for something. Wayne calmly asked: "What is this, a joke!?" Not answering, the firemen exited to the sound of my heartfelt "Thank you, thank you so much."

At Wayne's funeral in St Nicholas Russian Orthodox Cathedral, my unmarried twin son stood beside me while the other one was surrounded by his wife and her family. Other than church members, there were several men who at one time or another were Wayne's best friends and drinking buddies. These men carried his coffin to the hearse that was to deliver the body to the gravesite. Other close friends of our family followed in their own cars while my son drove our car. We had a small fender bender on the way, perhaps the result of our collective sorrow, which hindered concentration on the road.

When we returned home, I could not hold back my tears any longer, and I burst out sobbing. Our forty-two years of life together changed fast, and life as I knew it ended. Attached to Wayne and my firstborn son were concentrated emotions of my foreign past, my mother's unexpected death, and the pain of always trying to change myself to fit the local mold. Only my sons' presence gave me solace, and their genuine efforts to fill the emptiness left in my life by their father's death helped me eventually to get over my loss.

Starting life alone was greatly helped by my prayerful attendance at church on Sundays. I was fortunate to have been able to keep my teaching position at the community college as it also helped take my mind off my sorrow, and the head nurse at the health department called me back to continue my work as an interpreter. During the following Christmas vacations, I spent time on the East Coast at the home of the married daughter of my first and closest Russian friends in America. From their lovely home it was convenient for me to take the train to New York City and visit my oldest son and his family, something that was especially helpful in lifting my spirits.

The following year I went with a group of tourists to central Mexico, where the simple life of the local inhabitants took me back in time. This region was far inland from the ocean and was still inhabited by the original Indian population of Mexico. I liked their special kind of music and primitive, colorful costumes. I marveled at how a nation geographically so close to the United States was so untouched by modern progress. Some of those people still lived in caves, which we were able to visit as well as watch them knit and carve and raise darling children, who went to a local mission school that we visited. In some ways, the atmosphere around these Indians who lived next to a Christian mission school reminded me of my own impoverished childhood living and learning in a missionary school, and it felt soothing to remember it.

On the Volga to Valaam

In 2003, I took a cruise with one of my twin sons on a Russian ship along the Volga River from Moscow north to Lake Ladoga. Daily we disembarked on the shores of some small, historic town, until our ship reached Valaam Island, where we stopped for a picnic lunch. It had a Russian Orthodox monastery dating from the fourteenth century when it was an important frontier fortress, frequently attacked by the Swedes. The monastery developed model dairy and garden farming and was a place of pilgrimage. From the Russian Revolution until 1940, Valaam belonged to Finland, but after 1940 the area around it became part of the Soviet Union. The monastery was closed by the Communist government and used for military purposes. I had heard and read about this island and how famous it was before the revolution and always wanted to see it.

The ship let us off on the opposite side of the island from where the old monastery was situated. When we disembarked, we saw a monk passing by and I asked him how far it was to the monastery. "You need at least three hours round-trip on foot to make it there and back to the ship. If you hurry you will make it by midday," the monk told us. It was 9:00 a.m., and we had exactly three hours before the ship's departure at noon. My son's determination to walk there, as there was no other transportation, encouraged me, and we started to walk at a fast clip. On the way, we appreciated the island's natural beauty. On one side of the unpaved road, we could hear birds chirping in the woods. On the other side, looking down into a green valley we saw a young monk walking, and next to him a young colt was following its mother who was carrying containers of milk on her back. When they reached us, the monk told us he was on his way to the monastery from the dairy, where he milked the monastery cows.

Soon we saw the great walls of the ancient monastery and on entering the gate noticed it was being restored. There was a chapel open from where we could hear the sound of a service in progress and monks singing. As our time was very short, we attended only a few minutes of the service, and as we left stopped at a small monastery museum. Here on display were interesting building tools and photographs of monks at work using those ancient tools to build the church, the monks' cells, and a large refectory. My son was fascinated with the archaic tools and other implements used long ago.

On the way back, I was getting tired of the fast-paced walk and wondering if we would be able to make it back to the ship on time before its departure. However, my son was so encouraging and so pleased with this venture that I was energized and we made it back, but barely in time. The rest of

Russia we saw was also fascinating, but it was of a secular nature, the kind any ordinary tourist group is allowed to see. Perhaps the effort we applied to see this unique monastery was what made such a special impression on us.

Back at home, without Wayne the farm seemed to have little purpose in our lives, other than embodying memories of childhood and grandparents. It started to appear abandoned despite our attempts to keep it decent looking. There was no one to care for animals or grow a vegetable garden. We all worked and lived comfortably elsewhere, life kept moving forward, and we could not return to the past. All around the farm developments were growing fast as if trying to squeeze it out of existence. Yet I continued to feel some kind of loyalty to our family farm, something like the impoverished owners felt in Chekhov's play *The Cherry Orchard,* when they needed to consider selling it!

A New Friend

My keen awareness of being a widow was skillfully arrested by my kind young friend who helped me during my last days with Wayne before his death. One Sunday in church, she introduced me to her newly widowed brother-in-law. He was close to my age, had nice features with light blue eyes, and was pleasant to talk to. We started to see each other at church and at his brother's family parties, where their hospitality made me feel at home.

My new friend was born in Harbin, an old Russian town with a church on every crossroad. Harbin was established in 1894, when imperial Russia was building the railway to China. When he and his younger brother were born there, it was part of Manchuria but is now part of China. When in 1948 Soviet Communists occupied Manchuria, the family moved to Brazil, where their younger sister was born. A few years later, they were able to immigrate to America with the younger children. My new friend, at that time eighteen years old, was considered an adult and had to stay behind in Brazil awaiting his quota. Ten years later he was issued a visa that made it possible for him to unite with his family in America.

When I met him, he lived in Seattle in a house he owned, where now he was alone and trying to get over the recent death of his wife. His parents were dead and he had no children, only his younger brother and sister with their families. Most of his life in Seattle he spent working as a high-caliber machinist, and he belonged to the same parish, St Nicholas Cathedral, where his brother served as a *starosta* (warden). Here we became good friends, and I enjoyed driving together to our church services and to the Russian Community Center, where we did volunteer work. Our childhood and life in

America were quite different, but our common language and religion were the same. His childhood was totally immersed in Russian language and culture. Early in his life he lost his mother and regretted knowing so little about her; I felt the same about my father whom I also lost early in my childhood.

As a little boy, my friend spent several years living alone with his father. This was during the Japanese occupation of Manchuria when Russians were compelled to live on untilled soil in a distant province where there were no roads or buildings to live in. They brought with them the animals and tools they owned, and with hard work managed to make a home to live in, which was an underground dug-out house. For nourishment, they hunted wild boars, and at a very young age he learned to how to transport what they hunted back to their home. His father taught him to drive the horse and buggy, and their horse was their greatest helper and friend. Other Russian families at that time who found themselves in a similar situation had to live that way to survive.

To get wood, trees were cut down with a long, double-ended saw. With one person at each end, they pulled the saw back and forth against a huge tree trunk until it fell to the ground. This was how he and his father worked together to obtain lumber for building and wood for cooking, and in the winter, firewood for warming their home.

One evening during a snowstorm, their goat wandered away into the nearby forest. Father and son went to look for it and were forced to spend the night in the freezing cold in the forest, where they built a fire primarily to keep the wolves away. Next morning the lost goat was found, but my friend never forgot that winter night and how close they were to freezing to death or being attacked by wolves.

The Solovetsky Islands

A fascinating trip to Russia that my new friend and I took together with an international group of pilgrims, mostly of Russian descent, was in the company of Archbishop Hilarion (Kapral) who was at that time of Australia. I was impressed by his serenity, humility, and mellow personality. This was true especially of his ability to create a truly Christian atmosphere around him, without many words but rather with his attitude toward life. When several years later, upon the death of Metropolitan Laurus who was head of the Russian Church Abroad, Archbishop Hilarion was elected to take his place, I felt it happened with God's direct guidance.

The beautiful Solovetsky Islands in the White Sea are located in the farthest north of Russia. As we approached our destination, we could see in the distance the monumental stone structures of the Monastery of Our Savior's Transfiguration built on the shore of the sea, which only at this time of the year was not frozen solid. This historically famous place was surrounded by a magnificent wall built with rocks of massive proportions, and as we got closer, Russian-style church tops became visible. We were told the climate there was an unusual twenty-five degrees centigrade in summer and in winter rarely below minus twenty-five. It was founded in the fifteenth century, and for many years it was an important religious, cultural, and economic center of the Russian north. Also at one time it was used as a fortress and a place of banishment. During the Crimean War, it was shelled by the British troops, and after the Bolshevik Revolution, the monastery was abolished and was made into a concentration camp for religious and political offenders from where there was no possible escape.

The numerous surrounding islands constitute an archipelago. They have been united by the same history, which made their beauty at the same time tragic and attractive to pilgrims, who came here to purify their souls. There was an aesthetic and spiritual energy here that we felt as we disembarked and entered beyond the massive walls. What a treasure house of ancient culture was within! Yet the thought that this was a prison at one time, lost in the coldest, farthest sea in Russia, made me shudder. Since 1989, this monastery has been undergoing restoration, and volunteers, particularly from universities, spend summer vacations on these islands, helping with the restoration of churches and other buildings on the monastery grounds. It was believed in the distant past that voluntary entry by men into monastic life helped them find spiritual enlightenment, and they were able to withstand the rigors of nature around them.

Our hotel was nearby but outside of the monastery. We found out that it was recently constructed by builders from Finland. It was a charming place with two-story separate buildings big enough for only four couples to stay in each unit. They looked like log houses on the outside but were quite modern on the inside. There were enough of them to house all twenty of us in the group. We ate in a refectory closer to the monastery, where the food was healthy Russian food: borsht, kasha made from buckwheat, and fresh fish instead of meat. Attentive waiters wore Russian national costumes, and unlike how things were done in the Soviet Union where society did not follow the principle of serving the customer, here they did their best to please us with their service.

This was on the main island; the other islands were much smaller and had traces of early settlers from the Scandinavian countries. We saw places of punishment at one time used by Soviet jailers. One of these was a post to which in summer a victim was tied and left naked in a wooded area over-night. Summers in the northern regions of Russia abound in voracious mosquitoes so that by morning a person was found dead. The descriptions of other punishments gave me nightmares, but otherwise it was one of the most interesting places to visit, with fascinating architecture and magnificent natural beauty.

To return to St Petersburg, we would need to board a train somewhere in Karelia. To get to the mainland from the Solovetsky Islands, there was daily transportation on a small ship. On the last evening of our stay, we boarded this small ship. Some of us sat in the very bottom enclosure whereas others were in a semi-open upper level next to the captain's area. Soon the wind picked up speed and was getting stronger and stronger, making the waves get higher and higher as they crashed against the ship.

People started to feel sick to their stomach, and some were overcome with a feeling of pending doom. Someone asked the clergy on board to help us all pray together, and we did. The captain tried to calm us by saying that this was a natural occurrence in the White Sea and that very few shipwrecks and incidents of drowning occur, not more than once a year or so. Someone asked whether there was one yet this year. "Not yet," said the captain and added that the water is so cold in the White Sea, that if it happened to us we would not even have time to realize what had happened. These explanations, of course, did not help alleviate our genuine concern for our lives, and we sat shivering from the wet, cold feeling; but thank God, the storm slowly abated, and we safely arrived at our destination.

We walked across the train tracks to reach the platform where we would board our train, something that would never have been allowed in the United States, but here there was no other way. The interior of the train was nice; we were four to a room—the men slept on the top bunks and the women on the bottom ones, unless age or disability dictated otherwise. We had clean sheets and blankets, but the toilets had no toilet paper, without which we somehow survived. They served us hot tea in glasses placed in metal holders, with the Kremlin design on them, and at the first stop we were able to buy freshly baked *piroshky* and sweet rolls from the vendors outside.

I compared this trip to my very first trip to the Soviet Union in 1976. Great changes had taken place since then, the greatest of which was that one did not need to sneak into a church as during the Soviet regime. Beautiful, prayerful services and magnificent choirs now lifted the soul upon entry into a church. It was a great joy to see old monasteries being rebuilt and mutilated churches restored to their former beauty.

In the Footsteps of the Imperial Family

In 2005, one of my twin sons joined me and a group of Russian pilgrims on a trip in the company of Archbishop Hilarion of Australia before his appointment as metropolitan to New York City. This trip retraced the journey of Russia's last imperial family into exile in Siberia. We followed the same route by train, stopping in the towns where they stopped, including one where they lived for some time in a school building before arriving at what was known as the "house of special purpose," their last abode. Russians who were faithful to their memory sought the place of their remains, and only after many years with great difficulty were they located in the depths of a Siberian forest. Our group visited all the cities and memorial places built since *perestroika* and the rebirth of Russia. Looking at old photographs of the imperial family on display and contemplating their beautiful, calmly composed faces, I wondered what heartless persons could have wished them evil. Places where we made overnight stops were in locations rarely visited even by native Russians, let alone ordinary tourists.

We arrived in Tyumen, an area rich in deposits of gas; it was at one time a place of banishment and labor camps. From there we were transferred to a place closer to Tobolsk, where we settled for the night in a small rundown hotel with Lenin's bust on an old pedestal in the middle of a weed-infested front yard. It was early evening and already dark in the corridors as we entered the building in which the electricity was not working. Thanks to the small flashlight my son brought along, we were able to find our rooms and went groping down the hall to find a bathroom.

There was one big room for that purpose, the likes of which we had never seen before. A row of circular holes in the wooden floor of an elevated platform was what we were supposed to use as toilets with no walls enclosing them for individual privacy. Across from this communal toilet room, there was one with several sinks to wash in with only cold water available. This God-forsaken building, we were told, used to belong to the Soviet state, and now there was no electricity because the new private owners were unable to pay for it. The first floor was occupied by the homeless and poor drunks; the second floor was reserved for us guests. Fortunately we needed to spend only one night here, and to make us feel better after the tiring road travel, nuns from a nearby convent came over and offered us the use of a Russian *banya* (sauna), and afterwards they served us hot tea with bagels.

The next night was in Tobolsk, which at one time was the provincial capital of Siberia. Being a place of banishment during and after the revolution, Tsar Nicholas II and his family were sent here as well. We visited the museum called "the Tsar's prison," and not far from there was the Abalak Monastery. After prayer and a discussion of the local history, we dined in the monastery refectory and then took the train to Yekaterinburg. During the Soviet regime this big city was called Sverdlovsk, the family name of an outstanding Communist. It was situated on the eastern slopes of the Ural Mountains and the neighboring part of the western Siberian lowlands. Its population was chiefly Russian, and it was the principal economic and cultural center of the region.

Here we attended church services in what is called the Church on the Blood, built where once stood the Ipatiev House in which the Russian imperial family was executed. We also visited the chapel built in memory of the Grand Duchess Elizabeth, wife of Grand Duke Serge, both murdered during different periods of the revolution. There were monasteries and museums we visited in this city, and then we went to Ganina Yama on its outskirts to the pit where the remains of the imperial family were found. On the same grounds is a newly built monastery with wooden churches, recently built in memory of each member of the imperial family. Although it was a beautiful place and very interesting to see, it was also sorrowful and for me emotionally trying.

I thought of my grandfather, the general, who perished in the bloody revolution as did most of his sons, my uncles, whom I therefore never got to meet. The fact that both my parents were ready at that time to sacrifice their lives for Holy Russia and its tsar became very real and understandable for me. My youthful son, on the other hand, was more interested in the cultural aspect of the region and its beauty as expressed in the intricate carving on the natural wood structures built from locally grown timber from the surrounding thick forests. The Old Russian-style architecture, both religious and secular, fascinated him. He liked the Slavic designs carved on some of the nearby log houses and eateries in the villages. The stores sold colorful country handcrafts, and there was artistic woodwork done by artists we were able to watch at work.

During this trip to renewed Russia, we were fortunate to have been able to spend time in the old Diveyevo Monastery, a favorite place of the popular nineteenth-century Russian saint, St Seraphim of Sarov, whose biography was first written in English by my spiritual father and friend of my youth, Father Lazarus (Moore). We were visiting renovated monasteries and churches and were continuously impressed by the devoted hardworking young monks and nuns who were beginning to refill the convents and monasteries formerly assigned by the Communist government for use as military storage facilities.

One special event in this large, beautiful place made a strong impression on me. Toward evening, hundreds of pilgrims from near and distant Russian towns gathered in front of the Diveyevo Monastery Cathedral. It was summer but in this region it was getting dark early. Everybody stood still in total silence, even very small children with their parents. Then from the door of a nearby building, two nuns with lit candles in their hands walked up to the huge gathering of pilgrims. Everybody lit their candles from each other and followed the nuns whispering the Jesus Prayer: "Lord Jesus Christ, Son of God, have mercy on me a sinner." We walked in a procession within the convent walls around the edge of its territory on what is known as the "*Kanavka* (Ditch) Walk." During his life near here, the highly revered St Seraphim instructed the nuns to walk and pray this way in his memory.

It was a long, silent, orderly walk; parents carried their infants and older children walked whispering the prayer just as adults did. Hundreds of like-thinking people were walking in line for somewhat over an hour, and just as we were beginning to feel an element of fatigue, the brightly lit cathedral started to be visible in the distance, seeming only a little way ahead. Upon arriving, we sang together prayers to the Blessed Mother of God and slowly started to depart our different ways. There were smiles on people's faces as we looked at each other, and the warm feeling of being one big family of believers was something that made this experience especially memorable. I felt I was finally in a place like the Holy Russia of the distant past that Mother often mentioned in my childhood.

The other phenomenal change in Russia was the fact that people did not need to tell lies anymore in order to survive, as they were often compelled to do during the Soviet regime. It was amazing how much easier it was to ask them questions and get straightforward answers or to be questioned by them about life in our present home countries. Now people listened with interest when we spoke of where and how our grandparents lived in Russia before the revolution, and how they were forced to escape from the horrors in their once beloved native land. Now we were able to freely visit our parents' and grandparents' birthplaces and to see what was left of Russian culture so faithfully adhered to by them after they were forced to live abroad. Most of them, unfortunately, did not live long enough to see this rebirth of Russia.

CHAPTER 7

✠✠✠

Reflections and Return
to the City of Peace

I look back at my life and wonder: What have I learned from it? Above all, what was the purpose of all the joy and sorrow, failures and achievements in my life, or were those just coincidences not sent for a purpose? Did I follow my destiny when I chose to stay in America, giving up life in the Holy Land where I was raised and was loved? I realize mistakes I may have made not foreseeing possible consequences, but thanks to the efforts of my mother and those who helped her raise me, and the Orthodox philosophy of life they instilled in me, I overcame the bad in my life and remember only the good.

Are our children mirrors of our selves or of their environment? The time and place in which my children grew up was very different from mine; their father's world was much closer to theirs. They were not fortunate enough to have had a large extended family as so many other children had. There were no uncles, aunts, or cousins in their lives, just as there were none, for one reason or another, in mine or in my husband's childhood. There was no conveniently located organization for us to become part of or especially, to my regret, no Orthodox church near enough for regular attendance or a community to give moral support when needed. We ended up being simply one of America's numerous families who tried to be ordinary and avoided what would make us seem extraordinary.

When we were working at Birzeit University on the West Bank, we often visited the Russian Mount of Olives Convent and I introduced my children to my mother's old friends, the nuns, who played such a big role in my upbringing. They expressed surprise at how very American my sons were. "How could that be?" they asked, "When you were raised to be so very Russian Orthodox?" I did not try to explain to them that we lived in a very different and quite overwhelming society, where my presence alone in the family was not strong enough to overcome the multicultural, secular, materialistic environment in which my children grew up. Those who never lived outside their closed community would not have understood this.

Looking at it from another point of view, the only Russia known to young Americans at that time was the Soviet Union, and my "Russia" to them was just an old fairy tale. Also I wanted my children to grow up faithful to the country of their birth, and the necessity of this outlook was encouraged by their teachers in school. The Cold War was at its peak, and I was still adjusting to parenting in America. Being able to speak English when I arrived, it was easier for me to blend in and be understood by my family and neighbors. It even appeared to be "politically correct" to speak English at that time of competition between the two superpowers. Now that my sons are grown men and the reemergence and accessibility of Russia have become a reality, knowing Russian might have been a bonus for them, but alas they were born at a different time.

As far as the Palestinian side of me was concerned, that was a painful reality that I did not want to pass on in its entirety to my loved ones. In America, I was happy to be finally on the winning side, and my children to be inheritors of the secure feeling of belonging to a legitimate and powerful country, as I saw America to be. The day I went for the formal interview to receive my citizenship I took it very seriously. I liked the American way of life as I saw it and accepted things at their face value. But I asked questions about Native Americans, the answers to which American-born citizens did not always have. When I addressed my questions to the immigration officers, they seemed bewildered by them. I remember how well I answered all the questions on freedoms, but the judge said I forgot the most important freedom. I stopped to think for a minute and he reminded me that it was freedom of religion. "How could I forget that?" I questioned myself, and then thought that it was obviously because the religion I encountered in America was of a totally different brand than the three ancient religions I knew in the Holy Land. Religion there was a way of life, the primary reason for existing, and its precepts controlled our every action. However, I studied the required text from the U.S. Constitution, passed the test, and proudly received my American citizenship. I was told never to use my Hashemite Kingdom of Trans-Jordan passport but was allowed to keep it as a souvenir.

Knowing extra languages proved to be an asset in my life, something I discovered during my studies and work in America. After the first Iraqi war when groups of Iraqi refugees arrived in the Pacific Northwest, where I was living, I was working as a Russian interpreter for the local health department. A letter written in Arabic arrived in my supervisor's mailbox. She was concerned that it might be a threat or complaint, but when I happened to walk into her office and to her delight was able to translate it, she breathed a sigh of relief because it was a nice letter of thanks from an Iraqi patient grateful for the help given to his family. So I was able to do something that pleased my co-workers as well as those they had to work with. The Arab-speaking immigrants were happy to have me around to translate for them in the clinic and be able to soothe their children in their native tongue when they were being given immunization shots.

During a trip to Spain and Morocco, I remember the joy expressed by some Arab-speaking women farm workers when they discovered I spoke Arabic. They were on their way to a job picking berries somewhere near Gibraltar. The tourist group I was travelling with by bus stopped to use the same toilet facilities as did the Arab women. I was standing at the end of our group's line while the local women stood even further behind me in a long line. As I waited for my turn, I heard one of them in back of me tearfully telling her neighbor in Arabic that she felt so sick in the stomach she was simply unable to wait any longer. Without thinking, I turned to her and in Arabic offered her my place in line. The woman quickly ran into the toilet, but when she came out she was so thankful and excited about my giving up my place to her, especially because I did so in Arabic. Then the whole group surrounded me thankfully exclaiming, "You can speak like us, you are our sister." Then they proceeded to embrace me and kiss me so warmly that I needed to somehow extricate myself from their embraces, and rush to my bus so as not to be left behind by my group.

A friend once told me that life resembles handmade lace: some of it is simple and plain, and some of it is beautifully intricate. The intricate parts, she said, are like our travels and other joyfully interesting periods in our life. This became true of my life after age seventy, long past my childrearing and hardworking years, when with God's help I found myself able to take vacation trips abroad. One such trip was a cruise I took together with this friend to Greece with its beautiful islands, and to Turkey to see the remains of the Byzantine Empire. For Orthodox Christians like us, Constantinople, now called Istanbul, was of special interest, because Russian history and culture had spiritual roots in this place.

According to the history I was taught, the last Byzantine emperor was married to a Slavic princess, and therefore after the fall of Byzantium, imperial Russia inherited its double-headed eagle emblem. It received its Christian faith from Byzantium and its alphabet through the Greek monks Cyril and Methodius. Consequently Russia always believed that it was its destiny to protect Eastern Orthodox Christianity. My friend and I were especially impressed with the magnitude and superb architecture of Hagia Sophia [Holy Wisdom] in Istanbul. Built in the sixth century by the Byzantine Emperor Justinian, this formerly Christian Church was turned into an Islamic mosque by the conquerors of Constantinople, and is now a museum.

Upon looking up at the ceiling of the interior, the Turkish guide called our attention to the part where the cupola ceiling paint was being removed to expose the ancient Christian icons painted on it before the Ottoman Turkish invasion. Now was visible an icon of the Virgin Mary with the Christ Child in her lap. I noticed the word *Allah* in Arabic appeared below this icon, so I asked if this was all right with the Muslim faith. The guide's answer was that the Islamic inscriptions and the icons were of different historical periods. First there was Christianity, hence an icon was painted, and then it was covered over with white paint and superimposed was the Islamic word for God in Arabic, the original language of that faith. Both were equally important to preserve, he said and added that in any event Muslims also respect the Mother of Christ.

What we saw in Turkey reminded me of the ancient Christian churches in Palestine. One was built by the Byzantine Emperor Constantine after his conversion to Christianity. It happened when before one of his battles he looked at the sky and saw the Latin letters IHS under a cross formed by the clouds. Those three letters were an abbreviation of the Latin words meaning "with this sign you shall conquer." He took this prediction seriously, and upon being victorious, he converted to Christianity and became baptized. Consequently, with his mother Helena he built a magnificent church in Jerusalem that encompassed the places of Christ's crucifixion, burial, and resurrection. Here, underground, according to tradition, three crosses were found, which were believed to be those of Christ and the two robbers crucified on either side of Him. In Bethlehem, which to this day remains a Palestinian city, the Romanesque temple built by Emperor Justinian, over the cave of Christ's birthplace, continues to be a magnificent Christian church.

But as much as I enjoyed travelling and being with good friends, my sons remained my primary source of happiness. I am fortunate that two of them have settled in the same state where I live so we are able to visit on a regular basis. Our conversations give me an opportunity to enjoy listening to them and their responses to questions regarding life, its problems, and purpose. I respect them for trying to achieve honorable goals and to have put forth an effort to be educated and readers of worthwhile books. When good jobs were scarce or not available, they did not give up and were not afraid of hard work. They understood each in his own individual way that even if their growing up years did not expose them to all the possible wealth and opportunities of life in America, they were raised by parents who tried their best to pass on to them what they knew was good.

I am grateful for having worked at jobs I enjoyed, especially having had bright students who liked to study and did well. I treasured their thank you notes for having been patient with them, and some I have remained friends with to this day. Whether teaching Palestinian students at Birzeit University, or working with professors and students at the various universities and colleges in which I worked and studied in America, I enjoyed them all. I felt as if I was teaching my own children, which most of my students sensed and graciously accepted. One of the students in a class I taught wrote the following:

Dear Anya Derrick,

Thank you for your time and patience these last 3 quarters in Russian class! I have been very blessed to have you for my instructor here at the college. I pray God's best for you in the future! Spasibo! [Thank you.]

Penny

Another time, an older student planning a business trip to Russia after *perestroika* wrote:

To be the best we can be, in any capacity in Russia, we need to be able to communicate. A few phrases, a few songs and the opportunity to go are a great beginning. When we go we'd like to be able to talk with friends more and to learn some of what they can so richly teach us.

Anya, you are such a special person. You represent Russia so well. There must have been years when this wasn't so easy, yet your love for your country never faded and your knowledge of current affairs and history is incredible. I tell you because we see in you such strength of character and consistent kindness, and know it didn't "just happen." You are the result of many decisions. You are a constant reminder of the results of a disciplined life. You have become a pillar of strength to many. Responsibility rests on you in many areas. We'd like to give back to you a token of our gratefulness to you.

Sincerely Carolyn

Some say that in the end our personalities are determined by the place and time in which we were raised. Not having the opportunity to live closer to an Orthodox church earlier in my life in America, many years later when I became library director at a community college in Seattle, I was delighted to discover that my work was just a few blocks from St Nicholas Russian Orthodox Cathedral. After work in the late afternoon, I often stopped at the church for vespers. My husband and I became involved with church life, and I enjoyed singing in the choir as I did in my youth. At that time, the Bishop of Seattle was the youthful Bishop Kyrill (Dmitrieff). His thick black beard would soon turn white, after he became both the Archbishop of San Francisco and Western America, and the Secretary of the Synod of Bishops. Back in 1981–1982, while still only a priest monk, he lived in Jerusalem and taught at Bethany School. I felt that he understood my outlook on life, having experienced Jerusalem himself. The church, the bishop, and the choir: all these contributed to a sense of homecoming, a return to Jerusalem, the Mount of Olives, and Gethsemane.

I joined the church sisterhood and was elected head sister. Among our duties in the sisterhood were visiting and helping the sick and the elderly parishioners, and giving them rides to church when they no longer were able to drive. Teaching children and keeping the church and its grounds in good order were also among our duties. On Sundays and feast days, serving communal meals in the church hall was another duty to attend to. Parish life gave me the opportunity to be with new and old friends sharing our life experiences and our joys and sorrows. We treasured the time being all together in a setting that was so much a part of our native culture, enjoying the prayerful church services in our small and old but authentic Russian-style church, built with so much love and sacrifice by our predecessors who were some of the earliest Russian immigrants to America. St Nicholas Cathedral was also dedicated as a memorial to the martyred Russian imperial family.

At one time, our parish was relatively small and consisted mainly of the sons, daughters, and grandchildren of the first two generations of immigrants, who arrived in Seattle after World War I or because of the Russian Revolution. Then others came as displaced persons after World War II. Our joy was great when after the fall of Soviet Communism the way to the free world opened, and our church quickly filled up to capacity with Believers, верующий as they called themselves in Russian. It is a joy these days to be praying all together as old generations and new young families from Russia mingle together. We admire their devotion to their newly rekindled ancestral faith, Orthodox Christianity, that over a millennium ago gave birth to Russia's Christian nationhood.

Recently I received an invitation to return to Jerusalem and help complete a historic almanac of the Russian Orthodox communities on the West Bank, where I spent the period of my life that shaped my soul and made me who I am. I lived to be one of the few remaining witnesses of life in Palestine during the last decade of the British Mandate. The years after the British left and before my departure to America were in many ways particularly difficult for those remaining in what was left of Palestine. Survival was on everybody's mind, and the future was bleak. Those men and women who were carrying responsibilities for their monastic communities and Christian holy places had to be exceptionally strong and insightful leaders, whose identities should be etched in historic records. I was asked to come and share memories of my past experiences during that crucial time. There was a need to fill in remaining gaps of the already recorded history of Christianity in the Holy Land, particularly the Russian Orthodox presence in Jerusalem and the West Bank in general.

Our Turkish airplane arrived at Tel Aviv airport seven hours later than scheduled, and the two nuns who came to meet me and take me to the Gornia Russian Orthodox Convent were visibly exhausted as they approached me and gave me a warm hug. A whole lifetime had passed since I last was in Gornia. It was with my dear mother on the feast day commemorating the Virgin Mary's visit to her cousin Elizabeth to share with her the news of Christ's pending birth and Her motherhood. On this day, Russian pilgrims walked from Jerusalem to Gornia in the town of Ein Karem, a full day's walk, carrying the icon of the Mother of God. They prayed and sang along the way, and upon arrival after a short service in church where the icon was deposited, everybody gathered to share a meal in the monastic refectory. In preparation for that day, the nuns white-washed the convent buildings and planted flowering bushes in the surrounding area so they would be in full bloom at that time.

Many years have passed since the 1948 Arab–Israeli War separated the Russian Mission properties in the West Bank from those that ended up remaining in the eastern part of Israel as Gornia Convent did. I did not know what to expect to see there now, but I could remember the abbess who long ago came from a village in Old Russia and how very capable and hardworking she was. Usually she started the necessary physical work herself, and the nuns willingly followed her example. In addition, she was remarkably hospitable, approachable, and universally liked. Now I was told that the former Arab

5.1 Anya and her twins at Birzeit University near Ramallah on the West Bank.

5.2 Wayne Derrick, library director of Birzeit University.

5.3 Anya at work as reference librarian in the Serials/Acquisition Department at Birzeit University.

5.4 Part of Wayne's job included overseeing the building of the library. The completed university library is pictured here.

5.5 Student volunteers at the library building site.

5.6 Anya visits her mother's grave on the Mount of Olives.

5.7 Arab Orthodox nuns complete their beadwork at the Russian convent on the Mount of Olives.

5.8 Anya at the Damascus Gate, Jerusalem.

5.9 Wayne at the entrance of the Holy Sepulchre in Jerusalem.

5.10 Wayne in front of a mosque in Ramallah.

5.11 Anya's twins and their guides in the Sinai Desert.

5.12 Anya and students in front of Bethany School classrooms in the1980s.

Illustrations - Chapter 6

6.1 The graduation photo of Anya's father's youngest sister, Anna. She graduated from the Smolny Institute in St Petersburg.

6.2 Anya meets for the first time with relatives in Russia.

6.3 The author pictured at her first meeting with her Aunt Anna at age 92.

6.4 Aunt Anna's daughter Katia (the author's cousin) playing a favorite waltz of Anya's father.

6.5 Anya fishing with her relative Giorgy Bosniatsky, a well-known geologist.

6.6   Resting with Archbishop Hilarion whilst visiting a monastery in Russia.

6.7 The Church on the Blood, built where once stood the Ipatiev House in which the Russian imperial family was executed.

6.8 A monument in Yekaterinburg, Siberia, built in memory of the martyred imperial family.

6.9 Archbishop Hilarion visiting Orthodox brethren in Siberia.

6.10 Anya Derrick's children.

6.11 Anya's children as adults.

6.12 Anya's grandchildren.

6.13 Anya with her friend and former student of Russian language, Tamara Bogdanoff.

6.14 Anya and Yuri Bogdanoff travel along the Danube.

6.15 Anya's spiritual haven in the United States, the St Nicholas Russian Orthodox Cathedral in Seattle.

6.16 Anya with Archbishop Kirill (Dmitrieff) in 2013. Archbishop Kirill also taught at the Bethany School in Jerusalem.

6.17 The iconostasis of the St Nicholas Russian Orthodox Cathedral in Seattle.

6.18 Ink Sketch of Jerusalem by Georgi Alexandrovich Aleéff.

6.19 Door at the Mount of Olives Convent during the snowfall of 2013.
Tradition tells us that the Mother of God
stood in this place at the time of the Lord's ascension.

6.20 View of Jerusalem from the mount of Olives. 2012 © Anton Kudelin

town surrounding this convent was occupied by Jewish inhabitants, who in 1948 after the Palestinians were driven out transformed the place into a typical modern Israeli town. As it was already late, the nuns and I stopped on our way at a local eatery for an evening bite, and then drove to the convent guest house, which was to be my home for the next couple of weeks. From this well-kept place I could easily attend the church services and go to the refectory, but best of all was that it was conveniently located near a downhill path to my workplace. My time was to be spent with four nuns assigned to do research and work with me at the archive in the old library building erected in the nineteenth century.

Next day after attending the early liturgy, at about 9:00 a.m. we met at breakfast in the large refectory where icons hung on the central wall and food was sumptuously laden on four long tables, two for the nuns and two for the pilgrims. It was an appealing breakfast, without meat products; instead, as on all menus, we were served fish as well as lots of vegetables and fruit. After breakfast, the pilgrims took off in buses to Jerusalem's holy places as well as to distant monasteries built in locations of biblical interest, returning only in the evening for supper. Meanwhile the nuns and I descended to the archives for a day's work. We searched out documents and any materials familiar to me left behind during the Israelis' takeover of the Russian Mission complex in Jerusalem and later returned. I needed to verify and add dates of occurrences described, as well as to solve problems caused by incomprehensible handwriting and identify names and faces on old photographs about which the nuns had no way of knowing.

Comparatively speaking, the nuns were young and new to the area, mostly in their early forties and fifties, born and raised in the Soviet Union. They were interested in how Russian communities existed during and after the British Mandate, how they survived the Arab–Israeli War and then lived under the administration of the Hashemite Kingdom of Jordan. In the afternoons we did mostly oral history recording; notes were taken of my answers to questions and of my lengthy descriptions, and explanations were tape recorded. They said they were grateful for God's gift of long-term memory to the elderly, and to the fact that I saved and brought with me a collection of correspondence and photographs of places and individuals I knew and lived with in Jerusalem.

Since the fall of Communism, eighty-five nuns have resided in Gornia Convent, and only the abbess from a convent in Estonia was closer in age to me. They were eager to find out all they could about their predecessors, who came here from imperial Russia and managed to purchase and retain property in the Holy Land. The places they acquired were mostly close to where, according to the Gospel, our Savior spent time during His short life on earth. Now, as before the revolution, on a daily basis Russian pilgrims prayerfully filled the holy places and streets of Jerusalem, their faces glowing with a light of spiritual joy as they prayed at Golgotha and the Holy Sepulchre. In the *suq,* merchants repeated, "Russians are good for us, they support our economy, and anyway, just as our great-grandfathers liked the *Muscob* (Arabic for Muscovites), we like the Russians." In Bethlehem praying at the Church of Christ's Nativity, I felt hopeful for peace to prevail as long as Russian pilgrims continued to come to the Holy Land, where Arabs welcomed them and the Israelis graciously tolerated them.

I was pleasantly surprised to discover along a side street of this town a nice new building with the inscription in both Russian and Arabic: Russian Center of Culture and Learning. Here Palestinians, both Christian and Muslim, could come to study Russian language and culture as well as art, music, and dance, and participate in various sports. Inside the building on the main wall I saw engraved in Cyrillic the letters R.D.M. that are found on all Russian Mission properties I knew in Palestine. This is an acronym for the Russian Spiritual Mission, and next to this I saw a portrait of the Russian Patriarch Cyril. Close by there was a portrait of President Vladimir Putin and next to it the double-headed eagle emblem of Russia.

I was informed that Palestinians of all ages were welcome here and that they were able to attend all kinds of cultural programs in the large auditorium. It being only a week after Easter, I noticed traditional Easter themes in the children's and young people's art displayed in the hallway. Young Arab mothers who were on their way to a Russian language class expressed delight at having such a good place for them and their children to use freely. Others present in this center were fathers and their teenage sons, who told me that coming to spend time in this center has greatly improved their difficult life and helped lighten the stress of living under military occupation.

My whole stay in the Holy Land was short but contained meaningful experiences. Even now I find it difficult to put into words why this encounter with the local people and praying in the holy places with Russian pilgrims was so fulfilling for me. I always felt that leaving Jerusalem separated me from its fate and that of those among whom I lived; it was a painful feeling. Now I must live with the hope that there can be peace in Jerusalem and the territories around it. This is possible only if it remains an interfaith, international Holy City, accessible to those who treasure its ancient sanctuaries belonging to people of the three major faiths: Christianity, Judaism, and Islam. Its ancient Hebrew name Yerushalayim would then keep its true meaning: City of Peace.

NOTES
✛✛✛

Chapter 1

1. The Cadet Corps was an all-male, admission-based school with the express purpose of training future commissioned officers.

Chapter 2

1. Kuvuklia is the Greek term for the Holy Sepulchre.

2. In the late nineteenth century, the Russian imperial government purchased land from a Palestinian monastery in Jerusalem with the intention of building a consulate. In the process of digging foundations, a major archaeological site was discovered that is believed to be the site of the Judgment Gate, one of the seven gates in the city walls at the time of Christ. The site is close to the Holy Sepulchre and a chapel was erected above the excavations dedicated to the Russian Orthodox St Alexander Nevsky in memory of Tsar Alexander III. The site is commonly referred to as the Russian excavations or Raskopky.

Chapter 3

1. St Benedict's College merged with St Scholastica College in 1971 and was renamed Benedictine College.

2. King Abdullah was assassinated on July 20, 1951.

3. A mandiram is a Christian ashram (hermitage).

Chapter 4

1. Strictly speaking, the U.S. delegation in Hanoi at this time had no official status as America did not give diplomatic recognition to the newly independent North Vietnamese state after the withdrawal of the French colonial government in 1954. It is against the backdrop of this upheaval that Mac writes to Anya at Christmas 1954.

2. The period of mass immigration to the United States came to an end in 1924 with the passage of the Johnson-Reed Act. The new framework remained largely intact until 1965 when a new immigration act came into effect. In the intervening years, a quota for visas existed that from 1929 was fixed at 150,000 annually.

3. *Eleonskaya* is a Greek word with a Russian ending that refers to a female connected to the Mount of Olives.

Chapter 5

1. Wayne is being sarcastic. The Israelis call the part of the West Bank where they have settlements "Judea and Samaria." There the sanitation is better than the Arab-occupied parts of the West Bank where cholera is present.

2. Gush Emunim are ultra-religious Jews who believe they have divine authority to settle anywhere on the Palestinian West Bank without reference to the local population.

BIBLIOGRAPHY

Carter, Jimmy. *Palestine: Peace Not Apartheid.* New York: Simon & Schuster, 2006.

Carter, Jimmy. *We Can Have Peace in the Holy Land: A Plan That Will Work.* New York: Simon & Schuster, 2009.

Collins, Larry, and Dominique Lapierre. *O Jerusalem!* New York: Simon & Schuster, 1972.

Furlonge, Sir Geoffrey. *Palestine Is My Country: The Story of Musa Alami.* London: Geoffrey Furlonge, 1969.

Graham, Stephen. *With the Russian Pilgrims to Jerusalem.* London: Macmillan, 1913.

Mlechin, Leonid. *Pochemu Stalin Sozdal Izrail—Osobaya Papka* [Why Stalin created Israel: A special report]. Moscow: "YAUZA" "EKSMO", 2005.

Sennott, Charles M. *The Body and the Blood: The Middle East's Vanishing Christians and the Possibility for Peace.* New York: Public Affairs, 2001.

Sollogub, A. A. (ed.). *Russkaya Pravoslavnaya Tserkov Zagranitsei.1918–1968* [The Russian Orthodox Church Abroad: 1918–1968], Vol. I–II. New York: Russian Orthodox Church Abroad, 1968.

Sviataya Zemlya. *Istochniko-kulturnyi. Illustrirovanyi Almanakh. No1/2012 chast I-II.* [Holy Land, Historic/Cultural Illustrated Almanac]: Jerusalem: Russian Orthodox Mission, 2012.

INDEX
✠✠✠

The citations in parentheses following the page numbers refer to note numbers; for example 81(n4) refers to the text associated with note 4 on page 81. References to photographs in the illustration sections begin with "P"; for example, P2.3 refers to photograph 2.3.